REGNUM STUDIES IN MISSION

Leadership in a Slum

A Bangkok Case Study

REGNUM STUDIES IN MISSION

Series Preface

Regnum Studies in Mission are born from the lived experience of Christians and Christian communities in mission, especially but not solely in the fast growing churches among the poor of the world. These churches have more to tell than stories of growth. They are making significant impacts on their cultures in the cause of Christ. They are producing 'cultural products' which express the reality of Christian faith, hope and love in their societies.

Regnum Studies in Mission are the fruit often of rigorous research to the highest international standards and always of authentic Christian engagement in the transformation of people and societies. And these are for the world. The formation of Christian theology, missiology and practice in the twenty-first century will depend to a great extent on the active participation of growing churches contributing biblical and culturally appropriate expressions of Christian practice to inform World Christianity.

Series Editors

A full listing of titles in this series appears at the end of this book

REGNUM STUDIES IN MISSION

Leadership in a Slum

A Bangkok Case Study

Alan R. Johnson

Foreword by Suntaree Komin

First published 2009 by Regnum Books International

Regnum is an imprint of the Oxford Centre for Mission Studies
St. Philip and St. James Church
Woodstock Road
Oxford, OX2 6HR, UK
www.ocms.ac.uk/regnum

09 08 07 06 05 04 03 8 7 6 5 4 3 2 1

British Library Cataloguing in Publication Data
A catalogue record for this book is available from the British Library

ISBN: 978-1-506477-90-9

Distributed by 1517 Media in the US and Canada

To Lynette

You alone know the real truth of how I could never have completed this project without your unflagging support, willingness to lend a hand in editing, and most of all your comforting presence.

Contents

List of Tables

List of Figures

List of Photographs

List of Abbreviations

BMA	Bangkok Metropolitan Administration
BMR	Bangkok Metropolitan Region
CODI	Community Organizations Development Institute
CPB	Crown Property Bureau
ILT	Implicit Leadership Theory
LBDQ	Leader Behaviour Description Questionnaire
LWPW	Lang Wat Pathum Wanaram
NHA	National Housing Authority
NGO	Non-Governmental Organization
SAB	*Sakdi* Administrative Behaviour
SABLH	*Sakdi* Administrative Behaviour Leadership Heuristic
TLM	*Thuukjai* Leader Model
UCDO	Urban Community Development Office

Notes for the Reader

1. I have followed Thai convention by identifying Thais by their first name, and listing them by first name in citations and in the bibliography.

2. On transliterating Thai words in the text I have chosen to simplify the 1997 edition of the ALA-Library of Congress Romanization Tables for Thai with the goal of helping those who do not read Thai to have some sense of how the word sounds when spelled in Romanized script. The ALA-LC already leaves out tone markings, and I have not included the diacritical marks of that system. For those who read Thai, when a tone marking is critical I indicate it next to the term as mid, low, falling, rising, or high. In general I double long vowels and have used 'aw' for the Thai consonant อ. Exceptions to this are well-known names, places, or terms with spellings that are commonly used in English language publications.

3. In the bibliography, titles in Thai language are given in transliteration and then followed by an English translation in square brackets.

4. To simplify matters in the text and bibliography all dates are AD rather than the Buddhist Era (BE) which is 543 years more than AD dating (2006 AD is 2549 BE).

5. Thai currency is called baht and I have listed all amounts with this term, as in 2000 baht, followed by a US dollar amount in parentheses. For most of the time during the course of the research the exchange rate was around 40 baht to 1 US dollar.

6. I have chosen not to use any names when referring to people in Lang Wat Pathum Wanaram. People were often times uncomfortable sharing their name and I felt it would be more appropriate due to the sensitivity of the material to use either a unique record number for the interview or only a first initial in the case of those who became key sources. Where I share interview segments I represent myself as A. and the interviewee by their first initial. In some cases first initials overlapped and I use a second letter to identify the person, as in D. and De.

7. I used the Endnote program to organize all of my data and this program gives each entry a unique number in the database. In the text I identify any material by an abbreviation indicating the type of material and then a unique record number. The abbreviations that I use for the different types of data that appear in the text are listed below.

PO	participant observation
I	interview
DI	domain interview
LFRL	leader free-recall listing
NLFRL	nonleader free-recall listing
DQI	direct question interview (inquiring about leaders in the community)
DS	daily summary

8. Thai words and phrases are generally always translated in the text. Most of the time the English word or phrase appears first with the Thai in parentheses after it. In some cases for emphasis or to preserve some sense of how it was spoken I put the Thai first and its translation in parentheses. In the case of frequently used terms, the first time it appears it is translated and then used later in the text on its own. Any Thai term used repeatedly and standing alone in the text can be found with a translation in the glossary before the appendices.

Foreword

The issue of leadership and culture has been brought into focus towards the end of the 20th century through the rapid economic development and globalization - which triggered off the blooming of international business, international management, and thus the question of effective cross-cultural management for the academics to ponder. International business, especially where joint ventures or prolonged negotiations are involved, is fraught with difficulties. Apart from practical and technical problems (in which solutions are often readily found), it is the national cultural characteristics that frequently interfere at the executive level and the managing process, where decision-making and the process of managing people tend to be more complex than the practical accords reached between technicians. This phenomenon triggered off numerous studies focusing on the impact of socio-cultural factors on management for productivity. The success or failure of the manager depends on how effectively he manages his subordinates of a different cultural background in a different cultural context. Of course, there are a broad range of cultural factors in the cultural context that resulted from the studies. However, it all boils down to the focal issue of leadership in different cultures, particularly leadership in a specific cultural context, where even the latest developed cross-cultural scales cannot fully depict the richness of the related local cultural context involved. Here, the value of Johnson's work is that he systematically analyzes leadership in the Thai cultural context at a local community level.

Since leadership is a one of the major areas in the field of social psychology, it needs to be stated here that all the leadership theories developed in the West have been taken as universal, thus overlooking the cultural factors all along. It is not until the last two decades of the 20th century that indigenous psychology in Asian countries has developed, with the deep introspection of Asian psychologists, outgrowing its overwhelming dependence on the Western approach to studying and explaining human behaviour. The focus has shifted from merely adopting Western theories, conclusions and practices to one which cherishes the unique social and cultural factors influencing human behaviour and the applications of psychology for the Asian cultural context. Thus, several conferences have taken place with the focus on understanding the shared beliefs and value system of a culture, in order to promote the importance of social and cultural factors in both research and application. Consequently, with this awareness, leadership study which is one of the major areas of psychological contribution to the social sciences, has developed tremendously along this line, from research to application, resulting in the identification of specific cultural values, beliefs of specific cultures, as well as cross-cultural scales development and its application for cross-cultural management training, etc.

With the stated background of leadership study in mind, this present study is therefore valuable from the academic point of view - it combines the strength of the quantitative and scientific study of Thai value with the systematic, qualitative, intensive, and participative study from the anthropological perspective. Thus, the results provide the depth and richness of the sound knowledge of leadership in the Thai cultural context at the local community level with various dimensions of the leadership clearly identified. The value of this work cannot be sufficiently stated in a few sentences but rests in the full content of the book itself which is to be read and referred to. And finally, although it depicts the features of effective Thai leadership at the community level, it also reflects to some extent the pattern of Thai leadership at the broader social level as well.

Last but not least is the fact that admiration has to be given to the researcher's passion, motivation, total commitment, and perseverance that led to the success of this helpful work - one that marks the mileage of this leadership study in Thailand for all fields of social sciences, psychology, sociology, and anthropology, etc.

Suntaree Komin
Professor of Business Administration
National Institute of Development Administration (NIDA), Bangkok

Acknowledgements

The path that led to this book started with a conversation I had with Doug Petersen while sitting in a parked car in Southern California. I owe that conversation to the door-opening activity of Bob Houlihan who named me to serve on a committee of which Doug was the chairman. On that day Doug invited me to enter a doctoral program with the Oxford Centre for Mission Studies (OCMS), an idea that had not crossed my mind at all. Our brief talk led to a long journey which would not have been possible without the help of many people along the way. I have the deepest respect and appreciation for my two supervisors, Dr Peter Clarke and Dr Suntaree Komin. They both demonstrated a passion for their disciplines and a commitment to excellence that has modelled the true meaning of a life devoted to academics. Dr Craig Rusch served as a mentor, introduced me to the world of systematic data collection, and has become a valued friend. Dr Ben Knighton, my OCMS mentor, was the person who kept my head on straight throughout the entire process. When I ran into a problem or was discouraged, Ben was always there with a wise word to get me back on track. He never ceased to amaze me with his ability to meticulously read my work, cut to the critical issues, and problematize what I assumed was unproblematic. I will never write or read in the same way because of the things that I have learned under his tutelage. OCMS provided a wonderful learning environment that included enriching relationships with fellow students from around the world, and a staff always ready to spend time with us and challenge our thinking.

A host of friends provided invaluable support in a wide variety of ways ranging from timely words of encouragement, being supportive of my efforts to make time for research, solving technical problems, assisting with interviews and transcription, tracking down books in libraries, searching the internet, to photocopying—Dr Roger Heuser, Russ Turney, Jeff Dove, Niina Peltomaaki, James Wright, Jintana Ratritham, Brayun Maiwong, and Mark Rodli. I owe a deep debt of gratitude to the community committee and people of Lang Wat Pathum Wanaram for allowing me to work with them. With good humour they put up with my questions, exercises, and constant probing. When a new job assignment at the end of the writing made time an issue, Laura Snider, my married daughter, lent her eyes and editing skills to work through the material and help clean and tighten it. Becki Johnson, my youngest daughter, kept me at the keyboard with much needed back and neck massages whenever she was home. During the course of my research they both started and completed college, and we have taken turns cheering each other on in our studies. Finally, to

Lynette, my wife of 30 years, belongs gratitude for which there are no adequate words to express. She has patiently endured over the years my curiosity, passion for books, and more recently, long hours of writing.

Alan R. Johnson

CHAPTER 1

Introduction

Daily Summary 24 Jan 2003

I had made an appointment to do interviews with the committee at 7:00 PM....got in after 6:30.

D. [committee president] and L. [committee secretary] were at the table where D. always is at. She was singing and dancing with a group of her usual friends.

[Comment: This whole karaoke thing is interesting – there is a number of rather large women who hang around and they seem to drink and sing loudly. D. right in the middle of it. What does this mean?]

D. went with me to the med centre and got chairs. Interesting interchange between D. and L. – L. wanted to use the PA system to call people as they had been told about 7:00 PM. D. said people were not ready. She asked [me] "are you free another time" indicating that it was not convenient. I said I would work with whoever was free. There was a sharp interchange between D. and L. ... D. won out and said no. L. dropped it. Ta. the adviser [to the committee] came in.

Doing the Questions

They dived in before I could explain at all. All three were talking and confused. D. said it was a big headache. She did not seem very happy. I get a feeling like I'm disturbing her – much more from her than the others.

They did not let me explain the questions so I had to jump between people helping them. L. once she got it answered all easily, she is a high school grad. The more educated seemed to have the easiest time and generate more words.

D. had the most problems, only could give a single word or so....

Impression – everything is fluid. D. seems to have little control over the group. Can't call a meeting, people come and go as they please.

Left close to 10:00 PM.

The above, in a slightly edited form, is an excerpt from the log of daily summaries I kept during the time of my study in the Lang Wat Pathum Wanaram community. It was my first attempt at collecting some data using a form I developed that I thought would make things easier. As a method for collecting the data I wanted, it was a disaster. Any illusions I had about being able to easily collect data with pen and paper exercises were dashed.

Photograph 1 West entrance to Lang Wat Pathum Wanaram

Beyond the fact that this single experience let me know I needed to adjust my method, was my constant and utter sense of confusion through the whole process of data collection. How was D., a female in her mid-50s, with a fourth grade education, who sells food from her table near her home, chosen to serve as the community committee president? I had set out to study leadership in a slum. When I began, the slum was a background, the canvas on which I would paint a picture of leadership. But as I studied the slum – asking questions, probing for information, looking behind surface action – I found that in my own intellectual process the slum 'studied' me as well, challenging my assumptions about the nature of leading. At the end of the day I realized that to draw a picture of leadership using a social setting as a backdrop is to disembody it from what makes it leadership in its setting. To study leadership in the slum I found that I had to study the slum as a whole in terms of how things were done and who was allowed and entrusted to do them. Only then would D. as committee president make sense.

My interest in studying leadership was not purely theoretical. For the past 20 years I have worked with a Thai organization whose institutional survival is predicated on developing people who can lead well. In my own work with urban poor I am keenly aware that a major factor in improving the quality of life for people who live on the physical, economic, and social peripheries of their societies is effective local leadership. I undertook this study with the conviction that in order to strengthen local leadership, everyone involved, from the community level through to state agencies and the institutions of civil society such as non-governmental organizations, needs to know what both good and bad leadership looks like in their particular sociocultural setting. I will argue here that much of leadership happens at the implicit and non-discursive level of life; thus cultural values are deeply implicated in its conduct. Until we understand and grapple with the unseen parts of leadership perception and practise we will see little advance in leadership effectiveness by feeding people disembodied theory and principles derived from completely different social settings.

I believe that the data I collected and my analysis of it shows that the elements that are most powerful about practising good leadership, and thus the keys for improving it, are local, particular, and context bound. The results of grand theory, globalized, universal principle-seeking leadership research can be most profitably utilized when there is a solid understanding of the dynamics of leadership in a local setting. Thus leadership research is a both/and proposition requiring comparative studies and larger theoretical perspectives, as well as exploratory and lower level theoretical generation that explicates a single local setting. In this study I take up the latter task and develop an analysis that explicates leadership, broadly conceived of as the social influence processes involved in task accomplishment, in a single slum community in Bangkok, Lang Wat Pathum Wanaram (LWPW).

The Journey That Led to a Slum

It is an interesting literary device in writing up the results of study that what you do last, in terms of the chronology of the project, comes first in the final written presentation. While this is convenient for the reader in terms of laying out what will happen in the course of the document, this practise is dangerous for several reasons because of what it obscures. First, it hides the many twists, turns, and the sense of confusion that were all a part of the course of the study. All the correct spelling, proper grammar, and orderly headings create the appearance that I proceeded in an orderly fashion from A-Z. I doubt this is true of most ethnographic work, and it was manifestly not true of this one. Second, it helps to sustain the fiction that something hard and fast was gained here. I finished my investigation in the slum with more questions than I started with and the nagging feeling that if I could have asked another question or conducted another interview I would have discovered something else vital. The final product came about as I reluctantly crawled out of the stream of fieldwork and question-asking onto the banks in order to put some things on paper.

Ethnographic work does not grow out of a vacuum. I arrived in Thailand in 1986 to work with a Thai Christian organization. I do not really have any memory of ever thinking about 'leadership' before coming to Thailand. It was not very long however, before I was suddenly thrust into situations where I could 'see' leadership for the first time; it did not require vast amounts of social science training to see that Westerners and Thais had very different ideas and practises when it came to getting things done (or not done) in an organizational setting. I became fascinated by questions of why things work organizationally and why they fail, why some leaders can attract and sustain a following and others cannot. As an outsider I wanted to understand what the 'Thai' part of being a Thai leader was. It was these experiences more than any others that created the desire to one day conduct a serious investigation of leading in a Thai setting.

Delving into some of the classic ethnographic material on Thailand introduced me to the ideas of hierarchy and patron-client relations which gave some tools for understanding what I was seeing. An influential piece was Suntaree Komin's *The Psychology of the Thai People* (1990) which laid out nine Thai value orientations. This confirmed my feeling that cultural values were critical in understanding Thai leadership. In addition to this as I began to work through the not insignificant amount of leadership studies in Thailand, the majority revealed a marked bias for using quantitative approaches to do verification studies of Western-generated theory with subjects who are part of the highly educated globalized world. The tendency in such work is to treat culture as a kind of black box,[1] and when results are unusual, or confirm what is completely usual, 'culture' becomes the explanatory tool of choice. Searching this literature also made me realize that most studies of leadership in Thailand have been conducted among the globalized and highly educated.[2] These gaps in the knowledge base of Thai leadership provided an academic justification for seeking to understand the impact of Thai culture on their practise of leadership, and strengthened my conviction that there is a need for exploratory theory generation and investigation based in the perspective of local actors, and suggested a target population for the inquiry. I felt that looking at how leadership as it is practised among the urban poor could provide valuable insights into the nature of leading others in the Thai context as mediated through primary socialization without the external influences of

---

[1] I use the term 'black box' in the sense of 'a whimsical term for a device that does something, but whose inner workings are mysterious ... ' (Behe, 1996:6).

[2] A few examples will suffice; there is work on students (Rangsit, 1993), hospital administrators (Pongsin, 1993), principals (Rachanee, 1988; Sariya, 1980), military officers (Titie, 1997), business leaders (Pattarawalai, 1982), and bank executives (Pratana, 1999).

secondary socialization through advanced education and opportunities provided by a high socioeconomic status.

Framing an Approach to Solve a Puzzle

The original puzzle that started me on the road to this inquiry focused on trying to understand the 'Thai' part of leading in Thailand. My prior experiences in Thailand, which included learning the language and culture and working in a Thai organization, combined with my reading to lead me to a number of convictions. These include the need for more exploratory study to explicate the role of culture in Thai leadership, theory generation rather than a theory verification approach,[3] methods that are sensitive to the perspective of local actors, and the belief that to understand leadership in a particular setting, knowledge of the sociolinguistic terrain is invaluable.

Based on these commitments I made the decision to pursue my interest about Thai leadership by focusing my inquiry on a single slum community, Lang Wat Pathum Wanaram, with the goal of explicating social influence processes from a perspective that was sensitive to the dynamics of culture. At the end of the day, the framework I developed that became the engine to solve the puzzle focused on two goals. The first was to discern and explicate the models of leadership based emically in the perception of the people, and etically through observing behaviour. The second was to explain how these models and their component parts were utilized and enacted in social interactions. Thus the study was both descriptive (in developing the models) and explanatory (in explaining how the models work in social context). I felt an ethnographic approach using fieldwork that combined both systematic data collection[4] with participant observation and interviewing would be the most appropriate for this investigation.

---

[3] Punch notes that when a research area has a lot of unverified theory, a theory verification approach that starts with a theory and deduces hypotheses from it is appropriate. However when an area lacks appropriate theories then theory generation, where theory is built systematically from the data collected, is appropriate (Punch, 1998:16-17).

[4] Systematic data collection refers to systematic interviewing where each informant is asked the same set of questions (Weller & Romney, 1988:6). This approach is contrasted with open-ended interviewing where subjects give long explanatory answers to a variety of different questions and the researcher follows lines of interest in the questioning (1988:6). Structured interviewing makes use of standardized lists of items or a set of statements; it helps to minimize the problem of inconsistent or non-comparable data across informants, helps make systematic comparisons (Weller, 1998:365-6), and helps 'avoid researcher bias resulting from imposing prior categories that may not correspond to those of the people being studied' (Weller & Romney, 1988:6). Systematic data collection proceeds in two phases (Weller, 1998:365-6). The first stage is to make a descriptive exploration of the subject under study and develop a set of items relevant to the area of interest. The second takes these results and develops structured interviewing

From these goals the focal question of the inquiry became, 'What are the shared understandings that Thais in the target community have about the leader-follower relationship, and how are these understandings utilized and enacted in social contexts?' I then broke this down into three specific questions:

1. What are the perceptions that Thais in the target community have about the qualities and performances of leaders?

2. What are the meanings, components, and interrelationships of the terms that represent these perceptions?

3. How are these terms or major clusters of terms drawn upon and enacted in social interactions between leaders and followers in the target community?

Questions one and two were to form the first phase of the study. This included the development of the sociolinguistic terrain and then an explication of the connections and interrelationships between the terms and concepts of question one. Question three comprised the second phase, where through observation and interviewing, I was to show how the material from questions one and two played out in real life, on-the-ground leadership. It turned out that these questions were a good place to start but inadequate to finish. Within the framework imposed by these questions I could not create an account of leadership in LWPW that came anywhere close to integrating all of the data and experiences that I was acquiring. Actually starting the data collection brought to the surface some hidden assumptions that I had been unaware of as I designed my approach.

Two major problems emerged with my questions as originally conceived. The first was their inherent assumption of one kind of leadership, as if there existed a single, unitary, generic 'Thai' view of leadership out there. Theoretically I was open to seeing models plural, but when I set up my questions to use in the systematic data collection I automatically limited myself to developing just one model. What I could not see until I started collecting data was that the methodological limitation imposed on question one naturally flowed down the line to impact questions two and three. These questions could produce a model that was only a slice of what was happening in the community. The second problem was my assumption that one could study slum leadership solely in the context of the slum without reference to the broader world. I quickly learned that one cannot account for what is happening in LWPW without an understanding of the community's relation with the state and elite power.

---

materials for systematic examination. This can include general information, assessing knowledge, attitudes, how people classify things by making discriminations, and the beliefs of a group (1998:366-7).

After making necessary adjustments the inquiry fell into three major but overlapping phases. In the first, questions one and two became an investigation into the perceptions and practises of a culturally preferred leader using systematic data collection procedures. In the second phase, question three was broadened to seek connections between all the models that were emerging from the systematic data collection as well as the interview and observational materials. The final phase added a fourth question studying the relationship between the community and the state.

Organization of the Chapters

In the next chapter I set the study in the framework of larger issues by identifying a series of problematics from the literature beginning with Thai studies in general, then moving to Thai cultural values and social organization, the literature on Thai leadership and concluding with a look at Thai bureaucracy. Chapter 3 gives an overview of slums in Bangkok, examines the policy and practise of the government concerning the urban poor, and then looks in detail at the LWPW community with a special focus on its history from the point of view of leadership and governance in particular. Chapters 4 to 6 present the results of the study in a chronological fashion, showing how the material developed as my data collection and reflection progressed. In Chapter 4 I develop a culturally preferred model of leadership, called the *Thuukjai* Leader Model, and provide an interpretation of how this model builds interpersonal influence. In Chapter 5 I describe leadership on the ground in the community using three major themes: the Trustworthy Leader Model, the *Sakdi* Administrative Behaviour Leadership Heuristic, and leadership flowing through the group. Chapter 6 examines the relationship of the community and the state. Here I look at the various ways in which the community corroborates, ignores, rejects, and resists the views of the state and elite power. In the final chapter I examine insights from the fieldwork that relate to leadership in and outside of the Thai setting and for leadership training. In these points I connect both particulars from the data as well as methodological insights to suggest trajectories for improving leadership specifically in Thai settings and for the larger enterprise of understanding and seeking to improve the practise of leadership in other contexts.

CHAPTER 2

Issues in the Study of Thai Leadership

It was working with a Thai organization that stimulated my interest in a cultural account of how leadership operates in a Thai context.[1] Over time I had accumulated a growing number of questions through my own work-setting observations and experiences. Part of my search for answers was to look at the literature on Thai culture and leadership. What I discovered was that while there are substantial materials in both of these areas many of my particular questions remained unanswered or unexamined. My reading also made me aware that my very specific questions about aspects of Thai society were part of much larger areas of debate and tension points within the world of research about Thai culture and society. This chapter explores a series of issues that relate to the broader world of research on Thai culture and society and to the study of Thai leadership as well. At the end of each section I briefly summarize

[1] It is now a recognized oversimplification and weakness in many notions of 'culture' to assume that people 'do things because of their culture'. It is quite obvious that people do not automatically reproduce the ideals and values of their social setting in their behaviour. By my use of the idea of a cultural account of leadership I mean two things. The first is that it is an account that is sensitive to the dynamics of culture in the practise of leading, and second my understanding of culture is such that it allows for both reproduction and continuity as well as change, variation, and alternate views. Culture has proved to be a notoriously difficult concept to pin down, witness Kroeber and Kluckhohn's review four decades ago that listed 164 definitions in seven major groupings with eleven subcategories just for the English language (1963). Tylor's catch-all definition, 'that complex whole' (Butler & Martorella, 1979: 37) is a kind of catch-all that includes everything that is not inherited biologically. The challenge of recent years has been to come up with a definition with some boundaries that at the same time avoids the problems of reification, essentialism, and cultural determinism on one hand and extreme relativism and deconstructionism on the other. My conception of culture used in this study is influenced by Barth who proposes that rather than seeing culture as a thing in itself, the notion of idealist culture should be seen as one among many elements in the larger class of human action (2002:35). Thus the view of culture I am espousing draws together idealist notions of culture (as values, meanings, symbols, and ideas) and social structure (concerning social organizations, family, clan, legal systems, polity, and so on) so as to retain the unity between the social and cultural aspects of all human actions (Barth, 2002:34). Such a view roots human action in its socially embedded context and allows for both variation and consistency.

points that these issues raise for a study of leadership in Thai social settings. Exploring these issues sets this study in the larger framework of Thai studies and also makes explicit the problematics that drive it.

Issues from the Study of Thailand

While this is a study of Thai leadership in a community of urban poor in Bangkok, the broader context is Thailand. Thailand lies in the heart of peninsular Southeast Asia, covering approximately 514,000 square kilometres (somewhat smaller than Texas and about the size of France) and has an estimated population of 64,631,595 people (CIA World Factbook, 2006).[2] The population is roughly 75 per cent ethnic Thai[3] divided into four regional dialects (central Thai, taught in the public school system, northern, northeastern, and southern), 14 per cent Chinese, and 11 per cent comprised of Malay, Khmer, and a number of tribal groups that are referred to as hill people (*chao khao*) by the Thai. Early Tai settlements were centred on cities (*muang*) with villages nearby, and by the thirteenth century rulers (*jao*) of these *muang* began to expand and link *muang* into confederations that became distinct political zones (Baker & Pasuk, 2005:5-8). There were several of these federations of city-states but it is from Sukhothai that the Thai people of today trace the founding of their nation in 1238 AD. Buddhism came to the Chao Phraya river basin by the fifth century and underwent a renewal in the thirteenth century as Sri Lankan monks brought the Theravada tradition which began to be patronized by the rulers of the city-states (Baker & Pasuk, 2005:7-8). Today the country is around 95 per cent Buddhist and religion is a core part of Thai identity where to be Thai is to be Buddhist.[4]

Prior to World War II there was no organized research in or on Thailand, only the reports and observations of individuals (Ayal, 1978:x). Since the war there has been an explosion of Thai studies written both by foreign and Thai

---

[2] The last census was in 2000 and the population was 60,606,900 (Lahmeyer, 2002). Estimates for 2005 from the population statistics website was 68,422,000 (Lahmeyer, 2002). The CIA Factbook noted that the July 2006 estimate took into account excess mortality from HIV/AIDS

[3] The term Tai is used for Tai peoples in general who share a common linguistic and cultural identity and later differentiated into separate but related groups (Wyatt, 1984:1). 'Only over many centuries has a "Thai" culture, a civilization and identity, evolved as the product of interaction between Tai and indigenous and immigrant cultures' (1984:1). On the origins of the Tai and the movement of Tai peoples into what is now Thailand see Wyatt (1984:1-16), Baker and Pasuk (2005:1-10), and Terwiel (1991:11-12).

[4] Most numbers cited about religious adherents in Thailand list about 95 per cent Buddhist, somewhere around 4 per cent Muslim, somewhere less than 1 per cent Christian, a small Hindu community, and then various other religions. See http://www.cia.gov/cia/publications/factbook/geos/th.html#Issues and http://go.hrw.com /atlas-/norm_htm/thailand.htm for examples of these numbers.

scholars. Yet this now massive record presents challenges to those doing research there. Two issues in particular are relevant to this study. The first is that analyses of Thai life and culture are often contradictory in their conclusions and that Thai society itself appears full of contradictions (Slagter & Kerbo, 2000:x).[5] The tendency has been to respond in one of two ways to the dichotomies proposed: to see one as real or to see the dualities as givens, rooted in Thai culture (Anderson, 1978:232). Both of these responses have contributed to the reification of Thai culture, lending a kind of timelessness to key concepts.[6] Once concepts gain axiomatic status they are no longer questioned; variation and alternatives become either noise in the data or are written off to Thai uniqueness.

A second issue concerns the way that official viewpoints represent elite interests, and how both Thai and foreign scholars have based their ideas of Thai culture on these elitist conceptions. The standard version of Thai history commonly traces the origins of the current nation-state to the founding of the Sukhothai kingdom (1238-1488) in the northern part of central Thailand, followed by the rise of the Kingdom of Ayuthaya (1351-1767) and then after its destruction by the Burmese, the re-establishment by Taksin in Thonburi (1768-1782). In 1782 the capital was moved from the west side of the river to the east side inaugurating the Rattanakosin era and the Chakri dynasty that continues to the present. The 1855 Bowring treaty removed restrictions on trade and thus undercut both the sovereignty and economic monopolies of the Siamese kings resulting in an economic colonization rather than a political one (see Siffin's comment 1966:48, and Anderson, 1978:209). The treaty restructured the country's socio-economic system as they moved into the world economy (Brummelhuis & Kemp, 1984:11) and initiated a process that transformed Siam into a modern nation-state (Keyes, 1987:44). The conventional interpretation of the response of the Siamese kings to their contact with a world dominated by Western powers contains the ideas that Thailand by virtue of its non-colonization is unique, that it was able to avoid colonization due to its stable and flexible leaders, and that the Chakri kings played the role of modernizing national leaders (Anderson, 1978:198). In 1932 a military coup led by men who had been educated at the same institutions inside of and outside of Thailand brought an end to the absolute monarchy. The first permanent constitution was

---

[5] Cohen notes that contrasting conceptions of Thai society have been proposed (1991:11). Anderson, writing in 1978, notes the varying contradictory motifs that have been proposed for understanding Thai society: loose structure/rigid bureaucratic hierarchy, Buddhist activism/decline of the Sangha, dynamic rule/unchanging society, stability/instability, conservatism/decay (1978:231).

[6] See Anderson for examples of this tendency to reify Thai culture. He cites the example of the entourage model of Hanks that has been taken as a 'timeless reality' and 'uniquely Thai' rather than as a model (1978:216-17). In a similar note he argues that the axiomatic modernizing-monarchs = patriotic-national-heroes view has made it 'easy to assume that late Jakri "high culture" represented Thai national culture' (1978:227).

promulgated on 10 December 1932 with the military maintaining significant influence in the governance of the country.[7] In the years 1932-2006 there have been 31 different prime ministers, with the military dominating until the early 1990s, and 16 constitutions. The latest constitution, drafted in 1997, was the first to be written with input from a nationwide public consultation process (TPRD, 2000:40).

However the official and conventional account masks a number of other factors. This official version of history made up of a single tradition and a single unified nation has been consciously constructed since the reign of King Chulalongkorn (1868-1910) and represents 'the attempt to impose a dominant national ideology on the populace' (Keyes, 1987:201). Turton points out that the idea of a single historical legacy inherited by all Thais is not only inaccurate but ideological and that the ruling class has maintained its position and the apparent consent of the people by ideological and violently coercive forms (1984:22; see also Cohen, 1991:12).[8] Anderson sees the reforming policies of Ramas IV-VI not as the work of modernizing nationalist kings, but rather following on a small scale the patterns of European absolutism (1978:224-25). In this light, the coup of 1932 was not a decisive break with absolutism but a 'partial, mystified revolt ... of absolutism's own engine, the functionalized bureaucracy' (1978:225).[9]

These alternate accounts challenge received and elitist viewpoints and serve as a reminder that key concepts need to be freshly interrogated and not assumed

[7] Writing in 1984 Wyatt says, 'much of the history of Thailand since 1932 revolves around the participation of the military, who seem to have had the last word on nearly every issue' (1984:243). Ockey, writing in 2004, notes that while in recent years scholars have proclaimed the death of the 'bureaucratic polity', both the military and the civil bureaucracy still retain considerable power (2004a:146).

[8] On the diversity of the Thai and early history of the Tai people see Wyatt (1984:1ff.). Reynolds asks the question if there is something hegemonic about Thai identity in Thai consciousness (2002:26). In the end he rejects subscribing to a view of false consciousness, but the thrust of his chapter shows the role of the Thai elite in the formation of identity that exists today.

[9] Anderson questions the accepted view of the relationship between the monarchy and the modern Siamese nation, suggesting contradiction rather than 'harmonious lineal descent from one to the other' (1978:200). He argues that there has been a misinterpretation of the rationalizing and centralizing policies of Ramas IV-VI, reading the internal consolidation as identical with the development of the nation (1978:210). He sees in Thailand an example of 'official nationalism' defined as 'the willed merger of nation and dynastic empire' (Anderson, 1991:86) and 'an anticipatory strategy adopted by dominant groups which are threatened with marginalization or exclusion from an emerging nationally-imagined community' (1991:101). He argues that Siam had much more in common with the indirectly ruled principalities of Southeast Asia than it did with nationalist movements (1978:199-200), and that because it was the monarchy that constructed the centralizing colonial-style late nineteenth-century state, it actually inhibited the growth of true nationalist movements (1978:211).

to be unproblematic. They also show that a concept of culture is required that allows for a contested stability of meaning while avoiding essentialisms.

Issues from the Literature on Thai Cultural Values and Social Organization

Much has been written about Thai worldviews, values, behaviours, and interpretations of Thai society and its social organization.[10] While in a sense all cultural values impact the leader-follower relationship, this section focuses specifically on certain Thai values and aspects of social organization that are more critical to conceptions and practises of leadership and followership. In this section I examine notions of hierarchy, patron-client relations, and reciprocity and obligation.

Hierarchy and Patron-Client Relationships

The hierarchical structure of Thai interpersonal relations has been widely noted in the literature[11] and is a feature of critical importance to understanding leader-follower relationships. Cohen sees the notion of hierarchy as one of the fundamental cultural codes of Thai society (1991:42). Hierarchical social relations rooted in the *phuu yai-phuu noi*[12] distinction have clearly delineated roles in their idealized form. The superior is considered to be morally superior and should act in a manner that gains respect from inferiors. Calm, kind, generous, and protective behaviour is expected (Akin, 1975a:109). Age or

[10] See for example the numerous bibliographies on Thai studies which cover the classic works and give a sense of the depth and breadth of work on Thailand: AUA Language Center Library (1971), Aymot & Suthep (1965), Cornell Thailand Project (1967), Institute of Developing Economies (1972), Hart (1977), Keyes (1979b, 2006), Library of Congress (2006), Mason (1958), Nelson (2006), Sternstein (1973), Thrombley & Siffin (1972), Thrombley, Siffin, & Pensri (1967), Central Library of Chulalongkorn University (1960), Weber & Hofer (1974), Wyatt (1971).

[11] The pervasiveness of this principle in Thai socialization processes and throughout society is extensively documented. See for instance Kaufman (1978:49) and Akin (1975a:109). The emphasis on hierarchy finds expression in relationships that are 'characterized by relative superiority versus inferiority' (Mulder, 2000:85). For speculation on the origins of the hierarchical principle see discussion related to the Buddhist principle of merit (Akin, 1975a:103; Basham, 1989; Mulder, 2000:84-86; Thinapan, 1975:62), and Akin on the relationship of social structure and the environmental realities in the situation of abundant land and scarcity of manpower (1975a:94-5; 103-4).

[12] *Phuu yai* and *phuu noi* illustrate the hierarchical principle in social relations (Akin, 1975a:109). When *phuu yai* is used in contrast to a child it means a grown up, while in contexts where it is contrasted to *phuu noi* it takes on the idea of superior and *phuu noi* is the subordinate or inferior (1975a:108). Akin concludes that 'the *phuu yai-phuu noi* distinction pervaded the whole of Thai society' (1975a:109).

wealth alone do not guarantee respect, good Buddhist behaviour is necessary (Kaufman, 1960:32-3). While wealth puts one in the 'superior' position in a relationship, 'wealth without the proper behaviour results in contempt and malicious gossip, and receives only token respect ...' (Kaufman, 1960:36). Inferiors are to relate to superiors with politeness, compliance, and respect, and are not to discuss or argue matters with them (Thinapan, 1975:62). Their behaviour should be characterized by obedience, respect, not doing anything to displease the superior, and to avoid behaviour that would be appropriate with an equal or inferior (Akin, 1975a:108)

What complicates issues in the study of leadership in Thailand is the particular intellectual heritage in Thai studies that came to see hierarchy embodied in the specific form of patron-client relations[13] as the core of Thai social organization.[14] The consequence of this position is that all of leadership is subsumed under this rubric as well.[15] Such a view is problematic on several counts. The first is that by giving it universal relevance it loses all its analytical power. It becomes impossible to make distinctions between what is and is not patron-client (Arghiros, 2001:7; see also Kemp, 1982:156-7). Second, it obscures horizontal relations and differentiation, assuming beneficial relations between members of society and thus leaves no room for conflict between different strata in society (Arghiros, 2001:6). Finally, the breadth and scope of relationships between individuals in Thailand cannot fit the definition of

---

[13] Patron-client relationships, also referred to as clientship, 'refers to a dyadic relationship in which one party, the patron, is clearly superior to the other, the client; it is an instrumental friendship, in which striving for access to resources, whether natural or social, plays a vital part' (Akin, 1975a: 93). A concise definition in sociological terms comes from Wolf who sees patron-client ties as a type of instrumental friendship where access to resources both natural and social is central (1966:12) as opposed to emotional friendship, 'a relation between ego and alter in which each satisfies some emotional need in his opposite number' (1966:10). 'When instrumental friendship reaches a maximum point of imbalances so that one partner is clearly superior to the other in his capacity to grant goods and services, we approach the critical point where friendships give way to the patron-client tie' (1966:16).

[14] Arghiros traces this problem in part as a backlash to the early 'loose-structure' views of Thai society. In its place a similarly universal and exclusive model was proposed which conceptualized Thai society as 'a multitude of interlocking, asymmetrical, patron-client relationships' (2001:2). Terwiel sees three different responses to the applicability of patron-client relations to the study of Thai society: for some it is the basic organizing principle of all society; others see it as a key for understanding key aspects of Thai society; and finally there are those who are more cautious, seeing it as a help in understanding things Thai and having heuristic value (1984:20). In a historical analysis, Akin suggests this type of authority structure and stratification was the Thai response to the problem of scarce manpower (1975a:93-124).

[15] For examples of this see Henderson (1971:77), Hanks (1975:200 and 1962:1249), and Girling (1996:56).

patron-client relationships in its most abstract and comparative form (Kemp, 1982:151).[16]

I believe that making a clear distinction between the principle of hierarchy and patron-client relations is more analytically powerful than conflating the two, and that this distinction provides a better account for observed social life. Following Kemp, Arghiros, and Wolf, patron-client relations are dyadic, multifaceted, and asymmetrical, in an ongoing, personal, particularistic, and reciprocal relationship (Kemp, 1982:153; Arghiros, 2001:7; Wolf, 1966:16). By way of contrast, hierarchy is present in all Thai dyadic relations. It is helpful to think of dyadic relations on a continuum ranging from the very formal patron-client bond of the nineteenth century on one end and kinship relations on the other (Kemp, 1984:64-5).[17] Behaviour in hierarchical relations can be understood at one level as etiquettal role-play based on unwritten rules (Terwiel, 1984:23-28).[18] Finally, Arghiros makes what I consider to be a very important and helpful set of distinctions between true patron-client relations, and political patronage relations as asymmetrical relations of a specifically political kind. They are instrumental, short-term, and lack the personal component found in true patron-client relations. Politicians are adept at using the symbols and idioms of patron-client relations without entering into personal relations that require commitments on their part (Arghiros, 2001:37-8).

What are the issues that hierarchy and patron-client relations raise for this investigation of leadership in Lang Wat Pathum Wanaram (LWPW)? The first is to see if true patron-client relations do exist and if they are implicated in the leadership structure. At the same time I also need to be looking at horizontal relations and networks to see how they are involved in leadership. Do people in

---

[16] Kemp notes that it is difficult to justify the appropriation of patron-client or entourage terminology to describe long-term relations between individuals of different rank because these terms are generally much more restricted in their use to a more limited range of relationships and behaviours (1982:150). For more evidence in this regard see Millar (1971); Kemp's analysis of Moerman's (1969) work on village leaders and Akin (1975a) on *nai* and *phrai* relations (Kemp, 1982:147-154); Suntaree (1990:155); and Conner (1996:372-76, 401).

[17] Kemp sees these two poles as representing generalized reciprocity on the kinship side, where relations are not measured in terms of personal advantage, and giving is done without calculation of personal benefit, and negative reciprocity on the formal side, where 'an overlord attempts to wring the maximum service possible out of client freeman for the minimum return and the client does likewise in terms of the services offered by the *nai*' (1982:155). On this continuum, patron-client relations lie to the middle between the extremes of the poles because they are personalized and truly reciprocal (1982:155).

[18] Bilmes captures a similar idea in a different terminology. He introduces the idea of relationship templates that specify 'the orientation that actors have toward each other, general expectations regarding the other's behaviour' and by which social behaviour is judged (1996:3). In his opinion, hierarchical relations in the village he studied were mostly a matter of manners and not authority (1996:9).

the slum see themselves in terms of hierarchy or do they see themselves involved in more horizontal relations? Can relations between the state and the community be captured in the patron-client rubric? Finally, is there evidence of political forms of patronage or the use of patronage idiom within the slum or in its relations with the outside world?

Interpersonal Relationships: Reciprocity, Gratitude, and Obligation

Suntaree Komin's work on value study highlights the importance of obligation in the Thai social system (1990). What she calls the grateful relationship orientation ranks second out of nine major value clusters in terms of their order of importance in the Thai cognitive system. In a more socially embedded setting Arghiros connects his discussion of the use of the idioms and symbols of patronage to the cultural assumptions that villagers bring to the relationship – assumptions deeply rooted in the norms of reciprocity, gratitude, and moral indebtedness (2001:8-9). He goes so far as to say that these things underpin 'almost all social relations' and that 'giving creates an obligation to reciprocate on behalf of the recipient. No act of giving in Thailand is performed without expectation of future return in some form or other, and the morality of reciprocal obligation is present in all relationships – with peers as with subordinates and superiors' (2001:9).

Grateful relationships are based in the concepts of indebted goodness (*bunkhun*) and gratitude (*katanyuu*). *Bunkhun* is rendered by helping, doing favours, expressing goodness and so on, and the proper response is gratitude (*katanayu*) expressed in two dimensions on the part of the recipient. The first is to *ruu bunkhun*, which means to know, acknowledge, be constantly conscious of and bear in one's heart the kindness done; the second is to *tawb thaen bunkhun*, which means reciprocating the kindness whenever there is a possibility (1990:139).[19] Suntaree points out that Thais are brought up to value the process of reciprocity in goodness done and the ever-readiness to reciprocate. In a *bunkhun* relationship grateful reciprocation should be expressed on a continuous basis; it is not affected by time or distance, it cannot be measured quantitatively in material terms, and there are degrees of *bunkhun* 'depending largely on the subjective perception of the obligated person, the degree of need, the amount of help, and the degree of concern of the person who renders help' (1990:139). Her conclusion is that 'being Grateful to *Bunkhun* constitutes the root of any deep, meaningful relationship and friendship' (1990:139).

---

[19] '*Bunkhun* ... is a psychological bond between someone who, out of sheer kindness and sincerity, renders another person the needed helps and favours, and the latter's remembering of the goodness done and his ever-readiness to reciprocate the kindness' (Suntaree, 1990:139).

In his continuum of hierarchical relations Kemp introduces the dimension of reciprocity as well. The kinship pole is characterized by general reciprocity[20] and the formal relations (power) pole is characterized by negative reciprocity (1982:155).[21] Titaya suggests that role interactions vary from personal to impersonal based on whether or not a *bunkhun*-based grateful relationship is present (1976). Suntaree posits that the Thai easily compartmentalize themselves into the 'I' ego self and the 'Me' social self (1985:183). Impersonal relations draw on the social self and are transactional, 'etiquettal', and contractual. Psychologically invested relationships are based in *bunkhun* that connect with the 'I' ego self (Suntaree, 1985:183; 1990:5). Such relationships draw upon the values of gratitude, obligation, honesty, sincerity, and responsibility; while transactional relationships tap the values of 'responsive to circumstances and opportunities', polite, caring, considerate, self-control, and tolerance (1985:183). These are the values that make up Phillips' 'social cosmetic' and are the mechanisms by which relationships proceed smoothly (1965).[22] If the continuum of relationships represents the horizontal axis, the type of relationship is represented on the vertical axis. As you get closer to the kinship-generalized reciprocity end, you go higher on the relationship scale, with a stronger bond of interpersonal relations; conversely, the closer you get to the pole of power and negative reciprocity, the lower on the relationship scale you are, and relational bonds are very weak.

The issue in this study will be to see to what extent grateful relationships are important to leader-follower relations. Are followers in the community in some sense obligated to leaders, and if so how is that obligation formed? On the other hand if grateful relations are not observed as the basis for the leader-follower relationship, what is the motivation for followers to comply and cooperate with leaders? As I noted in the section above, horizontal relations have been obscured by the focus on patron-client as the basis of the social system. The question needs to be asked if there are relations that lie outside of the reciprocity-obligation nexus, and if such relations do exist, how do they affect issues of cooperation and compliance?

Issues from the Literature on Thai Leadership

In my view the most compelling case for additional investigation with a fresh approach on the subject of Thai leadership can be found right in the literature on that subject itself. While there is a fair amount of research on rural

[20] Generalized reciprocity is where relations are not measured in terms of personal advantage. Giving is done without the calculation of personal benefit.

[21] Negative reciprocity is where both sides attempt to maximize their benefits at the expense of the other.

[22] 'Smooth interpersonal relationships' ranked third overall in Komin's nine value clusters.

leadership and formal leadership studies, there remain large gaps and silences in the knowledge base. In this section I highlight the areas that remain as unexamined points in the literature and raise key questions that will be addressed by the approach I take in this study.

Rural Leadership

While the Thai monarchs were, theoretically, absolute rulers, in practise there were a variety of leadership patterns, ranging from the monarch in the centre to the villages on the periphery (Ockey, 2004b:3). The more remote the town or village, the less control was exercised by the nobility and the centre; it was at the village level that patterns of leadership were most different from the absolutism of the monarch (2004b:4). The two primary types of leaders were the village headmen (*phuu yai baan*) who were informally elected by the elders (*phuu yai*) and the bandit or *nakleng* types.[23] Turton documents three historical forms of unofficial leadership that were capable of influencing and mobilizing others. Such leaders tended to arise under the conditions of either absent or weak state power or where state power was being reasserted and was being opposed (1991:170-1). He divides them into three classes: informal ad hoc types of pioneer leaders who were often the founders of communities, outlaws such as bandits and robbers, and religious virtuosi, particularly millenarian leaders that can be subdivided into those with extraordinary power or exceptional merit (1991:171).

Traditionally village headmen came from among the leaders in the village communities themselves. However reforms during the reign of King Chulalongkorn (1869-1910) brought the state to the village and the new government administrative units did not necessarily coincide with local natural community structure of the village (Keyes, 1979a:225-27). This created a distinction between 'elders' (*phuu yai*) and headmen (*phuu yai baan*) based in two major types of sanction for authority at the village level. Elders are completely a part of the village social structure, sanctioned by peasant custom, and are not part of that which links the village to the nation.[24] Village headmen

---

[23] I discuss *nakleng* in more detail in Chapter 3. *Nakleng* has several nuances, but a general translation of bully or ruffian provides a sense of its meaning. Ockey notes that sometimes the elders and *nakleng* were merged into the same person, but most of the time the *nakleng* was a young tough (2004b:4-5).

[24] See Keyes (1979a:221 footnote 5) for an extensive bibliography of sources about anthropological studies of villages that touch on the role of elders. The work of elders includes management of community affairs such as maintaining important village structures like the temple or school, acting to solicit funds for needed projects, mediating in disputes, and in some places organizing home guard groups (Keyes, 1979a:221-22). 'Elders' are not really the most elderly, they are usually between age 35-55, while those who are truly old, though widely respected, are involved in more routine and religious affairs (1979a:222).

are sanctioned through national sources, whether the bureaucracy or through knowledge of the national marketing system (1979a:219). Yatsushiro observed this dual authority structure where the village headman is the centre of the official authority in the village representing the state, while the 'elders' are the recognized leaders who are consulted individually or as a group about important village affairs and who play an active role in solving community problems (1966:59,76).

I looked at a number of studies on rural leadership in relation to the kinds of factors that make a person potentially influential in the community.[25] Taken as a whole they provide a list of various factors that can be roughly divided into external qualities (such as education or wealth), personal qualities (such as honesty), and attributions made by others (such as being respected). These descriptive studies are helpful, but they lack a theoretical base on which to integrate the various factors that may be necessary but not sufficient for leadership emergence and wielding interpersonal influence. What is needed is a way to see how these traits, factors, qualities, and attributions are related and if there are important configurations that emerge. A second issue is that while describing cultural dimensions, they do not go beyond this point and give insight into how respect and acceptability develop and operate.

Formal Leadership Studies

The strengths and weaknesses of the literature on rural leadership and formal leadership studies dealing with educated subjects in the professional world are precisely opposite of each other. The rural material is descriptive and provides insights into how local culture impacts leadership, but it lacks a theoretical base. The problem with the majority of formal leadership studies is that they are too tied to theory and do not connect in a meaningful way to cultural issues. In the quantitative material I examined either in full text or the abstract works on verifying theory generated in the West, the sample populations under study are highly educated in professional careers, and the results do little to advance our understanding about how Thai leadership is conducted outside of the conceptual frames employed in the studies. There is very little here that gives insight into social influence processes. Culture is either ignored or treated as a black box and given unwarranted explanatory power.

Verification studies like these have two major limitations. They can only measure the constructs the preset questions are designed to measure, and when those constructs have been generated elsewhere it casts doubt on how well they can capture what is happening in a different social setting. They also face the problem of circularity in causality. Wright notes that when data on behaviour or

[25] Duncan (1980:135-6); Keyes (1979a); Manoonate (1981:40-2); Pira (1983:116); Radom (1980:217); Samphan, Bricha, & Chuun (1990); Somchai (1971:11-2); Wilson (1962:136); Yatsushiro (1966:37).

characteristics of leaders is collected at the same time as data on the hypothesized effects on followers, it becomes impossible to establish the direction of causality (see also Steers, Porter, & Bigley, 1996:170; 1996:4).

Literature with an explicit focus on leadership that does not take a quantitative approach is quite limited (Blanc Szanton, 1982; Conner, 1996; Sarote Phornprapha, 1995). There is more work on Thai political leaders, but this tends to be a better source for patron-client relations and issues at a national level.[26] From my perspective the most interesting and beneficial material comes from writers who sought to understand leadership in its cultural context. Hallinger and Pornkasem studied three schools that had successfully implemented education reforms and maintained them over a seven year period (2000). Contrary to the normal assumption of authoritarian leadership, they were surprised to find that principals' participatory leadership was a critical key to the change process. By relinquishing some of the authority given to them through the high power distance that normally adheres between a principal and staff they were able to overcome cultural values observed to work against the process of educational reforms in the country (2000).

Sarote used Misumi's (1985) performance (P) and maintenance (M) orientations as the framework for organizing data collected using critical incident methodology to study leadership style preferences in the operative staff of a restaurant chain in Bangkok (1995). Sacrifice, in the sense of helping employees outside of the formal work relationship, teaching, and coaching were all considered positive. Use of power, mismanagement of emotions, a lack of self-assertiveness, and bias were all negative. Unfortunately Sarote did not expand on the very rich qualitative data, devoting only four pages to relating that material to Thai culture (1995:261, 265-7).

Suntaree has applied her work on Thai values to issues of leadership and organizations. She explains that while there may be many universal leader traits, some traits of the Thai would not appear in other cultural groups (1994:35). One of these traits she suggests is *baramii*, which allows the leader to command respect, love, loyalty and sacrifice from others. She defines *baramii* in this context as 'the inherent goodness that the person has acquired as a result of years of good, respectable, and warm interactions with people' (1994:35). Conner interviewed leaders in five contexts (civilian government, military/police, Buddhist clergy, business and local community leaders) to try and understand what makes a good leader (1996). He discovered three key Thai concepts that form the foundations for leadership: authority (*amnaat*), influence (*ittipon*), and personal power (*baramii*) (1996:213). Conner's narrative

[26] Chakrit, (1981); McCargo, (1993); Montri, (1984); Ockey, (1996, 2004b); Surin, (1993); Yos, (1989, 1990). Michael Nelson, Center for the Study of Thai Politics and Democracy, King Prajadhipok Institute, Nonthaburi, Thailand in cooperation with the University of Leeds has developed an online bibliography of Western language sources on Thai politics (Nelson, 2006).

leadership profiles show a factor common to all three leadership foundations: the ability to influence others (1996:347). He concluded that *baramii*, which forms its power base through interpersonal moral goodness, is the culturally preferred foundation for leadership, at least in the northeastern Thai context (1996:274-76).

This review of leadership literature suggests a two-pronged approach: studying under-examined areas, and expanding upon what is already known. This includes working on theory generation, a qualitative approach, and using local actor perspectives among a sample population that is not highly educated. The goal should include expanding understanding of mechanisms of interpersonal influence. Finally, there should be an attempt to relate component parts meaningfully so that there are configurations of traits, behaviours, and qualities rather than just descriptive lists.

Issues from the Literature on Thai Bureaucracy

I came to the literature on Thai bureaucracy after I had already begun the data collection in LWPW. My original purpose was just to be thorough in finding sources of information that might shed light on understanding Thai leaders. What I discovered was that much of the behaviour that characterized Thai bureaucrats resonated with my own work environment experiences and what I was seeing in my fieldwork. It began to dawn on me that what was manifested as bureaucratic behaviour had roots that extended deep into the Thai social system.

Around this same time I was also undergoing a change in my thinking with regard to the conception of leadership that was to guide the study. During the data collection in LWPW I learned two things that made me seek out new ways to understand leading as a process. The first was that, although there were formal positional leaders in the community, it became quite obvious that the influence mechanisms by which tasks were accomplished were spread over a much broader group. Secondly, the issue of legitimacy came into focus because those who did have positions did not have any power to compel compliance. I found that although community committee members have a formal position they have no authority; the only way that they can secure cooperation or compliance is if the community members see them as having some level of legitimacy. Thus the issues of legitimacy and voluntary compliance strike at the heart of the process of leadership in the slum.

On the basis of these insights I broadened my definition of leadership to embrace the entire process whereby a group accomplishes a task through all the forms of interpersonal influence operating within that group. [27] I also found that

---

[27] Thus far I have used the term 'leadership' in an uncritical and casual fashion. The reality is that leadership is a highly contested concept. Leadership was once thought to be a relatively simple concept, but now is known to be incredibly complex. This

a perspective that fit well with my broad view of leadership as a process within a group was Weber's work on corporate groups, imperative coordination, and the issues of legitimacy and authority. For Weber, the distinguishing mark of a corporate group was the differentiation of roles in terms of authority (Parsons, 1947:56). Weber's work hits right at the critical issue when considering leadership as a process of interpersonal influence – legitimacy. Weber points out that systems of authority in groups always attempt 'to establish and to cultivate the belief in its "legitimacy"' (1947:325) and that 'a criterion of every true relation of imperative control... is a certain minimum of voluntary submission' (1947:324).

What produces that certain minimum of voluntary submission is a sense of the legitimacy of those wielding authority. Weber developed three pure or ideal types of legitimate authority: rational-legal, traditional, and charismatic.[28] These provided me with a tool for analysing what I was observing in LWPW in terms of the basis for compliance and cooperation. It also gave me a filter for looking at the Thai bureaucracy not just as a place to find random insights about leading, but in order to understand the type of legitimacy that undergirds the Thai bureaucratic system.

Weber's insight is that different forms of legitimacy produce different types of administrative staff to execute that authority (Weber, 1947:324-5), thus

---

complexity becomes quite clear when trying to define it. Bass and Stodgill's rough classification scheme identifies 12 different ways in which leadership has been conceived (1990:11-19). Leadership has been seen as a focus on group processes with the leader in the centre; as personality; as the art of inducing compliance; as influence to obtain goals; as an act of behaviour; as behaviour that results in others acting or responding in a shared direction; as a form of persuasion; as a power relation; as an instrument of goal achievement; as an emerging effect of interaction, which sees the leader as the effect and not the cause; as a differentiated role; as the initiation of structure; and combinations of all of these. The elements that are generally included in a definition are leaders and followers, group phenomena, interaction of two or more persons, intentional processes of influence by the leaders over the followers, and goal attainment (Bryman, 1992:1-2; Elliston, 1992:38; Hackman & Johnson, 2000:11-12; Northhouse, 2001:3). The problem with such definitions are that they assume the presence of leaders and followers and assume that formal position holders have an effect on those under their authority. The issues I have highlighted here have practical consequences for the study of leadership. The conflation of leaders with formal position holders means that much of the actual influence in a social setting can be missed. It also means that the leadership literature is weak in the area of how cooperation is rendered in situations where there is no positional power. My broadening of the notion of leadership to see it as a process diffused through a group or subgroups, alters the traditional sense of leaders and followers and puts the focus on the various interpersonal relationships where influence is occurring. Although I will continue to use the term 'leadership' because of its heuristic value in pointing to influence relations, it must be remembered that I am using the term in a very qualified and constrained sense as fluid influence relations that are part of the broader process of task accomplishment for the group.

[28] Weber (1947:328, 341).

traditional, rational-legal, and charismatic authority all have different forms of administration. As I began to work through the literature I found that although the type of legitimacy given to the ruling elite in Thailand has changed over time it has been the norm to use the term 'bureaucracy' to describe the administrative system from the Ayuthayan era to the present. It thus appears that the notion of bureaucracy as articulated by Weber[29] has been read back into history when describing the administrative reform of Trailok in the 1450s.[30] Descriptions of the administration of the Ayuthayan era show it to be patrimonial domination in the Weberian sense (see Weber, 1978:1010-15); the administrative staff was clearly not committed to an impersonal purpose or abstract norms but was directly the servant of the king (*kha ratchakan*). Siffin points out that the system developed by Trailok was both functional and social; he calls it a socio-bureaucratic organization that fused officialdom and society in an 'elaborate hierarchical plan' (1966:18-19).

The uncritical use of bureaucracy to apply to all forms and eras of Thai administration is problematic for two reasons. First, the misapplication of the Weberian concept of bureaucracy to describe Thai administration forms from Trailok to the present implies a continuity both in the forms of legitimacy and its associated administrative staff that is at odds with the empirical data.[31] Since the end of the absolute monarchy in 1932 the state has forged a legitimacy that in Weberian terms includes both traditional and legal elements, but as will be seen, not the rational. Turton observes that the state's monopoly on legitimacy has developed because of the close identification of the concepts of bureaucracy, the government, state, nation, monarchy, and religion (1984:21).[32] Weber's comment must be kept in mind here, that the basis of every system of authority and willingness to obey is a belief, and the composition of this belief

---

[29] The ideal type of a bureaucratic administrative staff is spelled out in detail in Weber (1947:333-36) and (1978:958-63). The claim to obedience is not to an individual but to an impersonal order (1947:330). Ideally, this type of administrative staff is productive, rational, and efficient (see Siffin, 1966:159).

[30] See for instance Chai-anan (1987b:15), Likhit (1973), Riggs (1966), Siffin (1966), and Jacobs (1971). In some instances caveats are made that this is not bureaucracy in the Weberian sense, but the tendency is to utilize the term broadly to refer to the type of administrative staff from the mid-1400s on.

[31] Turton identifies two broad approaches to explaining the relative weight of ideological elements and the extent to which they have been transformed or superseded (Turton, 1984:25). One stresses continuity while the other sees discontinuities, which he feels is the more convincing (1984:25). Turton warns that we should be wary of views that show Thai ideology and the traditional state in static or monolithic form (1984:28). My argument here is that at each nodal point there is a change in the way that legitimacy is conceived and this also impacts the formation of the administrative staff.

[32] See Pasuk and Sungsidh for a brief overview of the change in conceptions of legitimacy from the absolute monarchy to the post-1932 military leadership to the Sarit's revitalization of absolutism where governmental authority flows from the king (1994:134).

is not simple (1947:382). For most Thai this belief is a complex amalgamation of traditional and legal elements where the monarch functions as the symbolic centre that holds everything together. The use of the term 'bureaucracy' to describe the administrative staff that grows from this complex of traditional and legal elements risks bringing in other connotations than allowed by Weber that are not appropriate in the Thai setting.

The second reason is that uncritical use (even with caveats and qualifiers) of the term 'bureaucracy' from the mid-1400s to the present, with its Weberian overtones, obscures the presence of *sakdina* culture[33] and values that still adhere in Thai officialdom. It would be inaccurate to posit a continuity of patrimonial and *sakdina* values and practises in the administrative staff from the Ayuthayan era to the present. However, the documented characteristics and practises of the present day civil service show both persistence and creative reassembling under new conditions of such values. The *nai-phrai* (master-commoner) relationship no longer exists, the sense of *kha raatchakaan* (originally servant of the king) is now 'civil servant', and administrative staff are not patrimonial retainers of the King but salaried employees; yet elements of personalism, paternalism, hierarchicalism, seeing one's position as a personal possession, factionalism, and top-down decision making are still normative behaviours in Thai administration today.[34] Siffin points out that rationality, efficiency, functional performance, and emphasis on productivity are not highly valued in the system (1966:162). Pasuk and Sungsidh relate the weak concept of public office to current values influenced by the *sakdina* era practise of not providing the nobility (*khun nang*) with a stipend (1994:133-35). They had to extract their income in a variety of ways from those under them. Among the people, the diversion of a portion of the taxes and fees was not considered problematic, but for those who exploited their position the term *kin muang* (eating the state) was used (1994:7). While theoretically the state exists to serve the interests of the people (Turton, 1984:29), conceptions that have

---

[33] During the Ayuthaya era the kingdom was organized on the basis of *sakdina*. Most likely the original meaning of *sakdina* was 'power over rice fields' (*sakdi*-power as resources or energy and *naa*-rice fields) (Akin, 1975a:102; Terwiel, 1984:22) and the system was used to assign a number of points ranging from 100,000 for the crown prince down to 5 for a slave (Akin, 1975a:102). The entire kingdom was divided and organized by these dignity points into units of *nai* (master), consisting of the princes and nobles, and *phrai* who were mostly peasants. This made up the basic units for political and military organization for the country (Akin, 1975a:95, 97). This formal structure began to change in response to outside economic factors in the reign of Rama III. Akin documents the rise of three types of informal clientship which eventually 'rendered *sakdina* increasingly invalid as a map of the actual social stratification and, moreover, undermined the system of offices established by the king' (Akin, 1975a:120-23; see also Terwiel, 1984:21-3, and Jacobs, 1971:42, on the changes to the formal system).

[34] For details on Thai administrative behaviour see Jacobs (1971:79-89), Girling (1981:147), Rubin (1979; 1980), Siffin (1966:150-68), Chai-anan (1987a; 1987b:91-3), Mosel (1959), and Demaine (1986:106-109).

their roots in traditional values of deference and seeing government officials as masters and patrons have 'permitted government officials to exploit power and position for private gain' (Pasuk & Sungsidh, 1994:7).

When looking at issues of legitimacy and administrative values and behaviour, there is evidence of dynamism and discontinuity with the past. Yet even when differences are pronounced it is not so much a new creation as a fresh configuration reassembled and reinterpreted from cultural resources both past and present. The issues of legitimacy and administrative values and practises are important to this study because they touch upon the basis for voluntary cooperation and the perception of and response to varying leadership patterns within the community. In my thinking it is a weakness of the formal leadership literature that it has neglected to interact with the political science literature and its clearly documented patterns of behaviour among officialdom to see how it may impact leading and following both inside and outside government contexts.

I have suggested that using 'bureaucracy' to refer to the Thai administrative system is misleading, at least for the purposes of this inquiry.[35] My concern is not that of the political scientist who is trying to describe the Thai polity; rather it is on perception and conduct when people are in contexts of leading/following. Because administrative behaviour and values play an important role in the analysis chapters to come I am going to suggest a terminology that highlights issues that are germane to this study. I am drawing upon two ideas that I found in Siffin's work: the idea of the administrative system (he uses the term bureaucracy) as a social system, or at least a major subsystem of Thai society (1966:160), and his use of the term *sakdi* (rank, authority, status, pronounced 'sak') to describe the four-component system that indicated a person's rank and status (*sakdi*) in the Ayuthayan system (1966:19).[36] I will use '*sakdi* administrative behaviour' (SAB) to refer to Thai administrative behaviour as documented above with a particular emphasis on the way that acquiring status and rank affects a change in the way the rank holders see others and how others see them. I have purposely not used the idea

[35] There are casual uses of the term bureaucracy as a synonym for administration that could be acceptable when talking about the Thai government in broad terms, and this is not the focus of my argument. What is problematic is when legitimacy and the values of the administrative staff are under consideration, the use of bureaucracy can distort rather than clarify the Thai setting. The same problems adhere whether using Jacobs' terminology of 'patrimonial-bureaucracy' (Jacobs, 1971:5) or even the Thai term *sakdina*. In both cases there is the risk of implying that patrimonialism or *sakdina* as systems are still in place or that their values have simply come straight across over time.

[36] The entire system of rank and status indicators (a person's *sakdi*) was composed of four parts: the *sakdina* dignity mark system, *yasa* which were honourific titles, *rajadinama* that began as names assigned by the King and later became the name of the incumbents in the official posts, and *tamnaeng* which were terms indicating the grade of rank of the particular office (Siffin, 1966:18).

of *sakdina* culture or patrimonialism in order to create a sense of space from these historical systems to show that SAB is a new configuration in changed historical circumstances with elements of continuity with the past.[37]

Summary

In this chapter I have explored a series of issues that set the study in the broader framework of Thai studies, and provide both the rationale for such a study and the basic problematics that drive the inquiry and its approach. The first concerned the study of Thai society and culture in general and the tendency to reify and essentialize concepts into society-wide applicability and ignore the richness and diversity that exists in Thai social life. I then looked at key areas that are relevant to leading in the Thai social context from research on Thai culture and social organization. This material indicates a need for investigation into whether or not interpersonal influence exists outside of the parameters of patron-client relations and the reciprocity/obligation nexus.

The third issue related to gaps in the literature on Thai leadership. On the whole, studies tend to fall into two major categories. The first are verification studies using theoretical frameworks generated in the West, while the second are studies of rural leadership that are primarily descriptive and lack an integrating theoretical base. Findings are often explained by reference to an aspect of 'Thai culture' as if it were an unchanging and homogeneous reality. Leadership studies have also tended to focus on the elite of Thai society. They target groups with higher levels of education and those in the increasingly globalized managerial world. Finally, I examined the literature on Thai bureaucracy where I argued that well documented administrative behaviour patterns need to be connected with issues of leading outside of government contexts. In order to highlight the nature of those behaviour patterns I have coined the term '*sakdi* administrative behaviour' to emphasize the way that having rank and status in Thai society brings a change in values and conduct.

These four areas highlight the issues that form the problematics around which I shaped the lines of inquiry of this study. I chose to examine social influence processes at the margins of Thai society, among the urban poor. An ethnographic approach was used to answer the focal questions in terms of interpretive understanding, broadly conceived as the search for understanding 'the processes by which…meanings are created, negotiated, sustained, and modified within a specific context of human action' (Schwandt, 1998:225). The

[37] I am aware that there are a number of objections that could be raised to this analysis and the coining of a new term here. In choosing a new term with a Thai concept at its base I am not playing the 'Thailand is unique' card and asserting that Thai society cannot be analysed comparatively. There is a need for global comparison, but my point here is that the use of Western sociological terms can obscure more than they clarify in the Thai context.

approach focuses on theory generation rather than verification and the type of theory developed is along the lines of what is known as factor theory that seeks to identify networks of relations and configurations or patterns (Kaplan & Manners, 1972:16). A more detailed description of my approach to this study is found in Appendix 1.

In the next chapter I set the backdrop of the study by examining slums in Bangkok and then overview Lang Wat Pathum Wanaram specifically. Chapters 4 through 6 each examine different aspects of the results of the inquiry, beginning with a culturally preferred model of leadership, then looking at how leadership is played out on the ground in the community, and finally how the community relates to the power of the state.

CHAPTER 3

Slums, State Response, and the Lang Wat Pathum Wanaram Community

This study was conducted in a slum community called Lang Wat Pathum Wanaram (LWPW) located in the Pathum Wan district of Bangkok, Thailand.

While this is a single community study, the slum does not exist as an isolate within the city. This chapter introduces the broader setting of this investigation, the community itself, and key issues both external and internal to the slum that form the backdrop to the analysis that follows in Chapters 4 to 6. The first section focuses on the physical and material context by looking at Bangkok and its slum communities while the second highlights the atmosphere in which slum life is lived in terms of state policy regarding slums, the problem of land tenure, and eviction. The final section introduces LWPW and highlights key issues within the community that shape leadership patterns there.

Bangkok and Its Slum Communities

Bangkok, the capital of Thailand, is a primate city that functions as the economic, administrative, transportation, and education centre of the country (Askew, 1994; Sopon, 2003:3). It remains the heart of the economic engine that saw the most rapid expansion in the world between 1984 and 1994 (Unger, 1998:1). It is also home to over a million people who live in slum communities, and holds large disparities in income between the top and bottom of society (Pasuk & Baker, 1998:285; Somsook, 2005b:2). From its founding in 1782 through the end of World War II the population grew slowly to about 600,000 people. Two decades of fast growth was followed by two decades of slower growth so that the current registered population in the 50 districts that comprise the city limits is just under 7 million (BMA, 2006).[1]

[1] Bangkok is governed by a mixture of central management (*ratchakaan borihaan suan klaang*), territorial management, and local administration formed in 1972 and called the Bangkok Metropolitan Administration (BMA) (BMA, 1999:35; Tawil, 1982:xxi). The greater urbanized area centred in Bangkok and its surroundings is much larger than the administrative boundary of the BMA itself. The term Greater Bangkok usually includes the two provinces of Nonthaburi and Samut Prakan, while the term Bangkok Metropolitan Region (BMR) refers to the city plus the five surrounding provinces of

Some of this growth was the movement of rural poor into the city in search of jobs in the rapidly expanding economy. They became a part of the process transforming the city from a canal-based settlement that was home to the ruling elite, civil servants, and Chinese merchants to a 'concrete-and-asphalt automobile city whose crowded population represented people from all regions of the country, and whose unskilled workers were drawn disproportionately from its poorest provinces' (Askew, 1994:88). Slum formation was directly related to the role of private landowners who sought means of using their property profitably. One pattern of development was the construction of main roads that brought commercial development in the form of shophouses and suburban residences along *soi*, which are subsidiary streets or lanes that branch off the main roads. Landowners profited in three major ways: selling their land for development, building shophouses, or keeping land in tact, building cheap wooden houses on it, and renting them to people moving in from the provinces. This latter approach to profiting from land resulted in the formation of communities of the poor who were seeking inexpensive housing. In other cases it became more profitable for owners both private and public to rent out their land to the poor rather than do agriculture (Sopon, 1998:424-5). A third pattern was the movement of wealthier residents out of the declining *bang*, *baan*, and *trok* residential environments. When they left, they built more housing and converted rooms into small cubicles for rent (Askew, 1994:102).

The changes to the city also brought about changes in the conception of what constitutes proper housing and urban development. Johnson notes that there were some early efforts at welfare housing by the Thai government in the 1940s, but it was not until the late 1950s that the process of defining slum and squatter housing as a social problem began (1979:77; see also Sopon, 1998:442).[2] A turning point was the study published in 1960 by the architectural firm Litchfield, Whiting, Browne, and associates, who were asked by the Thai government to help develop the first city plan for Bangkok (BMA, 1999:141; CDO, 1996:1). They reported that 740,000 (46 per cent) of the 1.6 million people in the city lived in areas described as deteriorated housing (*laeng suam som*) that was in need of being rebuilt (CDO, 1996:1; Sopon, 1992:11). The Sarit government responded to the report by passing a piece of legislation called the Slum Clearance Act of 1960 (CDO, 1996:1; MOB, 1965:47; 1969:69).

Nonthaburi, Samut Brakan, Pathum Thani, Samut Sakhon, and Nakhon Pathom. When I refer to Bangkok I am using it in the narrow sense of the actual city limits administrated by the BMA and not in the broader sense of the BMR.

[2] Sopon notes, 'Prior to World War II, there was no such thing as a slum problem. The clustering of the ordinary people in makeshift thatch-roof dwellings was not considered a problem to the city. Although from time to time some of them were evicted or removed to pave the way for the construction of public infrastructure or commercial development, it was not a big deal' (1992:11).

These events and the sequence here are noteworthy for two reasons. First, it is part of a pattern where foreign gaze stimulates an elite response but does not substantially change elite values.[3] Second, it illustrates the ambiguity of the concept of 'slum' (Akimoto, 1998:9)[4] and how profoundly political slum definition is, with deep implications for both policy and practise. The 'discovery' of slums in Bangkok unleashed four decades of state response[5] that saw a continual increase of administrative structure designed to work with slums. It is a story of ad hoc policymaking, the development of a host of competing agencies, and the steady increase in bureaucratic layers dictated by elite decision makers.[6] Today the BMA has a Social Development Department and every district has its own Community Development Office.[7]

In this atmosphere terminology and counting have been far from straightforward. The initial word 'slum' was changed in 1981 by the National Housing Authority to 'densified community' (*chumchon ae at*) in order to relieve negative connotations (Nalini *et al.*, 1998:249; Sopon, 2003:14). In Thai the word *chumchon* generically means an assemblage of people and needs a qualifying term like *ae at* (dense, crowded) in order to clarify the reference, but it has now become a technical term used on its own to refer to slum

---

[3] I use the term 'elite' as a 'group of persons who in any society hold positions of eminence' (Travis, 1964:234). I use the term broadly, covering those who govern, the wealthy, and the highly respected. I use 'elite power' to speak of the elite who are capable of shaping decisions and policy whether inside of the formal government system or outside of it. In speaking of both the state and the elite I acknowledge that neither is monolithic; elements of the elite and reform-minded middle class have provided the leadership of the NGO movements that have done much to improve the conditions for the urban poor. I am using the ideas of state and elite power in a broad sense to paint a contrast between those who have power in the society and those who do not and to indicate the general overall trends in the relationship between the two.

[4] Akimoto cites the 1952 United Nations definition that emphasizes two elements, the physical and environmental conditions, and their impact on human life (1998:9). This definition notably leaves off any kind of economic indicators that would deal with poverty and focuses on the more tangible physical conditions of the housing. Slums can also be defined by governments in either a legal or an administrative fashion since the legality of the use of land is often at stake as with squatter settlements (Akimoto, 1998:11-12).

[5] My focus is on the state because LWPW has never had NGO involvement. For a brief history on the role of NGOs see Askew (2002:146-48; for a chronology of NGO involvement see the history of slum work in Nalini *et al.*, 1998:210-28).

[6] See the CDO publications (1996; 2002) and the BMA history (1999). Sopon has overviews of slum policy in his major works (1992; 1998; 2003).

[7] The other major state player in working with the urban poor is the National Housing Authority (NHA), which was founded in 1973 to provide housing for people of low and middle income and also to upgrade and demolish slums (NHA, 2006). At first all the power and responsibility for new housing and community improvements were placed under the NHA, but in 1975 this was transferred over to the BMA (CDO, 1996:7-8) under the oversight of the Division of Social Welfare, Bureau of Social Benefits.

communities. Both the BMA and NHA adopted a definition for a *chumchon ae at* (densified community, slum) that essentially incorporates the UN emphasis on the physical conditions of housing and its consequences for human life, specifying the minimum number of dwellings as 15 units per rai (CDO, 1996:14; n.d.:1).[8] Then the BMA changed and decided to bring five types of communities under their oversight and call them *chumchon*, each with a qualifying term.[9]

So how many slum communities are there in Bangkok? It depends on who is counting and why, the methodology used to count, and the borders counted within. One number that has a good level of agreement is from a 1990 BMA survey that found 981 slums with a population of nearly 947,000, which is 16.12 per cent of the population (CDO, 2002:44; Sopon, 1998:429).[10] At this point the BMA was focusing only on 'densified communities' and not the broader five-fold categorization. Starting in 1994 they began surveying based on their five categories and by 2002 had the following data for the three slum categories, representing communities registered with the BMA, which is a different figure than counting those that actually exist (CDO, 2002:44-9).

Table 1 Total number of slum communities in Bangkok

Year	Congested communities	Urban communities	Suburban villages	Total number
1994	511	264	401	1,176
1999	671	261	218	1,150
2001	796	168	327	1,291
2002	778	177	345	1,300

[8] 1 rai is equal to 166 square metres or 2.53 of an acre.

[9] Only three of these types are communities of urban poor: *chumchon ae at* (congested communities) are 15 units per rai, and *chumchon chaan muang* (suburban villages) and *chumchon muang* (urban communities) have less than 15 units per rai and are defined by their location on the edge or in the middle of the city (CDO, n.d; see Sopon, 2003:14-15 for discussion of types of slums and communities). The other two types of *chumchon* are housing estates (*mubaan jat san*) and NHA flats (*kaeha*).

[10] Sopon indicates where this figure comes from. In 1985 he did the first comprehensive survey which used aerial photographs and found 1,020 slums which included two adjacent provinces, with 943 being in Bangkok city proper. NHA based a 1988 survey on his work and used more aerial photographs including even more adjacent areas and found 1,529 slums with 1,001 in Bangkok city proper. He notes, 'In 1990, the BMA verified the above NHA data and concentrated on slums located in its own administration. Finally, 981 slums were found in Bangkok' (1998:430).

Thus despite rapid economic growth, major changes in the physical structure of the city, and several decades of government and NGO development work, slums and poverty still persist in Bangkok.

Upgrading and Eviction: The Two Faces of the State

In the previous section I introduced Bangkok and its slum communities, looking at their formation, definition, and numbers. The activities of defining and counting are pre-eminently the domain of the elite and the state. It presupposes the power and right to create or deny existence. The poor themselves are noticeably absent in these processes. This results in the existence of two radically different 'worlds' – one inside the slum and the other outside, each relating to the slum in a different way. The urban poor 'use' the slum literally: for some it is the only home they have ever known; for others it ranges from a place of survival, an entry point to employment in the city, or a location to thrive economically in a way they could not in a rural setting or on the edges of the greater urbanized area. The elite objectify the slum; it is something to be defined, a social problem to be corrected, something to count and measure on a host of variables, or the focus of a career. As a result slum dwellers live out their lives in a context that is defined for them rather than by them. They are counted or not counted, their communities are improved or not improved, and their tenure is declared legal or not legal by the state and elite power without their ever being consulted.

My argument in this section is that 'being defined' by powerful others who attempt to dictate the nature of the relationship forms the atmosphere in which poor communities live out their everyday existence on the economic and social periphery of Thai society. In order to set the stage for the analysis that follows, I explore here two primary connection points between the worlds of the elite and state power and slum dwellers. I will show that in the practises of slum upgrading and the elimination of slums as physical space, the state manifests itself to the urban poor in two distinct faces. The experience of these faces in the form of benevolence and indifference/hostility shapes the environment in which leadership in slum communities operates.

The government reaction to the 1960 Litchfield, Whiting, Browne, and associates report I noted earlier was the beginning of slum policy. The initial response was to clear out slums, but fairly quickly official policy changed and there was an increasingly sophisticated conceptual development tied closely to changes in thinking in developed countries and international organizations (see Sopon, 1998:441). Although the idea of slum elimination and clearance is no longer in the forefront of official policy, slum eviction manifestly continues.[11]

---

[11] On the fact of eviction see Evers & Korff (2000:239), Somsook (2005c, 2005a:3); for a history of major evictions see Nalini (1998 :243-47); for examples of rough estimates on numbers of places or units evicted see Vichai (2005:234-36), Bello (1998:108).

Askew notes the paradox of 'emerging state initiatives for the provision of facilities, basic infrastructure and resettlement…set against an increasing trend towards slum eviction in the inner city' (2002:146).

The urban poor experience this duality as the two faces of the state – both benefactor and indifferent guardian/hostile enemy – as market driven interests push them off the land they live on. In suggesting a duality, I am not saying that one face hides the 'real face'. Benevolence, indifference, and hostility are all real stances and are a major part of the complex linkage that connects the elite and slum worlds. Development that embraces the whole person, popular participation, and community-based problem solving are not just rhetoric; they no doubt reflect the sentiments and inform the practise of numbers of individuals who work inside the bureaucratic arms focused on the urban poor.[12] In the following sections I will briefly review some of the evidence for my assertion of the two faces of the state with regard to the urban poor.

Upgrading, Policy, and the Realities of Implementation

From an upgrading perspective the work of the community development arm of the government has accomplished a great deal.[13] Registered slums have the potential for access to a number of state generated funds for development. The Community Development Office of each district has a budget for work in the slums, and between 1980 and the late 1990s local ministers of parliament had access to development funds which were often used for building day care centres and local health clinics (Askew, 2002:146). The Bangkok Council and District Councils also have budgets for development in slums. All of these funds have resulted in registered slums getting concrete walkways, concrete or asphalted public areas for exercise and community programmes, children's play areas and equipment, fire fighting equipment, tables and chairs, public address systems, and so forth.

Slum upgrading, the formation of the National Housing Authority (NHA) that has built low-cost housing units (Chuanpis, 2004), and innovations like the Community Organizations Development Institute (CODI) capitalized with 1.25 million baht in 1992 by the NHA, combined with overall economic growth and

---

[12] However, by the same token, there are also those for whom it is a job, and who look down on the poor and treat them as social inferiors. In my own work among the urban poor, I have observed both of these types of civil servants, and I am very sympathetic to the reasons why the poor so dislike dealing with the government bureaucracy. Both of these 'faces' are present in relations with the urban poor and it is an important part of the context and tone for community-state relations.

[13] As an example Sriwan and Janphen compared communities inside of BMA that had been developed with those that had not (1988). They found that developed communities had better family planning; had lower infant and child mortality rates; were better in the areas of sanitary, health, and environmental issues; and were better organized with more community participation.

the work of NGOs, are significant developments. They have helped a large proportion of slum dwellers in Bangkok to live in improving conditions with the potential or hope for access to resources that will benefit their families in the long term.

But as Esterick points out, Thailand 'encourages an essentialism of appearances or surfaces' so that 'the surface is taken for the real,' leaving what is real out of sight and unchallenged (2000:4). Somsook, who directs CODI, says, 'On official paper and official tongues, words like participation, decentralization, transparency and partnership have entered the mainstream' (CODI, 2005). She then goes on to paint a picture of state institutions lagging behind opportunities, failed top-down efforts, real power flowing in ways that are not democratic, and the poor being cut out of the process of decision making about how resources are used (CODI, 2005).

Elite Attitudes towards the Poor

The rhetoric of concern and participation along with actual improvements for slum dwellers have to be balanced realistically against elite and state practises on the whole. If eviction represents the most hostile position against the poor, there is also a large body of evidence that points to an indifference toward their fate as well. Economics offers one example. Thailand has experienced strong economic growth over the last four decades and particularly since the 1980s when a series of more stable democratic governments were in place to create conditions for economic growth.[14] In many ways conditions for the poor have improved dramatically since the 1960s (Slagter & Kerbo, 2000:lx). In one sense it could be argued that by pursuing policies that have led to rapid economic growth the state has shown its concern for the welfare of its poorer citizens.

However, the evidence points in another direction. Unger argues that Thailand's choice of wealth producing market economic policies was nothing more than the 'serendipitous match' between Thais' low propensity for spontaneous sociability and the much stronger Chinese endowment of 'social capital necessary to thrive in business despite the absence of an effective framework of laws and institutions supporting a capitalist economy' (1998:175, 57). If the economic strategy was accidental, where the money ended up was not. Writing in the late 1990s Pasuk and Baker observed that the economic boom was more for the rich than anyone. The average income of the top ten per cent tripled in the last 20 years while income for the bottom 30 per cent stayed the same, and this was mostly true for the remaining 60 per cent as well (1998:285). By 2000, Pasuk and Baker said that by some estimates, half of all

[14] More recent works that focus on the Thai economy include Pasuk (1998), Pasuk (2000), Pasuk (1996b), Pasuk (1996a), Dixon (1999), Girling (1996), Warr & Bahanupong (1996), and Warr (1993).

the income gains during the boom years went to just 10 per cent of the population (2000:236).

Another area is the lack of an explicit policy or strategy to address urban poverty. Writing in a 1987 study on the urban poor, a group of Thammasat academics pointed out that the government's free-enterprise approach to economic management was either an intentional or an unintentional plan to:

> help the poor through market mechanisms or trickle-down process rather than through direct welfare assistance....There is no explicit policy that is designed to deal with urban poverty, and the prospect of that policy is not bright unless government decides it is about time the problems of urban poverty be tackled directly (Mehdi, Vorawoot, & Orathai, 1987:6-19).

A decade later Sopon observed that the government had not set up any recognized mechanisms to deal with slums and that there are very few documents with substantive policy toward slums (1998:444). He concluded that, 'Generally speaking, Thailand has no substantive and continuing policy for slum development....It could be said, that in the past government action tended to be on a one-off basis with no long-term vision' (1998:444).

Elites also reveal their attitudes towards slums and the urban poor through words, policies, and practises. In material documenting the history of development work by state agencies among slums – at the same time holistic development, local problem solving, and participation are coming into vogue – there is another track that sees slums as something to be contained and eliminated (the source material here is BMA, 1999:204; CDO, 1996:17-19, 22, 23, 26). Only registered slums are counted; the others do not 'exist' and thus do not show up in statistical tables; the parameters for upgrading are quite narrow (they cannot be illegally squatting, live on land slated for public infrastructure development, be too large, or have problems that are not too difficult to solve); no new congested communities are to be allowed to start; existing communities should not expand; local officials are to coordinate with community committees in examining and watching over communities to guard against expansion, new technologies like aerial photography are to be used for this purpose; it is recommended that laws be adjusted to control the building of housing for low-income people to keep it away from business and other types of housing; and a rule was passed regarding the development of congested communities that had four main principles: prevention, control, removal, and development.

In the early years of slum development up to the early 1970s a comment summarizes well the feelings of the elite regarding slums: they are deficient points lacking in proper qualities that need to be eliminated for the good of the city (*jut bokphrong thii tong kajat*) (CDO, 1996:6). While the rhetoric has changed, the attitude has not. When Bangkok hosted the World Bank/International Monetary Fund Conference in September of 1991, two slums near the venue were unable to be evicted in time. Officials constructed new walls to hide them and later moved city buses in to block these walls from view when one of the communities protested by painting murals on them (Askew, 2002:139). In 2003 Thailand hosted the Asian Pacific Economic Cooperation (APEC) summit in Bangkok. A half-kilometre long, 20 metre wide banner to welcome the delegates was commissioned by the governor of Bangkok and placed in such a way as to cover the Thai Tien slum across from the Navy headquarters (Cimatu, 2003).

Eviction

The patterns of attitudes and actions on the part of the state and elite power that I have illustrated above form the framework for the critical issue of eviction. It is here, in the practise of, and more importantly, the tolerance of eviction by others, that the attitudinal configuration of the elite to the presence of the poor in their midst is manifested.[15] While acknowledging the complicated nature of urban land use, eviction, relocation, and BMA/NHA efforts to secure tenancy, my major point lies in a different arena. It concerns at a broader level the way in which these issues have been approached concerning the urban poor. Elite power on the whole sees slums as physical entities that are a problem to be resolved by removing them without consideration for the people who inhabit them. The objectification of the slum in the end objectifies its residents, and they merge into the physical architecture of what needs to be eliminated, not treated as people with valid interests of their own.

Slum dwellers always rate land security as the most important issue they face.[16] This is not simply an impression on their part. A 1988 NHA survey on

---

[15] Slum eviction and relocation is highly complex. There are examples of successful relocations (where only 30 per cent of original settlers move away from the new site) and less successful ones (70 per cent leave) (Vichai, Perera, & Watanabe, 2005:251); more often than not the relocation sites are too far from people's employment, new employment opportunities are scarce, public services are lacking and people are in greater debt trying to pay for their homes, and defaulting on payments is the rule (Bello, Cunningham, & Pho, 1998:109-110; Somsook, 2005b:2-3). For a more realistic portrayal of the problems encountered by those who have been relocated to the edges of the city see Jareonrat's interview with community leader Somchai from Phet Khlong Jan (2005). Askew concludes that the realities of slum life prove to be disappointing to idealists as things like NHA housing alternatives and resettlement sites 'quickly changed hands as the poor sold occupation rights to better-off Bangkokians' and land sharing efforts while revealing 'considerable organizational capacity on the part of local community committees ... also exposed divisions among residents, and the different interests of renters, owners and squatters' (2002:147).

[16] Slum dwellers rank their biggest problems as dwelling security, vocational security, improved income, and the physical environment (CDO, 1996:25). This same document also admits later on that land security is the biggest issue for slum dwellers and that it leads to other problems such as not making improvements, environmental problems, and social and health problems (CDO, 1996:73-4).

eviction showed that 27 to 28 per cent of slums were under eviction pressure and that 71.5 per cent of all slum dwellers expressed a fear of eviction (Somsook, 2005c; Sopon, 1998:432). In addition to this, the BMA passed a regulation in 1997 to have all squatter communities located on waterways (*khlong*) eventually evicted (Jareonrat, 2005). The fear of eviction is well founded and a powerful influence in the formation of identity, planning for the future, and development.

What is it that causes eviction? In many parts of the world it boils down to competition among diverse interests for land use in inner city areas where land is difficult to obtain with the result that 'developers (both public and private) put pressure on low-income people to vacate the economically attractive land they are occupying' (Vichai *et al.*, 2005:232). This is certainly the case in Bangkok where land policy has been driven by individual owners (Askew, 1994:103, see also Nalini *et al.*, 1998).[17] In the past it was often more profitable for owners to rent land in and on the edges of Bangkok rather than do agriculture. However, with economic growth there are many more profitable uses, and this fuels the problem of private owners evicting long standing rental communities (see Evers & Korff, 2000:216-217; Sopon, 1998:424-25). The forces of the market have also driven public landowners. Public agencies such as the military, Crown Property Bureau, and the railway authority are the biggest landowners in Bangkok (Evers & Korff, 2000:213), and their ability to garner large rents on long-term contracts often puts them at odds with communities of the poor who generate miniscule amounts of income for them.

What is the state role in all of this? Evers and Korff assert that the state is always involved in the conflicts relating to urban land use, even when not playing the role of 'evictor' (Evers & Korff, 2000:240). I see two stances that emerge in the way that the urban poor experience the role of the state in eviction. The first is indifference because the entire bureaucratic arm responsible for slum upgrading and development, the Community Development Office of the BMA, has no authority to deal with the issue of land tenancy, which is the greatest need of the poor. When private or public interests want to use land the poor occupy, there is no entity within the state structure with the power or authority to protect the interests of the poor. Thus one part of the state system is relegated to watching while private owners or other state agencies appropriate the land. This leads directly to the second stance, which is the face of hostility. This antagonism is complex and layered; it is more subtle and manipulative than openly brutal. I am drawing here on a conceptualization that Turton makes regarding a 'secondary complex of predatory interests'.[18] These

[17] The land status for Bangkok slums is about 61 per cent on private land, another 25 per cent on public land through renting or squatting, 14 per cent on both private and public land, with illegal squatting being only around 17 per cent (Sopon, 1998:430-31).

[18] Turton draws this term from the work of Thompson (1978) on the exercise of state political power in eighteenth-century England. These configurations and concentrations

'local power structures' both support and form predatory complexes which themselves constitute much of the state (1984:29). He illustrates the varieties of such local concentrations of power from the village to the national level where people both within and without the official structure utilize wealth to develop networks of relations that wield influence and control to secure their own advantage in both legal and illegal ways (1984:30-3).

While a part of the state, these predatory complexes do not constitute the entire state, and this enables elite power to do two things. They can stand behind the state's ideological claim to serve the interests of 'the people' (Turton, 1984:29), and at the same time veneer their activities with a layer of legitimacy because they represent official interests. Thus the state can appear concerned for its poorer citizens with its official policy of up-to-date development rhetoric and upgrading practises, while carrying on an unofficial policy of elimination through these secondary complexes of predatory interests. This paradoxical duality has historical roots in the practise of maintaining an official discourse that is manifestly at odds with behaviour.[19] The official fiction is maintained while everyone goes about their own business. Here lies my major point in this section: that the paradoxes of upgrading and elimination, benevolence and hostility, and initiative and indifference form the broader environment in which slum dwellers live and that they participate in reproducing.

Chumchon Lang Wat Pathum Wanaram

In the previous two sections I have provided a macro-context for LWPW as a community in Bangkok by examining slums in general and their relation to elite power and the state. Here I will focus on the micro-context by looking specifically at LWPW and in the process highlight issues internal to the slum that are of importance to the analysis chapters that follow.

---

of local power structures are constituted by 'the complex overlapping and interpenetration of economic, political and cultural agencies, relations, and interests, and the combination of formal and informal, official and non-official, public and "private", legal and illegal activity' (1984:30).

[19] Siffin notes the paradoxical nature of the theoretical absolute power of the monarchy, yet the existence of other forms of authority in the system and the reality that the administrative staff served their own interests and not that of the monarch (1966:25). Another example is the way in which the *kin muang* (eat the state) system was set up so that nobles made their living from those under them, while at the same time there are documented exhortations from the monarchs to not oppress the people. 'To order the officials to stop oppressing the people or to devote their full time to their work were, in a sense, absurd in a socio-bureaucratic system with *kin muang* as a central premise and with no real differentiation between being an official and living one's life' (1966:37). The disjunction between official policy and practise regarding slums fits this pattern.

A Walking Tour through LWPW

When you get off at the Siam Square sky train stop and move through the bustling crowds down to street level heading east, the newly opened Siam Paragon shopping complex rises on your left. As you continue walking the wall changes to a distinctive decorative style alerting you that sandwiched here between the shopping malls and traffic is a Buddhist temple. Turning left through a small archway you are suddenly in a different world, but it is not the quiet of a temple as you may have expected. Mobile vendor carts, pouring smoke from charcoal fires, line the narrow path where adults, children, bikes, motorcycles, and the occasional motorized three-wheeler filled with vegetables compete for right of way. For the curious, another couple hundred metres walk leaves behind the quiet temple on your right and the cheerful voices of children playing at an elementary school on your left and completes the transformation: you have entered the world of a Bangkok slum. Dwarfed by skyscrapers, high rise condominiums, shopping centres, high tech plazas, the Saen Saeb canal on its north border, a temple to the south, and a royal residence on its western edge, LWPW is home to around 2,500 people.[20] Standing in the middle of this dense wood and cement block housing, it is hard to believe that this place was once a playground for kings and 60 years ago was still mostly agricultural land on what was the eastern edge of the city.

A walk through the L-shaped community provides a good introduction to its major features. The first 400 metres from the entrance to the canal shows a pattern of residence and the kinds of occupations common to the whole community. This first stretch running north-south is known as Ton Pho,[21] though residents at the southwestern entrance refer to themselves as *naa wat* because they are next to the temple. The entire community encompasses a total of 44 rai (73 hectares or 111 acres), 40 of which are on Crown Property Bureau (CPB) land and four of which belong to the Pathum Wanaram Temple. Though the land is owned by others there is a vigorous informal housing market where 'housing rights' are a commodity that can be purchased. Thus some people 'own' their homes or 'own' rental housing while others pay rent. The larger wooden or cement block homes tend to be 'owned' and rental housing is of the

---

[20] The primary source for the demographic and statistical material is a photocopied 2002 publication of the Pathum Wan District Community Development Office (2002). The map of the community it contained was much different than the actual community itself. I was later told that the District Office bases its statistics on dwellings with house numbers. This means that approximately a third of the actual community is not represented on the map, and I assume also in the various descriptive statistics. The number 2,500 that I use here is based on adding a third to the numbers in the document.

[21] This area is named Ton Pho because of the Pho tree located on the western end of the community. Alternately spelled as Bo or Bodhi, the pipal tree, *ficus religiosa*, is sacred to Buddhists because it is the tree under which Guatama Buddha received enlightenment. A small spirit shrine (*saan phra phuum*) is located at the base of the tree.

small cubicle variety where an owner has subdivided a larger building into smaller rooms.

The diversity of occupations in slums is noted in the literature (see Askew, 2002:141-3 for a review) and is clearly visible in this first segment of LWPW. People work both outside the slum and inside the slum in formal sector wage-earning occupations and informal sector work.[22] Outside the slum, people work in occupations such as guards, clerks, cleaners, construction workers, hotel employees, transportation workers, recyclables collectors, general labourers (*rab jaang*), and mobile food vendors who locate at the entrances of the community or on Ratchadamri Road. Inside the slum are a wide variety jobs for generating income like selling food, dry goods and snack shops, hair salons, motorcycle repair places, sewing stands, owning rental housing, and two open-air snooker shops. A more recent innovation sweeping Bangkok's slums is the commercial installation of public washing machines and public water dispensers.

Photograph 2 View of LWPW and its surroundings
Satellite imagery courtesy of DigitalGlobe

[22] Askew defines 'informal sector' enterprises as 'economic enterprises established outside the legal framework of registration, involving few formal skills and qualifications, and primarily maintained by family labour' (2002:141-2).

Those who are the local 'monitors' receive a portion of the income from these machines.

If you turn right at the Pho tree and head east about 150 metres you move from Ton Pho to the geographic and social centre of LWPW. Three features dominate here: a building that functions as a health clinic, meeting place, guest reception area, and communication centre; in front of this, a large asphalted area where community events are held; and to the west, three large five-story buildings known as 'the Flats'.[23] The history of the Flats is directly related to the connection of this land to the monarchy. Early in the reign of Rama IV (1851-1868) this was agricultural land farmed by a group of Laos who were taken prisoner in a rebellion sometime prior to this (Chulalongkorn University, 1999:16). The King wanted to build a place outside the city where he could relax, and apparently the area here was noted for its lotus flowers. Chinese labourers were hired and two lotus pools and a resting place were completed in 1857. The resting place was named Pathum Wan (which means lotus forest, *baa bua luang*), but the locals called it Wang Sra Pathum (lotus pool palace),[24] and the lotus pools Sra Pathum. After its completion the current temple was built there (Chulalongkorn University, 1999:16-17). At some point after this Wang Petchabun was built and served as the home of one of the princes.[25] Royal land is now managed by the CPB, and according to residents, it owns much of the land in the surrounding area, including that upon which the large businesses and shopping malls surrounding them are built.

Shortly before World War II Rama I/Ploenchit Road was a sparsely populated area, and the easternmost limit of the city was just past Ratchadamri at Wireless road. The transition of this area into a slum community seems to have happened gradually. The two palaces and temple drew in workers/staff associated with them; land use changed and the original farming people moved out. From the sketchy accounts given to me by older people the area behind the temple was filled in so that by the 1960s it was quite dense; two-storey wood

---

[23] There are 159 flats each with one bedroom and one bathroom, 24 square metres in size. This area is also sometimes called 'The Centre' because the title for the little health clinic starts in Thai with *sun* (centre). When I am referring in general to these buildings I will use 'flats' but when I refer to it as residents do in the sense of a geographic segment of LWPW I will use 'Flats'.

[24] Wang Sra Pathum is a 17 acre site (to the west of LWPW up against the Saen Saeb canal) where the current King and Queen were married, where the late Princess mother resided, and which has been recently renovated to serve as the residence for HRH Princess Maha Chakri Sirindhorn (2Bangkok.com, 2006).

[25] Wang Petchabun was the home of Prince Juthathuj's family and apparently was later taken over by the Wang Petchabun company owned by the Wanglee family. This company had a lease with the Crown Property Bureau to develop the World Trade Centre (WTC) but went bankrupt. Central Pattana, owners of the Central Department store chain, have now taken over the project and renamed it Central World Plaza (2Bangkok.com, 2006). A high-rise office building and five star hotel are currently being added to the site.

houses and wood walkways ran from the canal to the temple (I-128, 257, 203) and covered the areas now known as Ton Pho and the Flats. Older people in the community remember their parents paying rent for the use of the land to an official from the CPB, but nobody that I have spoken with remembers how the rental arrangements actually came about. There was a mix of social statuses and careers in the area including people connected with Wang Petchabun, lower level civil servants, city bus fare collectors, vendors, teachers, some career soldiers, police, as well as people from the provinces who had begun to come into the city (I-257).[26]

Photograph 3 View of LWPW

Satellite imagery courtesy of DigitalGlobe

By 1973 there were rumours of eviction and in the early morning hours of 5 December, the King's birthday, a major fire burned out the area around where

[26] The people I met who have been in LWPW the longest are Y.N. who told me that her family came there and staked out places to build right after World War II. Her family controls a large amount of rental housing in the Rua Khiaw area. I also met a woman whose mother is 67 and was born and raised in LWPW. Her mother (the grandmother of the woman I met) is now deceased and apparently came into LWPW sometime before World War II.

the flats now stand.[27] Before the fire most people in the community were either born there or were long-term residents, but post-fire the area east of the flats, sparsely populated before, now filled in with people from the provinces looking for work (I-302). By 1977 the CPB had completed the three buildings of rental flats for those who had lost their homes in the fire, and a new era of immigration was in full swing. In the 1980s, during the construction of the World Trade Centre, a green corrugated metal fence was put up separating the eastern side of the community from the construction. Residents started calling this area Rua Khiaw (green fence) and the name stuck even though the fence was later replaced by a concrete wall. While there is now a mix of owners and renters throughout the entire community, even in the flats, this area is primarily occupied by renters who have come from other provinces, the majority from the Northeast. Housing here is even more dense than elsewhere, and there is a greater proportion of wood shacks with corrugated metal roofs. Most of this area does not have house registration numbers and thus is not counted in the official statistics or placed on the maps in the district publication on LWPW.

Photograph 4 The Flats

Satellite imagery courtesy of DigitalGlobe

[27] The 1973 fire is critical to the development of LWPW both physically and socially. In the next section I will look at this event in detail.

While the housing is contiguous, historically Ton Pho, the Flats, and Rua Khiaw have each developed in a different manner; and this has created distinctions and divisions that will be discussed in the next section. In 1985 LWPW registered with the Pathum Wan district, extending the government administrative apparatus into the community and bringing them into contact with local politicians.[28] Registration formalized a community committee with two year terms and connected them to development funds for physical improvements to the community. Becoming on official *chumchon* has created, at least for some of the Bangkok-born residents, the ideal of a single united community expressed in the term *samakhii* (unity, harmony, accord). Harmonious unity as a concept is made visible in the celebration of festivals. The planning and conducting of these *ngaan* (literally work, it can also be used in a celebratory sense) is seen as one of the major roles of the committee. There are numerous religious and secular events throughout the course of the year in Thailand, and over time five have become traditions that are now considered community-wide celebrations. The five festivals celebrated are: Civil New Year; Children's Day the second weekend in January; Thai New Year in April; the Queen's birthday, known as Mother's Day, 12 August; and the King's birthday, known as Father's Day on 5 December. These events all take place in the large open area in front of the flats and health clinic. It is not uncommon at a community celebration like Children's Day or the King's birthday to have the local MP, the Bangkok Council, and District Council representatives make brief visits to say a few words and often pass out some kind of gift on the occasion. Community development officials and people from the local health district also frequently are present at community functions.

Life in LWPW has a great deal in common with other slum communities in Bangkok. The dwellings are crowded (averaging 8.0 persons per unit in Bangkok slums versus 3.75 per unit in the rest of Thailand), privacy limited, housing dilapidated and deteriorated, and the layout haphazard (Sopon, 2003:9, 13-14). Residents typically have a smaller number of income earners per household than the non-poor and tend to be older, less mobile, and less educated; their earning capacity reflects the lower educational levels of the household heads (Mehdi *et al.*, 1987:1-2 to 1-3, 1-5, 4-5 to 4-6, 4-19). Most of Bangkok's slums have water and electricity, and in LWPW residents pay 20 baht per month for garbage pickup by the city.[29] The impression that one gets

---

[28] There are two major parts of the BMA: the governor's office is responsible for the management of the city while the Bangkok Metropolitan Council (one member per 100,000 of population) is the law-making body and planning arm for the city and serves as representatives of the populace (BMA, n.d.:4-5). Each District also has an elected council with a minimum of seven members who serve four-year terms. Bangkok is divided into 37 constituencies for House seats so Ministers of Parliament generally cover slightly more than one district (Nattaya, 2006).

[29] Garbage pickup deals do not mean LWPW is 'clean' in the same way that outside the slum is clean. While there are not piles of rotting garbage everywhere, the area around

in walking through LWPW is that it is a place of vitality and dynamism, not desperation. The basic amenities are present, food is plentiful, the prosperity of economic growth over the last four decades has trickled into the slum in the form of motorcycles, televisions, refrigerators, and the ubiquitous cell phone. So the question could be asked how poor are the people in LWPW?

It is tempting when first seeing the rundown quality of housing, the crowded conditions, more garbage on the ground than elsewhere in the city, and the ever present rats, to make the assumption that everyone in a slum is poor. This is not true,[30] and Askew notes that from the beginning 'slums have been diverse social formations marked by internal differentiation,' calling them 'spaces of accumulation and inequality' (2002:143). Poverty indexes and minimum wage figures can provide statistical views of poverty, but they are unable to portray

---

and under housing tends to collect plastic bags and other garbage and people by habit throw things on the ground rather than in a bin. Data from the National Statistical Office in 1994 showed the availability of basic community necessities in slums: 99 per cent have electricity, 97 per cent have water supply, 58 per cent have garbage disposal, 52 per cent have drainage, 69 per cent have concrete walkways, 71 per cent with community committees, 69 per cent with a fire brigade, 19 per cent with a day care centre, and 89 per cent with household registration (Sopon, 2003:15). However Daniere, citing a USAID report of 1992, says that around 20 per cent of Bangkok residents 'live in settlements that have inadequate waste and sanitation facilities, contaminated water, and erratic and unsafe supplies of electricity. Data on the Bangkok region, from both NSO and Setchell surveys, ... suggest that slum households have access to few of the amenities typically available in formal housing' (1999:528).

[30] The Thammasat research showed that some 11 per cent of urban households in the country were poor by the poverty line established in 1987, with those in the BMR being the least poor (Mehdi *et al.*, 1987). Working with data from 1993 Sopon has developed a rough continuum of poverty in Bangkok that has three categories: the real poor, the typical poor, and the general low-income group (1998:437-38; 2003:17-18). The real poor consist of those who cannot afford three meals per day by his calculations of per capita income and consist of nine per cent of the Bangkok population and 15.65 per cent of slum dwellers. This means that 371,170 of the real poor live outside of slums. The typical poor he figures at two wage earners at minimum wage with two dependents and shows that this covers 47.28 per cent of slum dwellers (427,800 people), but 20.28 per cent of Bangkok (1.2 million people). This shows that that some 700,000 typically poor people in the city do not live in slums. Sopon's third category of general low-income group is comprised of those who cannot afford the least expensive house on the open market, which covers 76.62 per cent of slum dwellers. I certainly agree with Sopon's analysis that not all slum dwellers are poor, but taking a more subjective view based on my personal experiences with urban poor, what looks good on paper as numbers is a different reality on the ground. Even where there are two working adults with typical informal sector or low end formal jobs, if they have children or any other family members they are responsible for, life can be very challenging. While there may be enough income to eat every day and pay the rent, if anything goes wrong outside of these very narrow parameters, they are in trouble. Illness, loss of job, problems with family outside the city necessitating expensive travel, equipment breakdowns, and so on, all conspire to bring economic pressure and force many people to turn to money lenders who typically charge 240 per cent interest per year.

the social complexity that makes physical want a reality for many urban poor (see Iliffe, 1987:2).[31] Absolute poverty in the slums has decreased, while relative poverty continues to increase as the gap between rich and poor grows (on income disparity see 1998:285; Pasuk & Baker, 2000:236).[32] The inequalities seen in LWPW are intimately connected with family circumstances and not simply monthly income. Here Iliffe's distinction between two types of want is helpful.[33]

There are many in the community who do not have to struggle for their daily existence because their circumstances are such that they are able to put money aside for other uses. For instance, I spoke with a man from Chaiyaphum who has a mobile vending cart selling what he calls 'Japanese crepes'. Twenty years ago he bought the rights to a piece of land from a person born in the slum for 9,000 baht and built his own place on it. He is able to average 10,000 baht a month or more from his food sales and has built a house in Chaiyaphum where his children live (I-341). But for many people with comparable incomes in food selling, construction work, or hair cutting, they find themselves in a struggle for survival and cannot put any money aside for emergencies. It is a combination of paying rent, having to feed more people, and sending money to other family members out of their income.

When people fall short, the informal street loans run at 240 per cent annual interest, which only intensifies their difficulties. The idioms of the struggle to survive emerge as you talk with people about their work and incomes: 'enough to get by day by day' (*phaw yuu ben wan wan*), 'need to be industrious and frugal' (*tawng kayan tawng brayat*), 'enough to take care of the family but certainly not rich' (*phaw liang khrawb khrua tae mai ruay rawk*), and 'looking

---

[31] Figures from 1988-2002 show a nationwide drop in those living under the poverty line from 32.6 per cent to 9.8 per cent, with Bangkok having only 2 per cent under the poverty line (NESDB, 2006:8, 10-13). Both poverty lines and minimum wages are varied throughout the different regions of the country. In 2002 a new poverty line for the nation was established changing from 922 to 1,163 baht per capita per month which changed the poverty incidence level to 14.38 per cent. Bangkok's poverty line changed from 1,021 to 1,703 baht per capita per month (US$ 25 to 42) (NESDB, 2006:10-13). Bello, writing in 1998, had sources that showed 3.4 per cent of Bangkok's population under the poverty line, but notes that experts urge caution in handling these figures (Bello *et al.*, 1998:108). He cites Somsook from CODI who calculates that with a minimum of 3,000 baht per month to pay for food and energy some 1.2 to 1.5 million people are in poverty in the city, which is 22 to 27 per cent. Current minimum wage in Bangkok is 184 baht per day (Start, 2006).

[32] Absolute poverty is measured against the minimum that is necessary to maintain a person's physical efficiency. Relative poverty is measured against the average living standards of a particular society (Iliffe, 1987:2, 4).

[33] One type of want is found among those who must struggle continuously to preserve themselves from physical want. The second is comprised of those who fail at the first level and fall into chronic physical want and thus become the very poor or destitute (Iliffe, 1987:2).

for it in the morning, eating it at night' (*haa chao kin kham*). For some the struggle is more intense than others; one family collects recyclables as their primary source of income, making anywhere from 50 to 100 baht per day 'according to the stars and luck' (*laew tae duang tae choak*) (I-342).[34]

What I have been illustrating thus far can be described as economic deprivation, which is only one of five different types of 'deprivation', defined as 'any and all of the ways that an individual or group may be, or feel disadvantaged in comparison either to other individuals or groups or to an internalized standard' (see Glock & Stark, 1965:246-9).[35] While there are clear differentials both in income and the status of some people in LWPW, on the whole there is a sense of collective identity as being poor (*khon jon*). Glock and Stark's concept of social deprivation comes closest to capturing the feeling that people have of being on the margins of society, relatively powerless, and lacking in resources that others have. The presence of consumer goods does little to ameliorate the experience of social deprivation that people have living in a slum. From my observations and conversations with people there were five areas in particular that were salient in residents' experience of slum life. I will look at four of them here and discuss the fifth in a later section.

---

[34] Iliffe's distinction between structural and conjunctural poverty is helpful here as well. Structural poverty is the long-term poverty of an individual due to personal or social circumstances. Conjunctural poverty is the temporary poverty into which ordinarily self-sufficient people may be thrown by crisis. Structural poverty varies in different settings where resources, particularly land, are plentiful and where it is scarce (1987:4). Those who are poor in LWPW are primarily struggling to keep themselves from physical want in a form of structural poverty. Those who fall into chronic want and form the truly destitute are sometimes found in established slums but also seek refuge under bridges or on the street. Askew observes that 'poverty in the contemporary Thai metropolis takes a range of forms, and arguably a focus on slums excludes the most desperate of the urban poor' (2002:140).

[35] Economic deprivation arises from the differential distribution of income and the limited access to necessities and luxuries of life. It can be judged on subjective or objective measures. Social deprivation is the propensity of societies to value some attributes of individuals or groups more highly than others. Awards like prestige, power, status, and opportunities are distributed in a differential fashion, with the highly regarded getting more of these awards. Organismic deprivation is when a person is disadvantaged relative to others through physical or mental deformity or a stigmatizing trait. Ethical deprivation is where there are value conflicts between the ideals of society and those of individuals or groups, when people see a discrepancy between the ideal and real. Finally, psychic deprivation is when people find themselves without a meaningful system of values by which to organize and interpret their lives (Glock & Stark, 1965:246-248).

Photograph 5 Overlooking Rua Khiaw

There is a pervasive sense that slum dwellers' relative poverty makes them vulnerable to being taken advantage of and exploited. It is the rich, the police, and the legal system that take advantage because 'justice is money', respect is given to those with money, and the poor cannot be 'seen'. Thus people in the slum try to avoid interactions with the police and the official world and mind their own business. One person said, 'if you have money, what is wrong can be turned into not wrong' (I-342). Another major problem area is drugs and, for those with children, the fear that their children may get involved. People seemed to be resigned to the presence of drug use and selling because it is impossible to really eliminate. Residents acknowledged that Thaksin's efforts at suppression improved the situation for a time, but police are either seen as 'not being serious' about it or too outnumbered to impact the problem. This is a source of stress to parents whose children are users and a fear for parents in general.

Photograph 6 A lane in Rua Khiaw

A third area of deprivation comes from their awareness of the irony that LWPW is literally surrounded by incredible wealth. Some eke out their lives on the edges of this economy; they sell food or work as guards or clerks, forced to practise 'industry and frugality' to survive while watching the conspicuous consumption of the middle and upper classes. The people I interacted with in LWPW seem to be very realistic about their lot in life. It is very common in their speech for them to refer to themselves as the collectivity '*rao khon jon*' (we the poor) when talking about the world outside the slum. They are aware that the playing field is not level, and are highly sceptical about those in political power and in the government administrative structure who make so many demands of them for so little in return. It is interesting to me that in all my interactions with urban poor in several different settings, I rarely hear karma invoked as a reason for their condition of poverty.[36] Finally, for others slum life is not a matter of income, but a lack of options and the ability to choose. Many who could afford a home elsewhere if they were a wage earner

---

[36] Basham revisited the merit and power interpretation where the powerful have karmatic sanction for their power, with the practical result being the notion that authority deserves the loyalty of the subordinate (1989:127). His interview data asking about belief in merit and power found that of his urban respondents, less than half expressed belief in their connection. The explanations were based in much more pragmatic grounds such as power coming via wealth, ability, or connections (1989:131).

are locked into living in LWPW because it is the location that provides them their job and income. If they bought a house outside the slum they would not have the income from their informal economic activities which depend on the density of customers that LWPW offers both outside and inside the community.

Exploring the Inner Workings of LWPW

A walking tour through LWPW shows many of the prominent features, but there is much that cannot be seen from the surface level viewpoint. It is the things that are not apparent to the eye of the casual observer that are of most interest for this study. I have noted above that the way state and elite power relate to slum communities forms an issue external to the slum, part of the broader environment. In this section I will raise a series of issues that are primarily internal to LWPW and form the context for how leadership processes operate in the community.

Forces that Divide and Unite

Askew notes in the literature the varying representations that have been used to describe slums in Bangkok: the ideologically driven assertive picture as conflicts intensify over land use, the grass-roots development discourse of cooperative and equally poor people joining together to improve their situation and the environment, slum dwellers as individualistic opportunists, and the 'community of the poor' as a face-to-face society with close interpersonal ties and emotional linkage to a local area, which is used to garner public support and oppose eviction (2002:140). Each view can find empirical support, yet each tends to obscure and oversimplify the complexities that are found on the ground in any particular slum.

The first issue I want to raise in my representation of LWPW is to problematize the notion of LWPW as a 'community'. I have used the term unproblematically thus far as a convenient translation for the Thai *chumchon*, but there are actually multiple understandings of 'community' as a sociological term and of *chumchon* as it is used by people in LWPW. Definitions of community tend to cluster around three concepts: being a collectivity; a particular geographic location; and notions of social interaction, structured relations, and social cohesion (Keyes, 1978:3; Moerman, 1969:548; Winthrop, 1991:40-43). LWPW fits the second concept, but as seen through the eyes of its residents, the first and third are highly contested ideas. Residents' views of LWPW as a *chumchon* hinge on where they came from, their own sense of permanency in the community (related to renting or owning a place), and where they physically reside in the community. There are both centripetal and centrifugal forces at work in LWPW that are important for understanding leadership processes there, and these forces that pull apart and draw them together are closely related to events set in motion by the fire of 1973.

The fire serves as a nodal point for LWPW in terms of its physical structure, the distribution of power and wealth, the makeup of the residents, and the meaning people make of *chumchon*. When I first started working in LWPW I assumed it was a single community. It was registered with the District as a *chumchon*, and it was a bounded locality filled with dense housing. I saw the three divisions of Ton Pho, the Flats, and Rua Khiaw as being convenient physical descriptors. What emerged over time however was much more complex than that. Apparently even before the fire there were fine-grained distinctions based on locality, and the fire in some sense both intensified and dissolved these distinctions. Four pieces of evidence led me to this conclusion. The first had to do with the different names of the community in the past, where two were connected to the Ton Pho area.[37] The second was an incidental remark by an informant, who grew up in the area where the flats are now located, that there were fights between people who lived in his area and Ton Pho when he was a child back in the 1960s (I-303).[38] Another was how contradictory responses about the presence or absence of informal community committees prior to registration made sense when viewed through the lens of identity based in locality. Thus K. in Ton Pho said there was an informal committee (he was on it), while D. and L.P. from the Flats repeatedly insisted there was no committee until registration. Locality facilitates or inhibits seeing what others do as valid. Finally, certain celebrations are known to have their origin in a locality, with the oldest tradition being that Ton Pho puts on the annual Civil New Year's celebration.

When the fire happened in 1973 the physically altered landscape helped sharpen territorial distinctions, create new ones, and in some ways fostered a greater sense of community for at least parts of the *chumchon*. There are several different versions of what happened with the fire, but the consensus among residents is that it was not an accident. Sometime prior to the fire,

---

[37] Over the years the community was known by several names: *Trok Lang Wat Pathum* (a *trok* is a small lane); *Trok Pho* or *Chumchon Ton Pho*, because of the large pipal tree at the west end of the community; and *Lang Talaat Nai Lert* (behind the Nai Lert Market), because it sits to the south of what was formerly a well-known market across the canal, where a department store now stands (I-302, I-304).

[38] Normally, I would have passed over this comment as being part of the normal fighting that children do. However, at approximately the same time I began the study in LWPW, as a part of my job I also began working with a series of five contiguous slum communities. What I discovered there was how sharply delineated community lines were drawn in people's minds. The communities have separate names and leadership structures, and a distance of just a few metres makes a huge difference in identity. The distinctions are not only carried by the children who are very wary about interacting with children from another group, but adults as well. Most long-term residents are familiar with other long-term residents across all five communities but they definitely 'belong' to a certain community. It was this experience that opened my eyes to see that the geographical proximity of houses all stacked next to each other is not necessarily mirrored by a sense of being a unified community.

rumours about a coming eviction were strong enough to lead some people to take action (I-302). Bathiwat, a soldier living in the centre area, announced that he was planning a trip to go ask the King for permission to be allowed to stay on the land because it was owned by the CPB. He told everyone that he was leaving at 6:00 AM on the morning of the King's birthday, 5 December, to go to the royal residence at Hua Hin in Prajuab Khirikhan province. Those who wanted to go along were invited to join him. However, somewhere before 5:00 AM the fire started (I-302). K. noted that there were rumours in advance that a fire was coming. He was working outside the community, and when he came in that night someone told him there would be a fire; he did not sleep well (I-296). Bathiwat and a few others did make the trip to Hua Hin that day and met with an official of the King. A representative was dispatched to the scene and the King ordered that the flats be built to house those who had lost their homes. Temporary shelters were set up in the burned area so people could live, and by 1977 the three buildings of flats were completed.

In the aftermath of the fire there were four significant developments. The fire sharpened the distinction between Ton Pho and the burned area in the centre by creating differentiated housing that was not present before. People in other parts of the community now see the Flats as the locus of the committee and as the administrative and celebratory centre. The 2002-2004 committee that I first worked with had 11 members, and only three were from Ton Pho. They felt under-represented and cut out of the decision-making process. There was clearly a Ton Pho-Flats split in this group, and the change to a new committee in 2004 was seen as a chance to change the balance of power by adding people from Ton Pho. The 2004-2005 committee is now dominated by Ton Pho with 16 of the 17 members being from there.

The fire also changed the demographics of the community by creating the opportunity to build rental housing. Prior to the fire the Rua Khiaw area had some old wooden housing that was not burned. During the transition time after the fire, people born in LWPW or long-term residents staked out ground to build new rental housing on. In general people indicate that it was after the fire that people from the provinces, particularly the Northeast, moved into this new rental housing area. L.P. said that the influx did not really come till 1985 when the CPB moved people out of this area to Thep Lila. Again those born or long-term in the community took advantage to build rental housing and people moved back in, with the CPB apparently not opposing it at this point. The details of the influx are not as important as the fact that it created a new set of distinctions: renters and owners, those born in the slum and those who came from the outside. Whereas the Ton Pho-Flats distinction is nuanced and subtle, the renters/owners one is much sharper, and the strained relations between slum born people and the provincial renters will figure prominently in discussions about leadership in Chapter 5.

A third set of distinctions also emerged after the fire because of the opportunities that it created for amassing wealth. Those who built rental housing often held their claim to the land by the threat of force. Two family names were prominent in those that claimed land and built rental housing after the fire, and both had ruffian (*nakleng*) type family members who were able to keep others away from the land they had staked out (I-303, I-92). The wealth they generated then allowed them to become even more influential in the community in the future.

However, the fire not only heightened and created new distinctions, but also set into motion forces that served to lessen and obscure distinctions by promoting at least the ideal of the entire area being a single 'community', primarily among those who were born in the slum. After the fire another informal committee gathered around the issue of planning a large King's birthday celebration to show gratitude for building the flats for them (I-323). Although the King's birthday is a 'Flats' event, just as the Civil New Year's celebration is a 'Ton Pho' event, it is freely attended by people from the entire community area. By linking their own local history to a national celebration of the most respected institution in the country, that of the monarchy, the Flats created an event that embraced everyone and downplayed territorial and birthplace distinctions, bringing people together around their reverence for the King. One day I was talking with some Northeastern renters who sell food outside the wall at Rua Khiaw. I asked them if they were part of the *chumchon*, and they said no, 'we have no voice, no rights, all they want us to do is help.' So I asked them if they ever went to any of the festivals, and they said they attended the Queen's birthday and the King's birthday because 'you have to demonstrate your loyalty' (*tawng sadaeng jong rak phak dii*) (I-201). The presence of a large number of Rua Khiaw people for the merit making event on the morning of the King's birthday was noted as a good sign by committee members; they took it as an affirmation of their committee and leadership by these outsiders (PO-327).

Changing Views on Legitimate Leadership

In Chapter 2 I defined leadership in a processual sense as all the forms of interpersonal influence operating within a group that facilitate task accomplishment for the group. I noted that what is important in looking systemically at leadership processes across a group is the issue of legitimacy because this is directly related to how compliance and cooperation are gained by actors who may or may not have formal positions within the group. The critical issue in LWPW is securing the voluntary cooperation of others to help in events and tasks that are too big to do as an individual or small group (I-26, I-133). When buildings need to be cleaned, a festival put on, or a protest joined, people get involved on a voluntary basis and residents see this ability to mobilize as the defining mark of leadership. In both the informal pre-registration system and the formal community committee system that came with registration, the primary source of power to influence and mobilize others towards group task accomplishment is personal power rather than position. In this section I explore the patterns of leadership and bases of legitimacy in LWPW around the nodal point of community registration in 1985.

Legitimacy before Registration as a Chumchon

It would not be surprising to find some version of the traditional 'elders' and *nakleng* forms of village leadership in urban slums. Slum dwellers' roots, even when born in the slum, go back to rural areas. What needs to be discovered is how these forms are adapted and modified in the changed material and social conditions of the slum. Urban slum communities are not just simply reproductions of village life in the city (Sopon, 1992:82); the social cohesion of the village is broken down in urban life where there is no need for the defence and protection of the village as a unit. In the village, rice farming and irrigation necessitate forms of cooperation which are no longer present as people make their living through a variety means.[39] Akin's work, based on research in the late 1960s, found that *nakleng* were the community leaders;[40] Johnson in the early 1970s found elder type respected persons;[41] and Sopon observed that the well-to-do or communal tycoons are elected onto the committees when they are formed, so that the exploitative informal structure thus becomes the legalized structure as well (1992:111). All of these works are dated now, and new research needs to be done to provide fresh perspectives of the changed political, social, and economic conditions in slums. Johnson's narrow view of leadership and broad view of community obscures his ability to see alternative kinds of leadership,[42] and Sopon's observation is over-generalized and an oversimplification of the diversity that exists in Bangkok's slums.

---

[39] See Potter (1976:34-50) on village social groupings, particularly on cooperative labour-exchange groups.

[40] Akin's work in the late 1960s in Trok Tai identified three major cliques (*phuak*) whose leaders were *naklong* types, with one who had the ability to represent the entire community (1975b:283) and who commanded greater resources than the other faction leaders (1975b:301). In some circumstances it is possible for a single *nakleng* type leader to emerge as a community wide leader; there are also many other examples where influence does not extend much wider than their client group (see Ockey, 2004b Chapter 6 for examples of differing types of slum leadership).

[41] Johnson worked in slum development with the NHA in the 1970s. Trying to identify community leaders by both social survey and informants, they found only 20 per cent could identify someone they considered a community wide leader (1979:317). They were told that some leaders would not cooperate with other leaders because they belonged to different factions (1979:318). Others said they could mobilize people in the community for self-help projects, but this appeared to be exaggeration (1979:318). In a community of 2,000 people 15 leaders were identified and did not appear to represent the community but factions (1979:318). These leaders were long-term residents, occupied status positions, had reasonably good incomes, and were respected both because of their age and position (1979:318).

[42] Johnson concluded from his data collection among several slums that they were 'generally unorganized as communities' (1979:485). He noted that although community

Inquiring into the patterns of governance of the community prior to registration in 1985 was a very confusing process; it took me a long time to sort out and understand what was happening in the data. Four distinct perspectives emerged from my informants. The first sees no sense of community or leadership until the coming of formal registration in 1985. The picture painted is that of everyone being on their own, with individuals, families, and small groups pursuing their own interests without regard to others. The interviewees used Thai idioms to express the idea: *tua khrai tua man* and *tang khon tang yuu* (everyone for themselves).[43] However, in continuing dialogue with these same people two more perspectives became discernible. D. saw community tasks being handled within a group of people who were close to each other, had grown up together, trusted each other, and who as friends saw their relationship as horizontal rather than having large status differences (I-203). Here is a portion of my dialogue with D.:

> A. So what you are saying is that it was basically every person for themselves. So were there leaders (*phuu nam*) or not?
>
> D. There were no leaders. We watched over things ourselves. In the past there was no *chumchon* (here the administrative unit sense as not being registered with the BMA).
>
> A. So there was no committee?
>
> D. Right. There was none at all. There were no leaders/administrators (*phuu bokkhrong*). We administrated (*bokkhrong*) things ourselves.
>
> A. So you administrated things yourselves. Well surely that means that you must have had some people who were leader types or respected types?
>
> D. No, we did not have them at all. You see it was like we loved each other, we were together from the time we were little till we had grown up, we were able to associate with each other.

---

leaders existed, there was no formal structure, constituency, or stratification of the leaders. Religion and entertainment activities were segmented and not community wide (Johnson, 1979:308-9). His interests in community (defined as a geographic entity) led to the conclusion that 'slum communities and other low-income areas are not organized in a manner which allows them to operate as an entity' (1979:329).

[43] I asked a Thai friend for clarification of this term, and he explained it as each various person doing their own thing without any relationship, no coordination of activity, and not being interested in or interfering with others. L.P and D. used the idiom substituting 'groups' and 'homes' for the *tua* which references people. This gives the sense that various homes and groups were operating on their own with no relationship or coordination.

By way of contrast others saw decentralized *nakleng* as a kind of natural leadership. L.P. in describing the situation said that nobody was bold (*klaa*) enough to pull everyone together because they all thought of everybody as more or less equal. M. said that at that time there were people who had power, such as *nakleng*, but nobody had enough power to bring everyone together because their power was centred on the pursuit of their own interests (I-261).[44] Since Akin, who did his research nearly four decades ago, found that *nakleng* and the conception of *nakleng* were important to leadership in the community he studied I wanted to see how people construed *nakleng* in LWPW. So at this point, before picking up the fourth perspective on the pattern of community governance before registration I will digress for a moment to look at the conceptions of *nakleng* in LWPW.

Akin provides a detailed analysis of the *nakleng* in what is known as the *nakleng to* (big *nakleng*) form (1975b:253-69). While people in the community he studied said that there were no more *nakleng* like this (1975b:264), Akin concluded that the ideal conception of a leader in the community was modelled on the *nakleng to* and centred on the ability to give aid and protection, deeply valuing assisting friends and followers, and seeking to never lose one's *liam nakleng* (status, prestige of power) (1975b:287). In Table 2 I summarize the information collected from a number of informants covering most of the period of my data collection (I-16, I-68, DI-49, I-294, I-296, PO-18, I-300, I-341). What it shown is that in my informants understanding there were two main types of *nakleng*, those who were seen as positive and those seen as negative.

The positive conception of *nakleng* noted by Akin still exists, but it seems to me to be more of an ideal and not actually embodied in any real person. For instance, in LWPW nobody could identify a good *nakleng*. In Trok Tai where Akin studied there were people who others called *nakleng* and viewed them in a positive light. Today in LWPW people will admit that there are *nakleng* (although I could never get anyone to actually take me to meet one or point one out) but they are viewed completely in a negative fashion. Four names in particular came up when trying to find out about *nakleng* and those are well known in the community. There was a female moneylender named T. (no other details on her); H., the son of Grandma N., who was purported to be a 'right

[44] The perception of *nakleng* in the community in the past again depends on one's standpoint. D., as a woman who grew up in the community, admits to the presence of *nakleng* and does not like them, but in general has very fond and pleasant memories of her younger years. L.P., as an adult male who moved into the community as an outsider 40 years ago, was much more aware of the presence of *nakleng* as those who could do physical violence to others. Grandma N., one of the richest people in the community and whose son is the most well known *nakleng* in the community, insists that there are no *nakleng*. This kind of response resonates with what Akin experienced as well. He noted that in general people would say that *nakleng* were bad, yet they would try indirectly to convey with pride that they themselves were *nakleng* (1975b:253). Grandma N., due to the general image of *nakleng* as bad, would not want to admit that her son was one.

hand man' of Sia Baw, a well known godfather (*jao pho*) in the area; and Dh. and B., the uncle and father of the current community president who are both deceased.

Table 2 Views of *nakleng*

Positive view of *nakleng*	**Negative view of *nakleng***
Style: They have reasons and rationality (*mii hetpon*), they do not *riid tai* (extort, as in protection rackets) people, they do not bully people (*rang gae*).	Style: They operate by making others fear them (*kreng klua*), they threaten and oppress others.
Characteristics: bold, decisive, wide contacts (*kwaang*), they will struggle to the end (*jai suu*), resolute, determined (*naeow nae*), they do good with all sincerity, are fair, confident and bold to act.	Characteristics: They build a following through lending money, and build power centred on themselves, developing an entourage through the influence of money (*jaang boriwan*). They are *kaerae* (rogues) and have power. They *riid tai* (extort) from people in protection rackets, or force money from people by bullying.
Types: *nakleng dii* (good *nakleng*).	Type 1: The bully (*antaphaan*) has no money but is tough, beats people up, and is violent. The term *nakleng hua maay* (the wood head *nakleng*) may fall under this type; they speak abusively to others, beat people, and create problems. Type 2: Money lender, hired gun, right hand man for a gambling den operator, political level, mafia types.

Rental housing was a source of wealth although the men were considered *nakleng* before the fire of 1973. There are indications they were involved in drugs and money lending, and possibly one as a hired gun. The change over time in the acceptability of *nakleng* in community leadership is illustrated among this group. Table 3 was produced from L.P.'s memory and he was not clear at some points, but a general trend is discernible. Dh. was the most infamous *nakleng* in the community. He went on from community leadership to win an election to the District Council. He raised the funds to build the health clinic from people in the community and his own contacts. He was later shot to death in a rural area chasing down his wife whom another man had taken.

At one point in the community leadership history, although the details were murky, H. was elected to the committee and made the president by the others. If it was not H. then it was another *nakleng* whose name I do not know but who is still living. However there is a rule that you cannot have been in prison within the past five years, and apparently he had been and this was not checked out closely (or ignored) by the District. But people went and informed the District and he was removed. Since the late 1990s there have been no *nakleng* types and

T. who is from a family of *nakleng*, is considered acceptable for leadership because he is not a *nakleng* and is seen as 'good' and 'trustworthy'. This interview data shows a clear change in what constitutes acceptable community leadership in LWPW with there being a move away from the *nakleng* conception that Akin found in Trok Tai.

Table 3 Partial list of community presidents

Year	Election/Appointment	President of committee and type
1986	Appointment	B.-police officer, not a *nakleng*
1988	Election?	Dh.-*nakleng*
1990	Election?	"
1992	Appointment?	L.-*nakleng* to a degree
1994	Appointment?	"
1996	Election	Tu.-*nakleng*
1998	Election	L.P.-hotel worker, not a *nakleng*
2000	Election	"
2002	Appointment	D.-single woman, food seller, not a *nakleng*
2004	Appointment	T.-nephew of Dh., owns rental houses, not a *nakleng*

The fourth perspective on pre-registration patterns of governance came from K., a member of the current committee and long time resident of Ton Pho (I-296). When I mentioned to him that D. and L.P. said there was no leadership prior to community registration and that they had characterized it as every person for themselves, he disagreed. He said that in 1980 he had been part of an informal committee of around 15 older people who mutually respected each other. He was the youngest member, as he was able to do things like climb trees to trim branches, which the older men could no longer do. I brought this up to L.P. on another occasion, and he then admitted a committee formed in 1977 to put together the King's birthday celebration in gratitude for the building of the flats to replace the housing lost in the fire.

What do these accounts show? Clearly, there were traditional forms of legitimate authority operating as respected elders (as informal committees) and *nakleng* but with a very narrow locus. There was also another type of group made up of more horizontal relationships through friendship or mutual respect that was involved in tasks that benefited a wider circle than just their own group. This included putting on different kinds of festivals and celebrations, taking care of the environment of segments of the community, and handling issues that can be summed up in the term *bokkhrong* (governing). I want to suggest that the 'no community-no leadership' represented by D. and L.P. view reads back into history a newer perspective that is now shaping ideas of legitimacy in LWPW. This will be explored more in the next section. The fact that prior to the 1973 fire a small group was going to intercede with the King on behalf of their community points to some sense of a collective identity, at least for certain people, that belies the description of being 'everyone for themselves' (*tua khrai tua man*).

Legitimacy after Registration as a Chumchon

In trying to sort out the seemingly contradictory responses within and between the people I interviewed I came to the conclusion that the result of 20 years of formal registration with the state has changed the nature of legitimacy in LWPW and partially created a more comprehensive notion of community. This new notion is desired by some but difficult to obtain and maintain. In this section I will unpack the changed nature of legitimacy and its impact on the notion of community because of its importance to the analysis of Chapter 5.

While a decentralized structure of traditional leaders formed around small groups of kin, friends, locality, or *nakleng* seems to have been the rule, there were indicators that some people were able and willing to speak on behalf of a segment of LWPW broader than their own group. This was evident in those going to appeal to the King regarding their potential eviction in 1973 before the fire, the formation of an informal committee to plan the annual King's birthday celebration, and the 1985 registration of LWPW as an official *chumchon* with the Pathum Wan District.[45]

The functional centrepiece of registration is the community committee because it serves as the representative of the residents to the BMA. I will briefly overview the formal view of the committee and its work. The rules governing community committees are found in the *Handbook for the Work of Community Committees* (CDO, n.d.:22-8). There are six sections covering definitions of terms, the composition of the committee, eligibility rules for those running for a position and those voting, voting procedures, the work of the committee, the duties and responsibilities of the committee, and the guidelines for conducting their monthly meeting. The minimum number for a community committee is seven people, no matter how small the community, and the maximum is 25.[46] There are two routes by which people can become

---

[45] Registration of slums is not automatic. LWPW had to send representatives to initiate the process and show evidence of there being a willingness on the part of the people in the locality to register. Registration offers benefits in terms of connecting the community through a representative committee to the resources of the state to help with development projects. It is also the intention of the state that this representative committee act to mobilize the participation of the people to work for its own development (CDO, n.d.).

[46] If there are over 140 families, one position is added for every 20 families above that number up to 25. When I first started the data collection the committee had 11 members, with 15 being their allowable maximum. When it was time to choose a new committee

committee members, and the state controls and monitors both through the local District. A committee serves a two-year term, and the District CDO announces in advance the time frame when people can register as a candidate for the committee. Elections are held only when there are more applicants than the number of allowable slots. In such a case the people with the highest numbers of votes are taken to fill the slots. If less people apply than the number of allowable positions, then the CDO will announce the official appointment of those applicants (if they fit the required criteria) to the committee. Six positions are mandated by the regulations: president, vice-president, secretary, treasurer, registration, and information. These positions are chosen by the committee, which may create other portfolios as well. Any committee member who does not have a portfolio is simply a committee member-at-large. The committee chooses its advisers, who are able to attend meetings and give advice, but not vote.

The work of the committee as defined by the official regulations is as follows: to support democracy with the King as the head; to coordinate with public and private agencies that are working for the benefit of the community; to work for the development of the community physically, economically, and socially through the participation of the people and mobilization of community resources; to support *samakhii* (unity, harmony, accord) and *winai* (discipline); to support culture, arts, and beautiful customs; to watch over and care for the material assets of the community; and to make known, follow up on, and report to the Director of the District the activities and work of the various agencies and organizations involved in the community. A monthly meeting is to be held, and they can meet more frequently as necessary. The Director of the District also holds a monthly meeting for all of the community committee presidents with representatives from the various district agencies that are involved in the communities.[47] Representation, coordination, and mobilization are major themes in the state's view of what community leadership should be involved in. While the first two are shared by leaders and residents, the third is not, and this will be a subject of importance in Chapter 6. In the eyes of the community there are three important public functions: distributing items that are given to the community by outside agencies and politicians, planning and putting on the

in early 2004 they were told that they could have 23 slots, and in the end only 17 people applied and were accepted.

[47] I attended one district meeting. It was primarily information-giving from the various district agencies, and at the end there was time allotted for a representative from each *chumchon* to make a request to the District. Since I only attended one meeting I was not sure if the format was the same every time. One day while helping clean the concrete landing at the Saen Saeb canal I was able to spend some time with T. who was the current committee president. I brought up how I had attended a meeting once and narrated how it had been conducted. I asked if it was that way all the time, and he said yes (PO-306).

community festivals, and protecting their homes from eviction. All of these figure in the analysis chapters to follow.

How has registration impacted conceptions of legitimacy inside LWPW? In Chapter 2 I noted the complex nature of the way that the legitimacy of the Thai state is construed, calling it in Weberian terms a traditional-legal hybrid (see p. 23 above). Prior to registration, modified forms of the historical patterns of respected elders and *nakleng* existed in LWPW as traditional forms of legitimate authority. As the community entered into a relationship with the state via registration, the result over time was an increase in the 'legal' dimension of how they viewed legitimate leadership among themselves. What is now viewed as legitimate leadership in the community is closer to this traditional-legal hybrid accorded the state rather than pure traditional authority. This legal dimension I will term an 'officialization'[48] in the sense of authorizing and formalizing so that what now 'counts' as leadership must have an official basis as being sanctioned by the state. In using the idea of an increase in the 'legal' dimension, I am not using it in the sense of an increase in devotion to the impersonal law or the rule of law. As Unger notes, 'the most striking feature of Thai law is its weakness' (1998:175). The legal dimension means that officialdom is seen as legitimate, but it is officialdom conducting business in a personalistic and paternalistic fashion where law is bent to personal ends. I will first look at the evidence for this 'officialization' and then discuss its impact on views of legitimacy and conceptions of community in LWPW.

I first observed the officialization of the notion of leadership while conducting two different types of interviews as preparatory work for the free-

[48] I am coining a term here because I again want to avoid connecting what I am attempting to describe too tightly to the Weberian idea of legal-rational authority (see Weber, 1947:328-33) and thus introduce conceptions that are not present here in the case I am studying. I have already noted Weber's observation of the complexity of composition of the belief that constitutes the willingness to obey a system of authority (see page 23 above). In the same context he says, 'In the case of "legal authority," it is never purely legal. The belief in legality comes to be established and habitual, and this means it is partly traditional' (Weber, 1947:382). By using 'officialization' I am steering away from the sense of the legality as obedience to an impersonal order to highlight a movement towards a need for official sanction and its symbols in order to be seen as legitimate. Traditional bases such as being respected or a *nakleng* now require the augmentation of being 'official' in order to gain legitimacy and garner compliance and cooperation. Officialization is related to the rank and status values that I am emphasizing in *sakdi* administrative behaviour because there is law that operates through personalism. Individuals become the arbitrators and they justify something in terms of law if they want. However, if it is convenient they can use their status conferred through formal position to make their own decision. Thus there is a Thai saying with a play on words with a coarse pronoun '*kot ken kot kuu*' (there are laws, and then there is my law). Officialization means that 'officialdom' is seen as the legitimate carrier of authority, and at the same time officialdom uses its *sakdi* to make personalized decisions rather than conducting affairs by the impersonal rule of law.

recall listing.[49] In the first I asked directly who were formal leaders (*ben thaang kaan thii mii tamnaeng*) and who were informal leaders (*mai dai ben thaang kaan*), and in the second I explored who were considered respected, well-known, and acceptable in the community. In identifying formal leaders 19 of 24 respondents named either the committee as a collective whole, named a specific person who was on the committee, or admitted the existence of such leaders but said they did not know them personally yet. However, only three of 24 respondents could name an informal leader and, of the ones named, not a single one actually lived in the community. Similarly, the questions relating to the respected-well-known-acceptability complex showed that it was either people currently on the committee or former committee members who could be described in these terms. Leaders are clearly equated with official positions.

The importance of official sanction and the possession of the symbols of officialdom that confer legitimacy was clearly seen in the transition between committees in 2004 (PO-119). There were rumours in the community that enough people were applying to force an election. In the end only 17 people applied for 23 slots and thus were appointed in a formal meeting. Announcements were made over the loudspeakers that the new committee was going to be appointed. The meeting was directed by uniformed District Community Development Officers who read documents, brought papers that needed to be signed, and oversaw the process of issuing an official card to each new member. The entire palaver was done to show that this was an authorized transition of power. L.P. once made an observation in passing that indicates how important official recognition and its symbols are to the legitimacy of the committee. He was recalling the history of the different committees and noted that the very first group did not yet have official cards indicating they were approved community leaders like they have now. An official card serves as a symbol of the authority of the state; it legitimizes its holder and enables the person to act.[50]

The influence of the officialization process was also noticeable in the three primary ways that people used the word *chumchon*. The generic use draws upon the meaning of the word *chumchon* as an assemblage of people (Haas, 1964) and carries a spatial sense as a synonym for slum; this is *chumchon* as place. There is also as sense of *chumchon* as an administrative unit, a registered community with the BMA. This combines the spatial view of a bounded locality with the legality conferred by the government, creating an administrative unit where there was not one before (Evers & Korff, 2000:230). For instance I have been in unregistered communities and heard people refer to themselves as 'being a *chumchon*' (in the geographic/spatial sense) and then in

[49] See footnote 1 p. 71 for a definition of free-recall listing.

[50] I was also issued an official card by the National Research Council that had my picture, signature, name of the research project, and the dates that I was approved to collect data.

the same sentence say they are not a *chumchon* yet (in the registered with the government sense). One informant said, 'If you do not have a committee you are a *chumchon raang*' (an abandoned, forsaken, or neglected community) (I-114). D. reflected this official usage when she described the history of the community in these terms:

> Long ago (*samai kawn*) there was no *chumchon* here, we did not *khun gab chumchon* (meaning to be subject to, dependent upon the *chumchon*, here in the sense of officially registered with the BMA) ... we did not *khun ben chumchon* (in the sense of to start or begin to be a *chumchon*); there was no such thing. It was sort of like we were renting this land from the crown' (I-203).

A third sense has to do with the *chumchon* as an entity that one can belong to, or feel a part of, which has nothing to do with geography at all. This sense is expressed in two ways. First, there is an insider/outsider distinction that is relational and not connected to where one physically lives. In LWPW there are people who are renters but do not feel that they are part of the *chumchon* even though they live within the geographic boundaries of the community. People who live right next to the Flats will say that they are not part of the *chumchon*. There is also a geographic component in that people who live at the farthest edges of LWPW insist that they are not part of the *chumchon*. As an illustration, one man used *chumchon* twice in the same sentence with two distinct uses. I was asking who the leaders in the community were, and he said, 'There are no leaders here. The *chumchon* came afterwards. The *chumchon* does not reach to here' (DI-18). In the first use this man referred to a legal entity, which he clearly resides in; in the second he referred to a group to which he could belong. This second group is one that in his view is for the Flats people, and not for people like him, although he lives within 100 metres of the Flats.

In its broadest sense what I am terming officialization increased the importance of the perception of the need for legitimacy based in the formal sanction from the state. This shift has had a number of practical consequences on leadership processes and conceptions of community in LWPW. The major shift is the change in perception of who can lead in the community and the type of leader that is needed. In the first years after registration it was the traditional forms of leadership, respected elders and *nakleng*, that were acceptable, with more of the latter dominating the role of committee president (I-323). However, since the election of 1998 there have been no *nakleng* types to either win an election or even apply to stand for election or be appointed. During the course of my data collection people were emphatic that *nakleng* are not considered leaders by people in the community and would not be elected. Thus over time there has been a marginalization of *nakleng* style leadership so that while its presence in the community is acknowledged, it is not seen as official or appropriate for the community.[51] Whereas 40 years ago a *nakleng* type in the community Akin studied could mobilize the support of the whole community, this is less likely to happen today in LWPW for two reasons. First, *nakleng* are seen as pursuing personal rather than community benefit (I-261). Second, from L.P.'s perspective, with the election system in place, it gives people a chance to choose leaders that they like rather than those they fear (I-257).[52]

While the role of *nakleng* has been marginalized, 'officialization' has expanded the traditional role of respected elder beyond the kinds of decentralized small groups or localities that existed before registration and gives them *chumchon*-wide (in the legal and geographic sense) influence. The skill sets for leading the community have changed; it is no longer the wide (*kwaang*) contacts of the *nakleng* that are needed, but people who can interact with officialdom, have time to attend all the meetings, and work the administrative system (I-329) (see Ockey, 2004b:130). The role of group (*klum* and *phuak*) has also been elevated since people will apply for the committee as groups. These horizontal relationships provide mutual assistance and a labour pool for task accomplishment.

The process of officialization has ironically also played a part in decreasing the participation which is central to the democratic process, and heightened divisions between residents. The coming of the state administrative apparatus ostensibly brings democracy in its lowest levels into the community. However, the reality is that once a group has assumed official positions they do not feel the need to necessarily consult with others (PO-13), thus facilitating a model of leadership that actually is less participative than some of the traditional forms. (I will pick up this issue and discuss it in detail in Chapter 5). It is interesting that the officialization process has unleashed forces that work both towards uniting and dividing the community. For some, particularly those born in the slum, it is a natural step to move from the administrative unit version of

[51] Ockey has traced changes in the idea and practises of *nakleng* (see particularly 2004b:15-21; and 81-100 on the move from *nakleng* to *jaopho*). While his analysis focuses on larger figures in terms of money and a level of influence at a provincial or national political level, it appears that at the slum community level there have also been changes.

[52] Within the community people attribute the lessening of the influence of *nakleng* to changes in the political environment that in more recent years have suppressed criminal influences and, at least in the eyes of residents, broken the ability of the police to stand behind *nakleng*. In the past, according to K., *nakleng* were not touchable because of their relationship with the police (I-296). However, as M. points out, now it is possible for regular people to report suspicious or illegal activities to the police and something will be done about it (PO-324). Apparently, this lessens the sense of fear of those outside of the *phuak* (clique) of the *nakleng* and also circumscribes some of the activities of the *nakleng* themselves. Ockey argues that another factor bringing change to the *nakleng* form has been a trend toward the weakening of patron-client ties, which has contributed to a more restricted role for some types of *nakleng* (see 2004:6, 97, 131, 145).

chumchon to conclude that as they have been officially constituted a unity over a bounded geographic space, they are, and should be, a cohesive collectivity – a community – as well.[53] However, officialization has undercut this claim by raising but not fulfilling the expectations of people. Participating in decision-making, getting a share in distributions, and being able to vote for the community committee members are privileges theoretically present for all residents but not in practise. This creates an insider/outsider mentality and a lingering bitterness in some who live physically in LWPW but feel like they do not belong.

In spite of these divisive forces, the officialization view runs deep. When I interviewed people in Rua Khiaw they could not name an informal leader, and when asked if there were any formal leaders, some would respond with an emphatic no; then they would follow with a grudging admission that there was the community committee. Officialization brings a legal dimension to the idea of legitimacy; people may not like, trust, or respect the community committee, but the force of its legitimacy due to official sanction by the state has severely restrained other alternative claims to legitimacy.

Eviction and the Struggle to Survive

The theme of this section has been the exploration of some of the inner dynamics of LWPW that are not easily observable on the surface. Earlier I argued that one of the faces of the state towards the urban poor is an indifference/hostility that tolerates and at times pursues the elimination of slums as physical space. My point in making this argument was that this stance forms the operating environment for slum communities. This is certainly the case for LWPW. The current configuration of the community is for the most part a result of the erosion caused by evictions since the early 1970s. The fear of eviction hangs over the people in LWPW; it shapes their attitudes and actions and is a major part in their experience of poverty.

The gradual influx of people and increasing density of wooden housing on this CPB-owned land started after World War II. People rented the land from the CPB, and an official came in to collect rent each month. Most likely, in a process similar to what happened in other areas, long-term residents with more means moved out and divided up their homes into rooms for more rental housing. It is for certain that by 1973 there were rumours of eviction, and then the fire came, which in residents' minds was connected in some way to the

[53] Evers and Korff note that 'slums in Bangkok bear features of communality, partly based on existing social networks among neighbours, friends and informal sector activities … For larger slum areas of several thousand inhabitants we do regard it as impossible that the whole area is one community' (Evers & Korff, 2000:230). LWPW is large enough that claims of communality were not made prior to registration; instead local distinctions were highlighted. However, it is small enough that after registration its formation as an administrative unit led some people, notably those born in the community and who have served on the committee, to make a claim for communality.

eviction rumours. From one perspective the fire had the opposite of its intended effect because, with the King authorizing the building of flats to house the displaced, it rooted people by giving them more formal housing and registration numbers. Then, somewhere between 20 and 30 years ago, the CPB stopped collecting rent money on the land (I-65). To the residents this represented a methodology for allowing the legal owner to evict them for not paying rent. L.P. says that the community has been red-lined (I-128), and this opinion is shared by others who see a very limited future for the community. In inquiring about the possibility of eviction I never spoke with a single person who thought they would not be evicted. Everyone is sure it will happen; many are fearful because they are not sure what they would do and would like to get their family raised. Renters are less bothered by it because they feel like they will just go and rent somewhere else. They are usually in the city working and their families are living in the provinces.

In 1985 the CPB relocated people from the Rua Khiaw area to Thep Lila on Raamkhamhaeng Road; then around 1998 the housing that filled in the land immediately behind the temple was evicted in order to make room for the funerary structure used at Sanam Luang for the cremation of the Queen mother. There were two locations made available for people on the edges of the city at Wang Thong Lang and Rom Klaow (I-200). In the early 1990s LWPW was one of five communities that would have been eliminated in order to build a freeway exit along the Saen Saeb canal to bring cars down into the shopping centres there. However, they participated in the well documented and successful resistance campaign spearheaded by the Baan Khrua community against the Expressway Authority.[54] Although during the time of my data collection this issue was quiet, residents still feel that this can be revived at any time.

The level of uncertainty in the community has increased in recent years as the pressure for other more lucrative uses of the land grows. In 2000 the rent stopped being collected on the flats; then in 2005 a section on the west side was removed for a road that will run from the new Siam Paragon across to the World Trade Plaza. Residents next to the temple who paid rent in the past indicate that rent collection has stopped as well. They fended off a possible eviction for the expansion of the school that they live next to by sending their own representatives to talk with the District Director. A compromise was reached, and the school is being built on land behind the temple complex instead. Then in 2006 the cement company at the east entrance reached an agreement with the CPB to expand their operation and rent a portion of the land next to them. A major section of Rua Khiaw was evicted with higher prices being paid for their dwellings than normal since no relocation land was being offered. I spoke with a shopkeeper next to the evicted portion and asked if the

---

[54] See Ockey's summary of the protest effort in his chapter on slum leadership and eviction (2004b) and Askew (2002:295-9).

committee had been able to help. She said this was impossible because the housing in Rua Khiaw does not have registration numbers; if you have a house registration it is possible to fight, but if you do not, then it is very hard. This was why the people on the temple side were successful, because they had house registrations. She has heard rumours that when the new five-star hotel connected to the World Trade Plaza is finished they will evict the rest of the Rua Khiaw area to put in a park and walking area for the guests. In addition to not collecting rent, another technique used by owners of the land is to not sign off to allow for a house registration number (DS-2, I-254, I-327). M. explained that now after a fire the District (he did not say what particular group or office in the District) sends a representative and they take away the right to have a house number there. This then puts whoever will come and build on that spot in a vulnerable position when an eviction happens (I-341).

Eviction impacts leadership in LWPW because it is seen as a key role that the committee, as community representatives, must address. Protecting the community from eviction is high on the list of committee responsibilities, but is absent in any of the government descriptions of what the committee should do. Eviction also highlights divisions in the community because renters who do not have house registration numbers are easily evicted and the committee is unable to help them. In some cases the committee is seen as being uninterested as when the *naa wat* group sent their own representatives to the District to protest their eviction (I-341), or people are not sure if the committee is thinking ahead and working on this issue (I-302).

The residents of LWPW are surrounded by powerful interests that want to use the land they live on: from the Expressway Authority, to a cement company, to shopping malls. For some renters losing their place is not much of a problem, but for many people who were born in the community or who have lived there long-term, eviction is a serious dislocation for them and a disturbing future to contemplate. There is a mood of resignation among long-term residents, as they feel sooner or later the pressures of the surrounding interests will drive them away. It is not a matter of *if* it will happen but *when* in the minds of many. The constant insecurity in the face of eviction is perhaps the most painful part of poverty for the majority of residents. It is the social deprivation of looking up every day and seeing themselves encompassed by high-rise buildings that symbolize the wealth and commercial vigour of a city, and knowing that they are not wanted there.

Summary

LWPW is a place that easily hides its relational and social complexity under the surface homogeneity of slum life. An incident on my last trip through the community reminded me that what you see never tells the whole picture. I have walked by a wizened old man who collects garbage to recycle many times, stopping to chat on occasion and even interviewing him once. 'Uncle' has the wiry build, sweaty countenance, and greasy clothes that are so common to his career in Bangkok; he is always on the prowl, looking for bottles and cans and meticulously stacking and storing them away for sale in the future. Constant, methodical motion comes to mind when I think of him. I had noticed that near his storage area by the Pho tree a small room had been cemented in, an air conditioner installed, and it was now full of computers and children playing video games. An official looking piece of paper pasted to the wall grants permission for the establishment to operate. I had noticed the contrast before, and it always struck me: Uncle patiently stacking used bottles and sweating in the heat while children a few feet away explode monsters on a computer screen in an air conditioned room. It was the old and the new, the economy of the past next to the economy of the future, a picture of some of the paradoxes and divisions that exist in the slum. So on this last day I struck up a conversation with Uncle and casually asked about the owner of the video-game parlour. He smiled and said it was his daughter.

The garbage recycler and his entrepreneurial daughter are a picture of the contradictions in LWPW. To focus on either one is to exclude key facets of the community; to look at the 'surface' is to miss the linkages that lie below. In this chapter I have not only tried to show surfaces, but also to explore what lies beneath them and some of the points of connection. In the context of introducing the city of Bangkok, its slums, and LWPW in surface images, I have also raised a series of issues that are not plainly visible on a statistical tour or a walk-through. Behind smiling community development officials and politicians handing out gifts is the reality of state and elite power that wants to eliminate slums as physical space. I argued that these faces of benevolence and indifference/hostility form the environment in which slum residents live out their lives. I also looked beneath the surface conditions of slum life to highlight three issues that are of importance to leadership and interpersonal influence in LWPW. Forces of division based in locality and place of origin keep people apart; *chumchon* is a contested idea and communality cannot be assumed. The coming of the state administrative system into the slum has changed views of what constitutes legitimate leadership. I presented evidence that a process of 'officialization' has added a legal dimension to people's understanding of legitimate authority. The result has been to marginalize some forms of traditional leadership while expanding others, and at the same time fostering a sense of the *chumchon* as embracing everyone in its geographic locality while deepening existing divisions by narrowing participation rather than broadening it. Finally, eviction is not just a threat, but an ongoing reality. This has created in LWPW residents a sense of resignation as to the inevitability of being driven from their land by powerful interests outside the slum, and affects relationships within the slum and between the slum and the state.

The next three chapters present the results of the data collection and analysis set against the backdrop of key issues that have emerged here. In Chapter 4 I develop a model of preferred leadership that gives insights into the shared perceptions that people in LWPW have about the configurations of traits and associated behaviour that give someone the potential to have interpersonal influence. Chapter 5 moves from cultural ideals and values to develop models of how the process of leading in LWPW is worked out in real life, and includes a discussion of how the preferred model is drawn upon for actual leadership practises. Then in Chapter 6 I look at the relationship of the community to the state, examining how those tasked with representing the community negotiate their relations with the powerful.

CHAPTER 4

A Model of Preferred Leadership

In Chapter 2 I critiqued the literature on Thai leadership for not engaging with the Thai practise of leading in a way that indicates how Thai culture shapes that practise. In this chapter I address this underdeveloped area by focusing subquestions one and two to provide baseline sociolinguistic data rooted in the shared perspectives of local actors in Lang Wat Pathum Wanaram (LWPW). I then look for connections and configurations in the material to develop a model of preferred leadership. To answer these two questions I chose the technique of free-recall listing[1] and associated methods of analysis. Free-recall listing on a domain is a form of classification, where 'classification' refers to 'some kind of structured system of categories, most of them verbalized, constructing and labeling some universe of things, being, events or actions' (Tambiah, 1985:3). Tambiah points out that with classifications the tendency has been to see them as existing in some kind of unchanging fashion outside of everyday events or as at least part of the source of motivation of everyday action. In proposing here a model based on the classification of the qualities and performances of a preferred leader I want to avoid either of these positions. Following Tambiah, I see a classificatory system not only describing the world, but also entailing 'evaluations, and moral premises and emotional attitudes, translated into taboos, preferences, prescriptions and proscriptions' (1985:4). Such systems can be seen as designs for living that are used by local actors within specific situational contexts (Tambiah, 1985:4). There is no isomorphic relationship between the classificatory model and everyday life; the connection between the semantic and the pragmatic has to be carefully untangled.[2] As it applies to leadership, the semantic here relates to what Tambiah calls 'central collective

---

[1] Free-recall listing is an elicitation technique used to study a cultural domain (Bernard, 1995:239-40). The exercise is performed by asking respondents an open-ended question to get a list or partial set of items from informants about the domain under study (Weller, 1998:368). The responses are taken down verbatim and in order. If a response is given more than once, or in cases where multiple questions are being used to elicit that domain, a response that appears more than once in the entire set of questions is only counted once. The responses are tabulated by counting the number of respondents that mentioned each item (Weller & Romney, 1988:14).

[2] On a similar note, Quinn and Holland point out that cultural models do not translate simply and directly into behaviour, nor do cultural conceptualizations act as the sole determinants of behaviour (1987:6).

valuations and preferences' and the pragmatic to the issues of task and power/prestige in social interactions and contexts (see Tambiah, 1985:2 and his application to ritual). I will introduce the semantic element in this chapter and then will proceed to relate this to the pragmatic arena of how leadership is actually practised in the community in Chapter 5, and in its relation to the state in Chapter 6. In the first section I trace the procedural steps I used, explaining the decisions I made and the rationale for the particular directions I took in collecting the data, and share the results gained. In the next I interpret the results of the correspondence analysis of the data, and in the third section I move on to analysis of this material in the light of other leadership research. The final section concludes with a discussion of how the culturally preferred model developed here works to build interpersonal influence, relating this to two issues relevant to the study of Thai leadership, that of patron-client relations and the nature of reciprocation and obligation.

Free-recall Listing, Saliency Analysis, Paired Similarity Judgement, and Consensus Analysis

Free-recall Listing and Saliency Analysis

Preparation for a free-recall listing exercise involves testing questions on the semantic domain to be studied in order to construct questions that adequately cover the conceptual sphere of the domain, are meaningful to respondents, and are easy for respondents to answer. My initial thought was to examine residents' leadership perceptions of community committee members, but this was not feasible for a couple of reasons. My early conversations with people showed me that talking about community leadership was not going to be a neutral, intellectually stimulating exercise for residents, but a potentially volatile and emotionally charged one. This meant that, in addition to the fact that people would naturally be reticent to talk openly about someone they knew or lived nearby,[3] if someone was willing to talk critically about committee members it would jeopardize my relationship with the committee and make further data collection impossible. I chose to work around these obstacles by examining leadership perceptions in a relationship that many people in the community participate in, that between employer and employee.

This preparatory phase also raised the question of whether to study informant perceptions based on actual, real-life leaders, or on the perceptions of a culturally preferred leader. Since cultural models are conceptualized as the typical, stereotypical, salient, and ideal (Quinn & Holland, 1987:31), I decided

---

[3] Suntaree points out how the Thai value system which places high priority on both 'ego' and 'smooth interpersonal relationships' means that 'the Thai in general are more likely to dislike conflict' (1994:26). Because they feel uneasy about conflict they tend to avoid it or find indirect ways of handling it.

to do both. I had informants answer questions about leaders they knew personally and also about a culturally preferred leader.[4]

By the end of this preparation phase I was working with the following multi-part question:

> Think of a specific boss (*nai* or *hua naa*) you have worked with and then answer this question. This boss had what kind of *laksana* (characteristics), what kind of *nisai* (character), what kind of *bukalik* (personality), and what kind of *lila gaan nam* (style of leading)? For instance, what did they do (*khaow tham arai baang*), what kind of actions (*kaankratham*) did they do as a leader?

I found that each of these terms would yield new and unique responses if I asked them one at a time and waited to exhaust the term, before moving on to the next one. These same basic terms also worked well with a culturally preferred scenario of a work setting asking about the kind of boss that they would feel *thuukjai* (pleased, satisfied, to one's liking) with.

In structuring the free-recall listing exercise I decided to collect data from two groups. The first was to find as many informants as possible who were currently or had been involved in some kind of formal role or position within the community. The second group were those who have never held any kind of formal position. I was able to collect 18 from the first group and 30 from the second. For purposes of simplification and consistency I am using the terms 'leader' and 'follower' here in my English translations relating to the free-recall listing and its subsequent analyses. However, in the actual questions I used the Thai terms for boss (*hua naa*, *nai jaang*, or *nai*) and the word for an employee or subordinate (*luuk jaang* and *luuk nawng*). The specific context of these questions was that of a work setting and the relationship of superior/employer to subordinate/employee. Whenever I depart from that specific context in the discussion that follows I will always clarify the particular Thai terms that I used. For each of the 48 respondents I collected a list based on their perceptions of an actual leader they had worked with, and also their perceptions of a preferred leader they would like to work with. This left me with 96 lists which I then used the ANTHROPAC programme to run a saliency analysis on.[5]

---

[4] The idea for how to ask a question on preferred leadership came to me from an interviewee who made the statement that no leader can make everyone *thuukjai* (pleased, satisfied) all the time (I-42). I then developed a scenario using the same terms for questions on actual leaders and asked people to answer the questions, if the boss was someone who they were *thuukjai* with.

[5] A free-recall listing produces a list of terms in the order given them by the respondent. Frequency counts the number of times respondents have listed a term. Saliency is a measure that accounts for both frequency of occurrence and its rank order in the list. The formula for the salience (S) of a given term j is Sj=n-rj/n-1 where n equals the length of the respondent list (the total number of terms generated by the respondent) and rj is the rank of the particular term j (see Smith, Furbee, Maynard, Quick, & Ross, 1995).

What I discovered in this process of preparing for the free-recall and checking domain questions was that there were multiple conceptions of leadership present in the community but subquestion one and the free-recall listing exercise would only allow me to capture one perspective. The total effect of the two question scenarios, one for perceptions on actual leaders and one for perceptions on a culturally preferred (*thuukjai*) leader, was to provide an idealized and preferred view of leaders rather than real life practise. When doing actual leader perceptions I gave people a range of choices of the kind of experience they could reflect on; they virtually always defaulted to talk about good leaders, ones they enjoyed working for.[6] This tendency, combined with the question set on a *thuukjai* leader, means that the focus of the material in the free-recall listing is culturally preferred and idealized leadership.

Paired Similarity Judgement Exercise

With this data in hand the next step in preparation for analysis was to choose a set of terms from the most frequent and salient in the lists. These terms represent the most important concepts in the domain. I planned to do a paired similarity judgement[7] exercise where each term is paired against all the other terms in the chosen sample. I made the decision to work with 21 terms, which

---

[6] I asked respondents to rate their experience with the person under consideration on a five point scale (very good-*dii maak*, good-*dii*, adequate-*phaw chai dai*, not very good-*mai khoi dii*, and not good-*mai dii*). I also asked them to rate the effectiveness of their task accomplishment at work on the same scale. When given the choice of talking about a leader, people generally defaulted to a positive experience, so for the last ten interviews I began specifically asking people to tell me about negative leader experiences. In doing so I was able to get five people to share. In the end, by the five point rating system used, there were five negative leader interviews (not good, not good at all), 12 neutral interviews (*phaw chai dai* meaning 'adequate'), and 23 positive interviews (good, very good). I felt like my experiences here confirmed my decision to focus the free-recall on a more neutral working relationship that was outside of the community rather than on community leaders whom participants live near and interact with regularly. People still had difficulty focusing on negative aspects, even with someone external to their community, so this problem would have been greatly magnified when asking for perceptions of people inside the community. In the end I felt like I was unable to secure enough really negative experiences to obtain a good comparison, so I did not pursue separate analysis of these terms generated on people considered poor leaders.

[7] One structured interviewing technique to use with data about a domain (generally from having done a free-recall listing exercise) is to pair the items two at a time, present them to respondents, and ask them to make a judgement as to which is 'more' and which is 'less' (Weller & Romney, 1988:45). In the case of the terms I collected on leadership traits, the judgement involved an evaluation as to how terms were more alike (closer in meaning) or less alike (farther apart in meaning). The number of pairs that will be created from a list of items is calculated by the formula $m(m-1)/2$, where m is the number of items.

created a list of 210 pairs, because any more terms would make the questionnaire too large to be practical. Taking all 96 lists I ran a frequency and saliency analysis and then from the top 32 terms I chose 21. The short English translations next to each term are what will be used in the text, but it must be kept in mind that the actual meaning is much more nuanced and complex as I have tried to bring out in the definitions here.

NISAI DII - Good Character

This term was the most frequently used and salient term of all. In conducting the free-recall listing the idea of goodness was very prominent. The word *dii* (good) appeared as the second most frequent term and *khon dii* (a good person) was sixteenth. In choosing the final list of 21 terms I decided to drop 'good' as I felt from conducting the exercise that respondents often started their list when I was asking for the characteristics of the person by saying 'good'. In retrospect I was unsure if this was a characteristic or more of a summary saying they were a good leader. I left out 'good person' because good character would be a key component of being a good person. During my term interviews informants confirmed this connection.

Nisai carries the dictionary definition of habit, disposition, trait, character, or characteristic (Haas, 1964; So, 1984). Informants indicated that the person of 'good character' is the 'good person'; they do not take advantage of others (*aow briab*), do not cheat others (*kong*),[8] and do not steal from others. They have good human relational skills, get along well with others and are not self-centred. They are generous, kind and thoughtful, liberal in their help to others. In their speech they are not rough or coarse, not abusive or scolding, they do not talk about others. The person of good character will be respected.

T. said that good character stems from one's *sandaan*, which are the inborn traits and innate characteristics. This term is used for that part of character that is deepest inside a person and generally with a negative connotation, although not necessarily. He said that *nisai dii* equals *khunatham*, which is virtue, goodness, or moral principles (I-133). Another informant said that a person of good character is good to them, and expanded with the ideas of liberality and generosity, love, tenderness, and compassion (I-113). I spoke with D. and K. (I-70) about people of good character, how we know if people have it and how it is formed. The person of good character was one that you could associate with,

[8] The dictionary definition of *aow briab* is to take advantage of, while *kong* has a broader range covering to be bent, crooked; to cheat, deceive, take unfair advantage of others; defraud swindle, and to try and get out of one's commitment or avoid one's obligations (Haas, 1964). The two terms lie on a continuum with *aow briab* being lighter and *kong* heavier and broader. *Aow briab* starts where the concern for others is less than ourselves; it is putting ourselves first, and is not necessarily is either ethically or morally wrong. *Kong* involves what is wrong in method and ethics. To be *mai suusat* (dishonest) starts in taking advantage of others or a policy when we put our concerns first (*aow briab*), and it can then lead to *kong*.

be friends with, talk with and be understood, and whose disposition or temperament was not annoying and contradictory. In their expansion of this they noted that some people never follow along; they are always in opposition. You know that a person has good character by associating with them for a long time and through watching their behaviour. When I asked for an example of a person and why they thought he was *nisai dii* they said it was because he helped out, not with money but in being available to help and willing to help with events and work in the community. They felt that it was not possible to teach a person how to have good character; rather it was something that was inside of them already.

D. and K. also brought out a distinction that is important in terms of leadership and which plays a part in some of these terms. While in general many of these terms link together and relate to each other, it is possible to make separations that from my observations seem to have to do with two dimensions: one's own group versus others, and the reason for performing a particular action. Normally the person with good character is a good person, but they noted that it is possible to be considered a good person (*khon dii*) and yet not have good character. Their illustration, which is relevant to the situation in the slum, is the example of the person who helps her friends, but will not help others in the broader community. Such a person is considered a good person by their own circle, but others outside that circle would not think of them as having good character. They also noted that it is possible to be *jai dii* (kind) but not have good character. Here their example was based in the motive that led a person to do something. If a group of outsiders came and you fed them, you would be showing yourself to be kind, but if you did not try to help people in your own community, you showed that your kindness was only to build your own face, rather than being based in good character (I-70).

CHUUAYLUA LUUK NAWNG - Helps Followers

This was the second of four terms with representation across all of the lists for both actual and ideal leaders on perceptions by both leaders and nonleaders. The root idea is that when those under this leader are in trouble, face difficulties, or have a problem, whether at work or in their personal life, this type of person is one who will help them out. This help will often take tangible form as in financial assistance, but it can include counsel, encouragement, or problem solving as well. Informants noted that this kind of help is done with a pure heart and does not expect anything in return. T. said that 'help' was part of *namjai* (having compassion, understanding, and friendliness) which is *uafua* (obliging generosity, helping support) (I-133).

BEN GAN ENG - Informal, Approachable

This was the third of the four terms with representation across all of the lists for both actual and ideal leaders on perceptions by both leaders and nonleaders. When asked to define this word informants often responded with *mai thuu tua* first. To *thuu tua* is to be proud of oneself, to have a high opinion of oneself, and to hold oneself aloof. *Mai* is the negation term, so *ben kan eng* leaders do not stay aloof from those under them. This is expressed in speech in that you can talk easily with them, in eating together with subordinates, in being friendly and treating people like family, and in getting along well with people. This term is connected very closely with *bruksaa dai* (able to go to for counsel). B. said that if you are *ben kan eng* you are *bruksaa dai*, while the opposite is a person who is *bokbit* (closed) and *thuu tua*. The person who is *ben kan eng* does not show their power so that others will feel comfortable, and this makes followers feel that they can come to them for counsel. The voluntary lowering of formality by the leader opens the door to communication.

SUUSAT - Honest

In the free-recall listing *suusat* appeared only three times among the perceptions about leaders lists. In a pilot study where I had asked a more educated group of people about the *khunasombat* (qualities, properties) of leaders, *suusat* was more prominent (Johnson, 2002). I left it in for the paired similarity because I felt that it might not have appeared because it was subsumed under the idea of 'good character' and the 'good person'. Support for this came later on as I worked on term definitions. When asked to define what makes up a 'good person' *suusat* was included as a component along with good human relational skills and good character (I-133, I-129, I-137). B. was of the opinion that *suusat* was most of the time associated with good character, but not always. He felt that it did not appear in the leader lists because it is usually connected with money and not so much with work. This was born out in the term definition interviews where respondents noted that a *suusat* leader would pay workers on time. B. noted that in *chumchon* relations, *suusat* would be more prominent because of the responsibility of leaders to distribute material items that are given to the community and because they must handle the budget for development projects (I-117).

As a follower construct, *suusat* carries the idea of being loyal to a respected person. As a leader construct it refers to honesty in the sense of not being corrupt or dishonest. Informants said that the *suusat* person was a 'good person' and that they are not *khotgong*, which carries the idea of cheating, swindling, taking unfair advantage of others, being crooked. The *suusat* leader does not seek out personal benefit, is an example to others, and pays his employees on time. It means to have a pure heart as applied to both leaders and followers (I-117).

KAYAN - Industrious

The *kayan* leader is one who goes ahead of followers in the work, looks after followers, comes on time, does not stop working frequently, is not lazy, does everything, and is interested in the work.

MII HETPON - Reasonable

A *hetpon* is a reason for doing something, and I have chosen to translate it with the sense of being reasonable. The opposite expression is *mai mii hetpon* and carries the sense of unreasonable. Informants see the unreasonable person as using their moods as a basis for decision making, or always following their own thoughts rather than listening to others. The leader characterized as *mii hetpon* listens to others and sorts out which side is right and wrong, considers things before deciding, thinks before acting, and is capable of explaining what is happening to subordinates.

JAI DII - Kind

This is the final term of the four (*nisai dii*, *chuaylua*, *ben kan eng*, and *jai dii*) with representation across all of the lists for both actual and ideal leaders on perceptions by both leaders and nonleaders. Based on informant interviews it was very difficult to come up with a distinct meaning between this term and *namjai* (literally 'water from the heart' and translated as compassion, understanding, friendliness). While being helpful and giving are central in both and some informants made them virtually synonymous, there are distinctions that can be made and this was confirmed in the graphic representation of the metric scaling (see Figure 1). Illustrations from informants showed that *jai dii* could be expressed across three dimensions: speech, giving, and behaviour. The speech and behavioural elements are closely related; a *jai dii* leader is not overly harsh or scolding when a subordinate makes a mistake, does not come down too hard on others, forgives or lets things go, is merciful, and will help to solve problems. As it relates to giving, the key distinction between *jai dii* and *namjai* is that the former has to do with giving if asked or if the need is somehow made known. With the latter, the giving is generated by the concern the leader has for the other person and the initiation lies with the leader. *Jai dii* can also be seen as a term that is broader than *namjai*. Being *jai dii* can be shown through expressions of *namjai* or helping; there are many ways that is can be expressed. However, *jai dii* as kind behaviour does not necessarily mean concern, as a person can be playing out an expected role and not be truly interested or concerned in the other. *Namjai*, on the other hand, is the expression of concern when it has not been asked for.[9] T. made the following distinction between *jai dii* and *namjai*. *Namjai* has to do with helping someone else out, such as helping an old person in walking, helping someone who has

[9] Moore, in his popular treatment of 'heart' terms, makes *jai dii* the term for giving that is done without it being requested (1992:45-6; 84-5), and some of my informants made a similar statement. Moore's treatment of *namjai* made it the expression of consideration and appreciation, for example through small gifts (1992:50). While this smaller type of action is certainly present in *namjai*, my informants showed that it also can carry a much stronger idea of helping without the hope of getting anything in return, sacrificing for others, and assisting and being generous and liberal with those who are in trouble and struggling. It can include money, speech, and other actions.

fallen, or a group taking an offering up for a person who has had a relative die. *Jai dii* has to do with giving (*gaan hai*) (I-133, I-134).

KHAOWJAI LUUK NAWNG - Understands Followers

Understanding is expressed by listening to them, knowing their situation and their needs both at work and personally, giving counsel, forgiving them, and helping to solve problems. The person who understands also does not take advantage of others.

RAK LUUK NAWNG - Loves Followers

The terms in which love was expressed were often closely related to some of the other words in the list of 21 terms. This leader is informal and approachable, helps when a follower is in trouble (this was equated with being *namjai* as having compassion, understanding, and friendliness), shows interest in others, watches out over followers, protects them, is sympathetic, and greets and talks with followers.

RABPIDCHAWB - Responsible

This term was only weakly represented but I left it in because it was probably assumed on the part of those making leader perceptions, and there were also other terms that were related to this such as 'loving work' and being serious about work. My feeling about its importance to leadership was confirmed in three ways. First, informants were able to describe it quite easily in terms of being a leader characteristic. Second, when I experimented with a few pile sorts, getting local people to categorize the terms and indicate which were the most important for being an effective leader, responsibility always was high on the list. Finally, *kayan* (industrious) was often described in terms very similar to 'responsible'. Informants described responsibility in terms of watching over the work and the followers, performing their duty, working from the beginning to the end of a project, making sure things are right and orderly, and making sure there is no deficiency in the work.

YUTITHAM - Fair, Just

This characteristic was described as loving followers equally, listening to both sides and deciding which is right and wrong, understanding both sides, treating people equally, not deciding on their own, being straightforward, not deceiving or lying, not treating people as favourites.

SAWN LUUK NAWNG - Teaches Followers

This has to do both with giving words of advice and counsel, as well as instruction about the actual work. It involves being a good example, and not being harsh or scolding.

TRONG TAW WEELAA - On Time

This leader comes on time, comes before the work, comes to appointments on time, and is not late. This term did not appear in the terms on the ideal leader, but rather on actual leaders that people have experienced. It was pointed out to me that the reason why people said that being on time was important was because status is associated with time. If you come on time, this lowers your status; if you are of high status you come late and make others wait on you. This is frustrating to people but they cannot say anything about it to higher status people; so it is a quality that is desired by people. In their experiences with actual leaders this quality was noted and appreciated.

CHUUAY THAM NGAAN - Helps Followers with the Work

Informants related this to not taking advantage of the follower, and not holding oneself aloof as a boss. Instead, if the follower cannot get the job done, the leader helps, or if the work is too heavy they help. If the leader's work is finished he may come and help the follower. If the worker does not understand his work, this leader will counsel with them and give advice to help with the work.

BRUKSAA DAI - Able to Go to for Counsel

This means that when you have a problem or are in trouble, related to either your work or personal life, you can go and consult with this type of leader. They are open to being consulted on every kind of problem, from money to family problems. It is not necessary for them to give anything but they can just advise. *Bruksaa dai* is closely related to *ben kan eng*. The leader who is informal and familiar is not aloof, so this opens the door for the follower to come for counsel and advice.

RIABRAWY - Well Mannered, Polite

There were three terms primarily defined in terms of each other: *riabrawy*, *suphaap*, and *phuud jaa dii*. *Suphaap* (polite) is the broader term and *riabrawy* carries the idea of being well mannered, polite, neat, tidy, and in good order. You can work, dress, and behave *riabrawy*. Informants defined the characteristics of the *riabrawy* person as being detailed in their work, cautious, proper in dress, not dirty, being quiet in their motions and actions, having nothing in their work or person that can be criticized.

NAMJAI - literally 'water from the heart', translated here as having or showing compassion, understanding, friendliness, thoughtfulness, consideration and goodwill expressed, sincere concern.[10]

---

[10] Throughout the text I will refer to *namjai* using only the first three terms as a complex (compassion-understanding-friendliness), but it should be remembered that all of the

Namjai is one of the most difficult terms to translate. It was in attempts to understand terms like *namjai* and *jai dii* where I encountered the idea of different kinds of 'giving' that relate to the expectation of the giver. On the part of those receiving, giving creates a sense of obligation that varies in strength depending in part on the expectations of the giver in giving, either to hope for something in return (*wang sing tawb thaen*) or not hope for something in return. While some will equate *jai dii* and *namjai* (I-117), others will make the distinction that *namjai* has to do with giving that is from a heart of goodness and virtue (I-134) and does not expect anything in return. The *jai dii* person gives because the need may be made known, but with *namjai* the initiation lies with the person who sees the need and without a request seeks to meet it. The critical distinction between *namjai* and *jai dii* is that *namjai* grows out of consideration for the other. The giving of *namjai* encompasses not just tangible material giving but also in speech and actions, sacrificing for the other person. As I noted above, *namjai* has a 'thoughtfulness' kind of dimension where small kindnesses shown to another are *namjai* but it also has this deeper dimension of helping and supporting with kindness, generated by the initiative of the giver in response to the need of the other.

SUPHAAP - Polite

Informants defined this as *riabrawy* and in terms of speaking politely (*phuud jaa suphaap*). The polite person gives honour to others, is not disrespectful, and does not lie. As the broader term *suphaap* has three dimensions, that of speech, one's manner or bearing (*thaa thaang*), and one's countenance or look (*naa taa*). *Riabrawy* has two dimensions, that of manner or bearing and how a person dresses. Finally, *phuudjaa dii* has only one dimension, that of speaking.

DEDKAAD - Decisive

The decisive leader is serious in what he does, makes decisions and does not change or vacillate, and takes responsibility.

PHUUDJAA DII - literally 'speaking good', translated here as 'friendly speech'

Phuud jaa is colloquial for speaking and talking and this literally means to speak good. It was defined in terms of speaking politely and being polite and well mannered. Informants indicated that the person who is *phuudjaa dii* does not use coarse or low language, does not scold others, uses politeness particles in their speech,[11] speaks with reasons, speaks beautifully, is not aloof from

ideas listed above come into play in trying to express *namjai* in English (see Suntaree, 1990; 1994:45).

[11] For examples see Haas' listing of the numerous different nuances associated with the particle *na* (high tone), *na* (falling tone), *kha* (high tone), *kha* (falling tone), and *khrab* (1964). This includes making an utterance milder, indicating a mild question, coaxing,

others, is informal and familiar, submits to the authority of others, is respectful and mindful of others, and is humble.

MANUDSAMPHAN THII DII - Good Human Relational Skills

Informants related this very closely to speech. The person with good human relational skills is one who you can converse with, while the opposite is to be sullen, not greet others, and not talk. This person is one who is easy to get along with, interested in others, welcomes others, and is informal and familiar. The triad of *suphaap* (polite), *riabrawy* (well mannered and polite), and *phuud jaa dii* (friendly speech) are all related to good human relational skills because it is a part of being friendly as a means of interaction with others with the goal of getting along with others, which is an important part of having good character.

Using the questionnaire with the 210 pairs of terms for discrimination, I collected a total of 50 responses. Each respondent generated 210 answers in the form of a number ranging from one (not similar at all) to five (very similar). The answers were put into a text file organized by respondent, listing all their choices for the 210 discriminations, and this file was used to generate two types of analysis in ANTHROPAC, a consensus analysis and a correspondence analysis.

Consensus Analysis

Consensus analysis is a method designed to find out the percentage of agreement among a group of respondents where the answers are not known (Borgatti, 1990:40-4; Romney, Weller, & Batchelder, 1986). In this case I am trying to find out how much agreement there is among my informants on the interrelationships between the 21 terms. The assumption in consensus analysis is that cultural patterns are high consensus codes (Romney *et al.*, 1986:332) and therefore you want to see high informant-by-informant correlations with the first factor being several times larger than the second in order to have confidence to say that a cultural model is present (Borgatti, 1990:44; Romney *et al.*, 1986:332). Borgatti notes that the rule of thumb is, if the ratio between the first and second value is less than three to one, the assumption of there being a single cultural pattern is indefensible (1990:44). The higher the average informant-by-informant correlation, the stronger the patterning (Romney *et al.*, 1986:332), with 50 per cent and higher being considered a high level of agreement (Weller & Romney, 1988:76).

The results show a weak cultural pattern, which was not a surprise to me. I believe that the existence of even weak patterning is indicative that these terms actually represent shared material that is widely agreed upon. I base this assertion on my observations from collecting the paired similarity data.

---

expressing mild reproach, urging, acceptance, requesting, emphasizing, intimating, use in a command or question, as agreement, and so on.

Watching how people handled the exercise I was sceptical that there would be any patterning at all. Consensus analysis is based on the assumption of independence, which in an anthropological context means that 'the only force drawing people to a given answer is the culturally correct answer' (Borgatti, 1990:44). This assumption was violated in LWPW because of the low educational backgrounds of people and the physical and social context of the slum. People in the slum who have limited education feel that they cannot answer questions, and this leads them to draw in others to help them. The density of people in the community insured that privacy was virtually impossible in interview settings which were done outside of their dwellings. The novelty of a foreign researcher would often draw a group as well, and I observed that debates would break out on how dissimilar or similar two terms were. Completely different lines of reasoning would manifest so that answers were very diverse. Many people found it difficult to understand and would read into the exercise, thinking they were rating some kind of actual person rather than comparing terms. Finally, with 210 questions it was obvious that people became bored and started marking answers without making discriminations. I believe that a weak cultural pattern is not indicative of multiple patterns in the data but is related to the challenges encountered in collecting data among this type of population.

The Results of the Correspondence Analysis

Correspondence analysis is a tool that falls under the rubric of metric or multidimensional scaling. It provides a visual representation of similarities of a set of objects, allowing us to look at a complex set of relationships at a glance (Borgatti, 1990:28, 30), and serves as a tool for the descriptive task 'of revealing the structure of the data and providing a scaled model of that structure' (Weller & Romney, 1990:7). I analysed the paired similarity data using the correspondence analysis function in ANTHROPAC and then graphed the results with the Statistical Program for the Social Sciences (SPSS) programme. Figure 1 shows the results along two dimensions. Correspondence analysis produces a point rather than vector model so that the degree of similarity between items is related to how close the points are in the space of the diagram (Weller & Romney, 1990:12). In this sense the points on the diagram represent the relationship between terms in the psychological space of the aggregation of the informants. In this section I present an interpretation of the visual representation of the data provided by the correspondence analysis.

The Nature of the Representation of the 21 Terms

What precisely is the nature of this visual representation? The result of the methods applied and seen here in Figure 1 is the raw material of an implicit theory of culturally preferred leadership among the people of LWPW in the specific context of the relationships between an employer/superior and employee/subordinate in a work setting. The terms represent implicit leadership traits[12] based on the personal characteristics and attributes that followers expect from leaders (Ling, Chia, & Fang, 2000:730). They provide a window to how people in this community conceive of a prototypical leader, and help elucidate the social influence processes that cause others to see a person as a leader or potential leader (Yukl, 2002:129). This is baseline sociolinguistic data that gives insight into the conceptual structure and discourse used to construct culturally preferred forms of interpersonal influence.

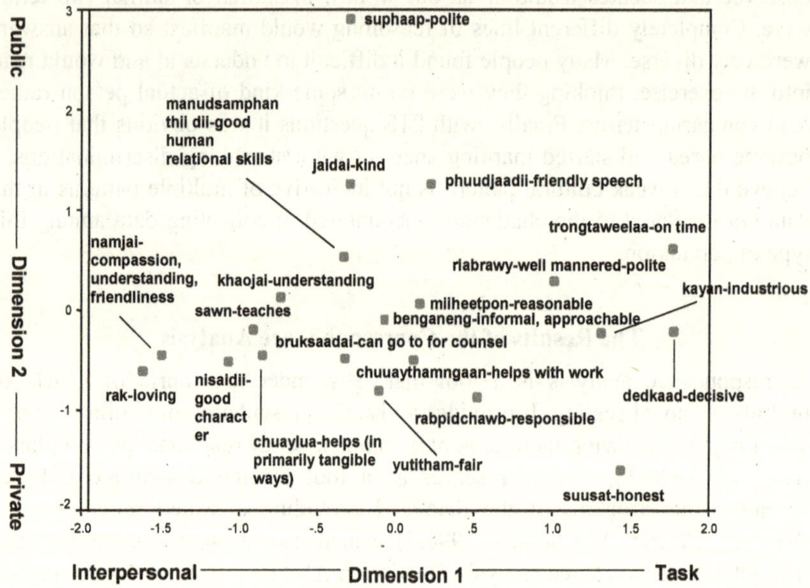

Figure 1 Correspondence analysis of the 21 terms on two dimensions

In working with this material there are a few points to keep in mind. It was generated in the specific context of working relationships with a specific set of questions. The type of question used affected the terms generated; a different

---

[12] The concept of traits stems from the attempt to account for consistencies within personality (Cattell, 1968:123). Personality traits, as 'relatively stable dispositions to behave in a particular way' (Yukl, 2002:175) include constellations of behaviours, operate over a wide variety of situations, and contain that notion of being a characteristic that a person can have more or less of (Cattell, 1968:123-4, 126). The 21 terms generated from the free-recall listing can be best thought of as traits, representing characteristics and associated behaviour which taken together as a whole form a prototypical view of a culturally preferred leader.

set of questions worded in a different fashion would certainly have yielded some different terms. It is important to keep in focus that these terms in the aggregate do not represent any single leader, but rather indicate what a prototypical leader looks like. This is not *the* single model of culturally preferred leadership; rather it is a construction specific to the context and types of questions that were asked. The 21 terms are representative of key concepts but do not capture everything that existed within the free-recall listing exercise. They were chosen from a larger pool of terms because of limitations inherent in the paired similarity judgement exercise, which becomes too long to expect people to complete if beyond 21 terms.

Interpretation of the Correspondence Analysis

In analyzing a map produced by correspondence analysis it is important to remember that the axes are by themselves meaningless and the orientation is arbitrary; what is significant is which points are close to other points (Borgatti, 1990:34). The contribution of the visual representation is in terms of identifying dimensions and clusters (Borgatti, 1990:34-5). Borgatti defines dimensions as 'attributes that seem to order the items in the map along a continuum' and which theoretically are 'thought to "explain" the perceived similarity between items' (1990:35). Clusters are groups of items that are closer to each other on the map (1990:34).

Since the consensus analysis showed only a weak cultural patterning, I decided to investigate other methods that might be easier for people in the community to work with than the paired similarity. I developed the interpretation offered here from three major sources: the visual representation of the correspondence analysis, hierarchical clustering of pile sort data[13], and interviews on term definitions and relationships. These multiple sources of analysis create a triangulation of data that lends more weight to the interpretation than any single source would have provided.

---

[13] Pile sorting is a form of classification, showing which things go together. I used it with the 21 terms to produce a matrix showing the percentage of informant agreement as to how often respondents placed two terms together. This matrix can be analysed using consensus, correspondence analysis, or hierarchical clustering. When the items in a domain have been identified they can be put on a card and then informants can be asked to sort them into piles so that similar items are in the same pile (Weller, 1998:386). There are many versions of pile sorting and I used the unconstrained version that does not limit the number of piles. The only rule is that there must be two or more items in a pile; singles are not allowed. Clustering analysis is useful for finding out what goes with what and to what degree (Handwerker & Borgatti, 1998:556). In the matrix that I have analysed the levels of clustering are the rows, expressed in terms of the percentage how often the two terms were placed together, and the terms are the columns (see Borgatti, 1990:27-9).

I begin with the results of the pile sorting and hierarchical clustering because these are procedures that help us see what terms go together and to what degree (Handwerker & Borgatti, 1998:556). As I mentioned above, the logic of the consensus analysis is that strong cultural patterning exists at anything over 50 per cent of informant-by-informant agreement.

Figure 2 is a hierarchical clustering of pile sort data taken from 30 respondents in LWPW. The 21 terms are listed across the top in abbreviated form (the number below them was assigned for the pile sort), and the per cent of agreement among informants is on the left. This analysis confirms and illuminates the relationships between items in the visual representation of the correspondence analysis in Figure 1. At the 47 to 50 per cent level and above four major groupings are seen:

- cluster one: good character, friendly speech, well mannered-polite, polite
- cluster two: loving, understanding, teaching
- cluster three: helps with work, industrious
- cluster four: responsible, on time, honest, fair, reasonable, decisive

Three of these clusters match closely with the way the visual representation of the correspondence analysis divides on the horizontal axis. Dimension 1 in Figure 1 is a continuum of task related behaviour (to the right) and interpersonal behaviour (on the left). The terms of clusters one and two are located on the left side of Figure 1, while cluster four lies on the right. The clustering analysis also clarifies and enhances understanding of the relations between terms in the interpersonal side and connections between the interpersonal and task poles. Cluster two suggests further differentiation among the interpersonal terms, linking behaviour directed specifically towards the subordinate. Cluster three suggests that some interpersonal behaviour can be linked to task accomplishment as well on the interpersonal side of the map.

Dimension 2 on the vertical axis in Figure 1 is a continuum from public behaviour located on the upper half to the private internal world on the lower half. The public pole has to do with behaviour that is observable to others; this includes politeness, friendly speech, human relational skills, manners, kindness, and being on time. The private pole includes good character, helping others, and being fair, responsible, and honest. These traits are not simply internal, as they are also expressed in behaviour, but they speak to what is more deeply rooted and indicative of character. Note however that cluster one shows that on the private pole good character is closely link with public behaviour in the minds of informants, the external flowing from the internal.

```
JOHNSON'S HIERARCHICAL CLUSTERING

Input dataset:                  C:\PROGRA~1\ANTHRO~1\AGPRO
Method:                         AVERAGE
Type of Data:                   Similarities

HIERARCHICAL CLUSTERING

            C             U
          H O             N
          U M             D     I   I   R
          M P   F W       E     N   N   E       R
          R U   R E       R   H D   F   S       E
          E N G I L       S T E U   A   P       A D
          L D O E L       T E L S H P C O       S E
          S F O N M P   L A A P T E P O N O H   O C
          K R D D A O   O N C S R L R U S N O   N I
          I I C L N L K V D H W I P O N I T N F A S
          L E H Y P I I I I I O O I A S B I E A B I
          L N A S O T N N N N R U N C E L M S I L V
          S D R P L E D G G G K S G H L E E T R E E

                        1 1 1   1 1   1 1 2 1 1 1 2
 Level    3 2 1 5 6 7 8 1 2 4 9 9 0 4 3 8 0 6 7 5 1
------    - - - - - - - - - - - - - - - - - - - - -
0.7000    . . . . . . . . . . . . . . . . . XXX . .
0.6667    . . . . XXX . . . . . . . . . . . XXX . .
0.6000    . . . . XXX . XXX . XXX . . . . . XXX . .
0.5667    . . XXX XXX . XXX . XXX . . . . . XXX . .
0.5333    . . XXX XXX . XXXXX XXX . . . . . XXX XXX
0.5148    . . XXX XXX . XXXXX XXX . . . . . XXXXXXX
0.5037    . . XXXXXXX . XXXXX XXX . . . . . XXXXXXX
0.5000    . . XXXXXXX . XXXXX XXX . . . XXX XXXXXXX
0.4778    . . XXXXXXX . XXXXX XXX . . . XXXXXXXXXXX
0.4756    . . XXXXXXX XXXXXXX XXX . . . XXXXXXXXXXX
0.4333    . . XXXXXXX XXXXXXX XXX . XXX XXXXXXXXXXX
0.3778    . . XXXXXXX XXXXXXX XXX XXXXX XXXXXXXXXXX
0.3741    . XXXXXXXXX XXXXXXX XXX XXXXX XXXXXXXXXXX
0.3407    XXXXXXXXXXX XXXXXXX XXX XXXXX XXXXXXXXXXX
0.3229    XXXXXXXXXXX XXXXXXX XXX XXXXXXXXXXXXXXXXX
0.3138    XXXXXXXXXXX XXXXXXXXXXX XXXXXXXXXXXXXXXXX
0.2446    XXXXXXXXXXX XXXXXXXXXXXXXXXXXXXXXXXXXXXXX
0.2107    XXXXXXXXXXXXXXXXXXXXXXXXXXXXXXXXXXXXXXXXX
```

Figure 2 Hierarchical clustering analysis from 30 respondents in LWPW

I want to draw all of this material together now to offer a model[14] illustrated in a graphic representation that is based on the term definitions, correspondence analysis, and hierarchical clustering, but goes beyond these as an interpretation of it as a whole. This model represents an implicit theory of culturally preferred leadership in LWPW, which I call the *Thuukjai* Leader Model (TLM).[15]

---

[14] I use the idea of model here in the sense that Jacobs defines it, as a 'series of logically interrelated statements about reality; the statements serve as blueprints for the analysis of that reality' (1971:5). He points out that models are not designed to be comprehensive, but rather they are judged on how well they provide understanding of the reality being studied (1971:5-6).

[15] Naming this model was not an easy task. I worked through a number of different options before deciding to use the Thai word *thuukjai* (satisfying, pleasing) which was part of the question terminology in the free-recall listing scenario on a preferred or ideal leader. In the end I chose to utilize *thuukjai* in keeping with my emphasis throughout on trying to elucidate Thai conceptualizations rather than setting the Thai material into a broader framework of sociological terms.

I attempt to show how the various terms connect together and relate in the larger framework of the public, private, task, and interpersonal dimensions.[16] A superior who makes subordinates feel pleased and satisfied (*thuukjai*) is strong in both task and interpersonal relations. The behaviour cluster that relates to work very clearly reveals Thai cultural preferences and values. The *thuukjai* leader makes sure the job is done but not at the expense of relationships with subordinates. The term definitions show that people do not make a sharp separation between work and personal life, thus 'helping' and 'loving' can be expressed to a subordinate outside of the work context when they are having problems. This behaviour configuration happens in dyadic relations and is a key to motivation for subordinates in the Thai context (this idea will be explored further in Chapter 6).

There is another set of publicly observable traits, but I have placed these at the upper side of the private dimension. They represent the public self that others see but are rooted in private character, expressed in the ideas of good character and honesty, the deepest levels of the private self.[17] The critical connector that has much to do with causing subordinates to feel *thuukjai* is the informal-approachable (*ben kan eng*) trait. The public self that others see is brought into action in dyadic relations by being informal-approachable, someone who can be sought out for counsel, who helps in time of need, who gets involved helping people with their work. Being informal-approachable operationalizes the publicly observable image into warm dyadic relations.

---

[16] Two points of clarification are needed here. First, I am making a shift in the use of the term 'dimension'. In the visual representation of the correspondence analysis a dimension represents a continuum of attributes which can be used to explain the similarity and differences of the items (see Borgatti, 1990:35). In the TLM I am using dimension in a slightly different fashion, the four 'dimensions' being elements or component parts of the whole. At the same time they retain their sense of being a continuum as well so that it can be said there is a public-private dimension and a task-interpersonal dimension. The second point is that in order to develop this analytical model I have had to separate and make distinctions between items that are not always separable. The value of the model here is not that it captures every single relationship between terms, but that it provides a broader heuristic for understanding how major configurations connect to create interpersonal influence.

[17] The notion of public self and private self was suggested to me by Dr. Suntaree while we were discussing ways of representing this implicit leadership theory model. The idea of the self having a public and private side helps to capture the publicly observable 'face' that others see and to separate it analytically from the strong cluster that emerged which was also public and interpersonal (what I have termed 'work related relational behaviour').

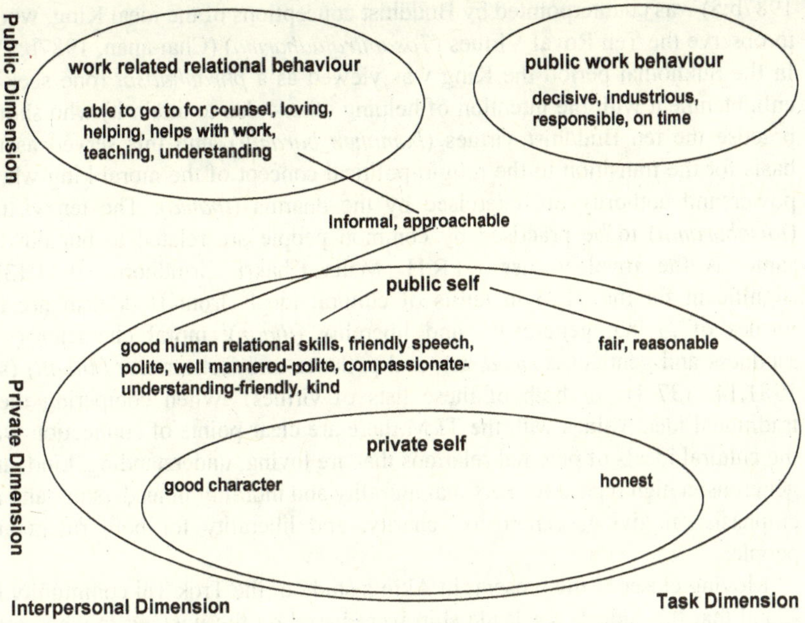

Figure 3 Major dimensions of the *Thuukjai* Leader Model

The TLM and Thai Leadership Ideals

The question arises as to the relationship of the TLM, developed in a very specific context, to any types of known leadership patterns or leadership ideals in the Thai social structure. I find in the literature five potential points of contact with this model, though none are isomorphic with it. The ideals represented in the model have antecedents in traditional values of idealized superior-subordinate relationships, concepts of ideal monarchy, principles of Buddhist virtue, elements of the positive view of the traditional form of *nakleng* leadership, and changes in the political culture in terms of what constitutes morally acceptable leadership.

Idealized superior behaviour in the superior-subordinate (*phuu yai-phuu noi*) dyad is to act calm, be kind, generous, and protecting (Akin, 1975a:109). In terms of ideal conceptions of monarchy, the Sukhothai and Ayuthayan periods provided values that have shaped ideals regarding leadership. In the Sukhothai era the style was that of patriarchal monarchy, where the King was seen as the father of all his people (Thinapan, 1987:168, see page 191 footnote 5 for a list of historical sources; Wyatt, 1984:54). In the Ayuthayan era the Hindu-

Brahmanical[18] ideology that emphasized the ruler as a warrior-king (Chai-anan, 1987b:5) was counterpointed by Buddhist conceptions of the ideal King, who is to observe the Ten Royal Virtues (*Tosapitrajadharma*) (Chai-anan, 1987b:9).[19] In the Sukhothai period the King was viewed as a *phraphotisat* (one seeking enlightenment with the intention of helping others also to attain it) who should practise the ten Buddhist virtues (*bamphen_baramii*), and this served as the basis for the transition to the religio-political concept of the moral king whose power and authority are exercised by the dharma (*thama*). The ten virtues (*totsabaramii*) to be practised by common people are related to but not the same as the royal virtues (H.R.H. Maha Chakri Sirindhorn, 1981:137). Significant for the TLM in terms of cultural ideals from Buddhism are the virtues of giving, generosity, and liberality (*thaan*); moral character (*sil*); kindness and gentleness (*medtaa*); and patience and forbearance (*khanti*) (see 1981:14, 137-41 for both of these lists of virtues). When comparing these traditional ideal values with the TLM there are clear points of connection with the cultural ideals of paternal relations that are loving, understanding, kind, and generous; a high regard for personal morality and morality in leadership; and an emphasis on giving, generosity, charity, and liberality for both rulers and people.

Moving closer to the present, in Akin's study of the Trok Tai community he found that their ideals for leadership were based on the *nakleng to* who could give aid, protection, and help (1975b:287). Associated with this was also the positive view of the heart of the *nakleng* which is expressed by a willingness to give up everything for friends and followers without hesitation (1975b:287). Ockey cites interview data indicating that people feel that in order to be successful in politics one must be bold and decisive, which are traits associated with the idea of having the heart (*jai*) of a *nakleng* (2004b:79-80). Again the dual themes of giving, helping, and loving combined with decisiveness match well with values in the TLM. Ockey has also traced changes in the political culture through recent decades and argues that *nakleng* type Prime Ministers were historically more successful prior to the 1970s, while *phuu dii* (good

---

[18] Chai-anan points out that both the Hindu and Buddhist philosophical streams were present as cultural and political foundations well before the Sukhothai kingdom and that what is referred to as the 'Indianization' of Ayuthaya was a process begun in the Sukhothai era (1987b:8).

[19] The ten duties of the King are as follows: liberality, charity, generosity (*dana*), high moral character (*sila*), sacrificing everything for the good of the people (*pariccaga*), honesty and integrity (*ajjava*), kindness and gentleness (*maddava*), austerity in habits (*tapa*), freedom from hatred, ill-will, enmity (*akkadha*); non-violence (*avihimsa*), patience, forbearance, tolerance, understanding (*khanti*); non-opposition, non-obstruction, in the sense of not to oppose the will of the people or measures that help the welfare of the people (*avirodha*) (Shin, 1989:101-2).

person) style leaders have been more successful since (2004b:8).[20] He sees the *phuu dii* as being associated with moral goodness (*khunna*) and believes that this indicates a change in political culture as regards the nature of legitimate leadership (2004b:8). The TLM seems to track with Ockey's observations about the change in what is deemed legitimate leadership. Forty years ago in the slum Akin studied, it was the idealized version of *nakleng* that provided the model, and actual *nakleng* formed the leadership structure. Today in LWPW *nakleng* are not seen as legitimate leaders and leadership ideals focus on moral qualities like 'good character' (*nisai dii*), which was the most frequent and salient term in the combined list from all the free-recall listings.

The TLM and Issues in Thai Leadership

I now want to move beyond the description of the TLM and seek to understand how it works to create interpersonal influence. This analysis will be done in light of some key issues in the area of Thai leadership studies. In Chapter 3 I pointed out that from the perspective of residents, the critical issue for *chumchon* leadership is the ability to secure cooperation for a variety of different kinds of tasks, events, and activities. Because of the voluntary nature of the community leader-resident relationship, there being very limited positional power or ability to use reward or sanctions to gain cooperation, it is personal power that leaders must rely on. This touches upon the realm of interpersonal relations in Thai society, how various relations are formed, and the kinds of obligations entailed in each.

I have already noted above that the TLM represents how people in the community perceive a person who has the potential for interpersonal influence. The model also gives insight into the dynamics of influence, showing patterns of behaviour that are linked together. However from the beginning of the data collection process it was clear that there are multiple bases for interpersonal influence and that the TLM represents one type among several.[21] This raises the question of how the TLM actually works and why it is an ideal and preferred model in contrast to other bases of interpersonal influence. Asking this question leads to the issue of patron-client relations and the nature of reciprocity and obligation. In Chapter 2 I traced the debate over how to understand patron-client relations in Thai society; one line of thought has seen patron-client relations as the master key for understanding Thai social organization, to the

---

[20] *Phuu dii* means literally 'good person' and was originally used to describe members of the aristocracy. While retaining this connotation it also refers to 'well-mannered' and 'good' people in general (Ockey, 2004b:7-8).

[21] People's comments about leadership generally fell into four basic categories: descriptions in terms of a positive or negative experience, differentiating types of leadership based on how leaders gain cooperation, the scarcity of those they considered to be good leaders, and the impact of good leaders on work performance.

point that virtually all dyadic relations are seen in this light. If this is the case then all forms of leadership simply become a manifestation of such relations. In order to offer an answer to these questions in light of my findings I will first begin with what appears to be a digression into other bases for influence, add some findings on the subject of reciprocity and obligation, and finally return to the TLM to draw some conclusions regarding how this model works to build influence in the voluntary cooperation setting of the slum, and how it relates to patron-client relations.

Examining Other Bases for Interpersonal Influence

In Chapter 2 I introduced the work of Suntaree on personal power as expressed in the term *baramii*, and Conner's development of three foundations for interpersonal influence: power (*amnaat*), influence (*ittipon*), and *baramii*. In Chapter 7 of his thesis Conner examines in detail these three foundations and notes that each one elicits a variety of responses in other people. In my own interactions with people in the community, as with Conner and his informants, I observed a fluidity of use regarding these terms, a kind of polarity where native speakers could use a term with a positive or negative connotation depending on the circumstances. Thus with both the leadership foundation terms and the terms used to express response to those foundations, the same terms can be used in different contexts to mean different things, or to express different nuances of meaning. The polyvalence seen here should signal some caution in attempting to formulate a framework based on a stable meaning for a particular term. In my opinion a problematic point in Conner's analysis was that in his attempt to systematize a leadership foundations continuum with clear cut boundaries, he had to downplay or dismiss evidence of linguistic diversity and multiplex usages, particularly as it relates to *baramii*.[22] In the material that follows I draw upon Conner, but attempt to move beyond his three foundations rubric to embrace more of the nuances found in interpersonal influence. Whereas the idea of follower response to another person exhibiting one of these three foundations was somewhat peripheral to his work, it is central to what I am doing in trying to understand how cooperation and compliance are given or withheld in the voluntary relational setting of the slum. My ultimate goal here

---

[22] Some of Conner's informants suggested that *baramii* could be used in a negative sense to describe mafia type godfathers (*jao pho*) (1996:261). He notes that his informants disagreed among each other with some asserting the term could be used in this fashion, and others arguing that it represented a misunderstanding of the term (1996:238 footnote 17). In the end he argued that when local people use the term in a negative sense it is an incomplete attribution that should be corrected (1996:307) I feel uncomfortable with telling native speakers what is the correct understanding of a term that they seem to have quite definite ideas about. The necessity to bend local meaning to conform to an attempt at systematization is an indicator of other factors that should be taken into consideration.

is to increase understanding of how the TLM 'works' in terms of being a preferred style and a prototype for being a person able to influence others.

Without attempting to replicate the detailed work that Connor did on these three foundations of influence, I will draw upon his and Suntaree's work, and my informants' comments, to point out the major polarities of usage of the terms *amnaat* (power), *ittipon* (influence), and *baramii* (personal power). With this information as a baseline I will then examine the nature of the relational bonds that are formed through these different bases, how these bonds impact the building of influence in the kind of voluntary relations seen between community leaders and residents, and see whether or not other bases for securing cooperation are possible.

Working with focus groups of native speakers both inside and outside the slum who were primarily, though not exclusively, urban poor, I collected data on the different ways people use the words *amnaat*, *ittipon*, and *baramii*. I find that both power and influence have positive and negative views, while *baramii* has four different views: an ideal moral sense, a prestige sense, a negative sense in which it is used to refer to *jao pho* (godfather types), and a charismatic sense as used by Weber. My impression was that in the community, generally *amnaat* and *ittipon* were used in a more negative sense to refer to *nakleng* types. *Baramii* rarely came up in conversations in the community, but when it did it was used more in the prestige sense than the ideal sense. People would often qualify their use of the term by saying it was a 'type' (*baeb*) of *baramii* or by equating it with money.

As I noted earlier, Conner points out that each of these bases for interpersonal influence elicit a response on the part of other people, such as polite deference (*kreng jai*), fear (*kreng klua*), and grateful obligation (*bunkhun*). While I was familiar with these terms, it was not until much later in the data collection process that I became aware of two key points regarding these response concepts. First, it became clear that in the eyes of residents, both those with formal positions and those with no position, the crux of community leadership was the ability to gain cooperation from others. The second was that people were framing their explanations of why they or others would cooperate with a person based on these ideas of deference, fear, and gratitude.[23] While these concepts cover more territory than just compliance, cooperation, or obeying a command, there is a part that includes that potential within them. What this means in a practical sense is that any given instance of cooperation can be generated from a number of different response motives. This leads naturally to the question of whether or not the concepts of *amnaat*, *ittipon*, and

---

[23] In working on explaining *kreng jai* for outsiders Suntaree has provided a number of behavioural examples (1994:45). One of them was being *kreng jai* to refuse complying with others' wishes or requests. This is precisely the way that the interviewees I worked with framed their explanations of why they would cooperate or join with the giving party.

baramii comprehensively cover all possible forms of response, or if there are other bases upon which to build cooperation. It also raises the question of where the TLM sits in its relation to these leadership foundations.

I set up a method to investigate these questions based on disparate observations that coalesced later on in my study. One thing that emerged from looking broadly at the preferred model was the centrality of some form of giving. In working on defining the 21 terms it became clear that many of them are operationalized in some form of giving. This is generally conceived of in tangible terms such as financial assistance, but may be intangible. The giving can include providing emotional support, understanding, and counsel. As I delved deeper into these concepts I also learned that forms of giving not only produce a response inside of those receiving, but also that the response varies based on the receiver's perception of the motive of the giver as expressed in the idea of hoping for something in return (*wang sing tawb thaen*) or giving freely without any interest in personal benefit (*mai wang sing tawb thaen*).

The response that giving creates inside the receiving party partly contains a sense of obligation back to the giving party. Thus I began by thinking in terms of a continuum expressing the sense of obligation that one person has to another. This sense of obligation represents a potential to cooperate with another person, should that person invite her, or be in a position to require help. Theoretically the continuum ranges from the highest sense of obligation on one end all the way down to no obligation at all on the other, as in tit-for-tat economic exchanges. I then set up with interviewees sets of scenarios of dyadic relationships where person A was involved in some form of giving to person B. I would often draw an A-B relationship at the bottom of a sheet of paper, representing a transaction in which there was no need for reciprocation (such as the purchase of an item at a store) and than draw an A-B relationship at the top of the paper, asking interviewees to think of a relationship which carried the maximum sense of obligation they could conceive. With this in place I would then explore the different types of possible relationships that could exist with a focus on the kind of response that was generated inside of the receiving party. After doing this for a while and getting a feel for some of the parameters, I would create scenarios of specific relationships (such as professor to student) and vary their status, the closeness of the relationship, and the type of giving to see how it affected the sense of obligation inside the receiving party. I would also create the scenario of community leadership and inquire specifically as to how this particular sense of obligation would impact a request for or perception of the need for cooperation. In setting up the scenarios of dyadic relations I limited myself at two points. I excluded dyadic relations where one person had formal positional power that would require the subordinate to comply whether they wanted to or not or else face some kind of sanctions, since this type of situation did not exist in LWPW. I also excluded relations between kin because the situation in the community required leaders to mobilize more than just family members.

Working through these scenarios gave me a number of insights into the nature of obligation and reciprocity, which in turn brought a sharper focus to the dynamics of the TLM. In the next two sections I summarize my findings in two ways: first as a series of general points, and second as a set of factors that people take into consideration when calculating the type of obligation they have to another person. I then conclude the chapter by looking at how these findings connect to the TLM.

General Insights on Reciprocity and Obligation

The Same Response Terms are Used for All Relationships

Terms used to describe the response evoked inside of a recipient to an act of giving, such as *kreng jai*, *kreng klua*, and *bunkhun* are utilized across the gamut of social relationships. At every level and type of relationship people were able to make fine distinctions between and among these terms. In the section that follows where I discuss a number of factors I will look at some of these criteria for making distinctions.

People are Aware of the Scope of Their Obligations to Others

I found that in a particular relationship people are aware of what that relationship requires in terms of reciprocity and obligation. They can define its parameters, quantify it, and make choices about behaviour based on their sense of who they owe relatively more obligation and need for reciprocation. Recipients are active agents in making attributions about giver motives and adjust their sense of obligation based on their evaluation of the situation.

Not All Relations are Patron-Client

The basic rules of hierarchical relations between social superiors and inferiors apply at all times and at different levels of status. I argued in Chapter 2 that hierarchical relations are not in and of themselves patron-client relations, which are a specific type of relationship. In the community there are patron-client relations of the type known as *nakleng* and *luuk nawng*. *Nakleng* are those who have *ittipon* (influence) and, as was explained to me, in the history of Lang Wat Pathum Wanaram (LWPW) they were often leaders because they had the ability to *jat klum* (form a group); in L.P.'s words, '*khaw ma tawng ma*' (if they ask you to come, you have to come) (I-323). In general, informants say that the sense of obligation in such a relationship is rooted in being *kreng klua*, which in this context carries the idea of literally being afraid. *Kreng klua* covers the range of fear, from being in awe of, to reverence and respect (So, 1984).[24] With

[24] As with the English term fear, this term can apply to both positive and negative situations. You can have fear in a positive sense of the King or of parents, and you can have fear of physical harm as with *nakleng*.

the *nakleng*, actual fear is present because as a person who has 'influence' the *nakleng* can use their influence to threaten and actually carry out physical harm.

People in the community were very clear that acts of giving between a social superior and inferior in and of themselves do not constitute a patron-client relationship of the type known as *luuk phii-luuk nawng.*[25] There are other discriminating factors (I discuss these below) that enter into the equation that will dictate whether the relations turn into that of patron and client.

Personal Power Embraces More Than *Baramii*

Both Suntaree and Conner have proposed *baramii* as a Thai concept that falls under the area of leadership studies dealing with leader power, and specifically that of personal power.[26] I want to suggest here in a preliminary fashion, and then pick up the theme in more detail in Chapter 5, that there are other forms of personal power besides *baramii.* My investigations on dyadic relations showed that there are types of relations that do not partake of *amnaat* or *ittipon*, but at the same time do not fit any of the three types of *baramii* that I have described above. In light of the diverse use of *baramii* and the difficulties with classifications of power, it may be more useful to track these indigenous concepts in the Weberian scheme of legitimate authority. Rather than attempting a clean systematization of the Thai concepts, which is difficult due to polyvalent meanings, it could be more insightful to map them against Weber's ideal types. As Weber notes, in the real world we seldom find these pure types (1947:110), but they do provide a useful framework for placing these different concepts. *Amnaat* (power) clearly has legal overtones in one of its forms, while *ittipon* (influence), particularly in the *nakleng* as ruffian leader sense, and *baramii* represent traditional forms of authority. As Conner notes, *ittipon* can shadow or parallel *amnaat*, drawing upon positional power to increase influence in this negative sense (1996:239). Similarly *amnaat* can be built from *ittipon* as a traditional form of leadership outside of the legitimation of a formal position on a legal basis. While pure *baramii* could certainly be a part of charismatic authority in the case of the monarch, in general use it is a

---

[25] Akin says that the patron-client relationship is expressed in the term *luuk phii-luuk nawng*. The dictionary definition is cousins (literally 'child of older sibling-child of younger sibling') but it carries a range of meanings. I inquired about this in LWPW and people explained that it can be used in three ways. It can refer literally to family, it can be used in the context of a boss-employee relationship, and it can also refer to a *nakleng*-follower relationship (I-294).

[26] I will use personal power in its broader sense as potential influence based in friendship and loyalty, as contrasted to position power that grows from legitimate authority, control over resources, rewards, punishment, information, and the work environment (Yukl, 2002:144). For definitions of various types of power and classificatory schemes see Dahl (1968:412); French and Raven's five types: reward, coercive, legitimate, expert, and referent (1959); Bass (1990:228); Yukl (2002:144-5); Dubrin (1998:163).

traditional form of leadership based on the moral character of the leader. At this point I think it would be more helpful within the frame of traditional leadership to see *baramii* as part of a continuum of concepts that includes respect and trust. I introduce this issue here because of its relationship to the discussion of the TLM that will follow, but in Chapter 5 I will develop the evidence for this assertion in more detail.

Not All Compliance is Based in Reciprocation and Obligation

Because the tendency has been to focus on status differentials and patron-client relations in Thai studies I wanted to particularly examine relationships that are more horizontal in nature, like those found in groups (*klum*), cliques (*phak phuak*), and between friends (*phuan*). While there is less difference in status in horizontal relations, *kreng jai* still applies, and as I noted above, expressions of help and goodwill increase the sense of *kreng jai*. One focus group noted that within a clique there is informality and mutual sharing, and the closer people become, the fewer boundaries or limitations they have in helping each other (I-325). This points to a key direction where the relational bond in horizontal relationships is different from vertical relationships in the arena of helping others. In relationships of larger difference in status the discourse is based on *kreng jai* and *bunkhun*, and the corresponding idea of reciprocation (*tawb thaen*). With groups, cliques, and friends it is possible to have the same dynamics built through expressions of giving, however, there are also other bases for cooperation that can be activated that are different from reciprocation based on gratitude and polite deference. Cooperation is rendered because a person might *hen kae* (look out for the sake of, act out of consideration for) another person, know the other person well, or help out because he is part of a group. Voluntary cooperation can also grow from trust or respect, or the perception of mutual benefit. One of my Thai friends explained, 'Relationship can occur, not because of an individual, but because of joint benefit' (Wirachai Kowae, 2006). In the case of friends, the reason given for helping out was the feeling of friendship (*mitraphaap*). In the case of being part of a group, such as the *chumchon*, it can be described as a sense of group solidarity, *rao ben chumchon diaow* (we are one *chumchon*), or being a part of the *chumchon* (*rao ben suan khawng chumchon*).

Factors that Influence a Person's Sense of Obligation

In the section above I made some general observations regarding reciprocity and obligation based on my interview data regarding dyadic relations where some form of giving is expressed from a social superior to an inferior. In this section I summarize a series of factors that I drew out of this interview material about what a receiving party takes into account in order to determine the type and level of obligation they have to the giving party.

Factor # 1: What is the Motive of the Person Giving?

A key insight from one informant was that it is the element of *choice* on the part of the giving party that forms the basis for a sense of obligation. A pure business transaction, such as with a bank or a loan department is governed by rules and regulations, so there is no choice or personal opinion in the matter (I-307). However, in the realm of personal relations, the decision to let a person rent a place to live from you or the decision to release money at interest for a loan, represents a choice of that particular person over a field of many possible receivers. This then is an expression of goodwill (*namjai*), being kind (*jai dii*), or helping (*chuay*) in a time of need, and it forms the core of the feeling of a need to reciprocate.

However, once the giving person makes the choice to give in some way, the receiving person immediately starts an evaluative process that seeks to determine if the motive for giving was to get something in return (*wang sing tawb thaen*) or to not expect anything in return (*mai wang sing tawb thaen*). It is this perception of motive that is a determining factor in the sense of the level of obligation due. I have already noted the work of Suntaree on *bunkhun* (grateful) relationships and the distinction between psychologically invested relationships and those that are transactional (1985:183). She notes that there is a subtle distinction between the two, one based in true feelings of gratitude and the other in a friendly but non-committal relationship (1985:184). Among my informants there seemed to be a level of disagreement regarding *bunkhun* and its formation, which may reflect a cultural value in transition. For some, the presence of virtually any giving was capable of building a sense of gratitude defined as *bunkhun*, such as Bangkok City Council or District Council politicians coming into the slum and passing out gifts on a special day like Children's Day (I-67). As one informant put it, 'this is the character of Thai people – giving even just a little bit builds *bunkhun*, and they will think about (*nukthung*) *bunkhun*' (I-226). However, when I tried to gain some understanding of the sense of obligation created by the practise of vote-buying by politicians I got a different picture. People noted that in past times to receive and not reciprocate made a person feel like they were *thambaab* (sinning) (I-300, I-319). While some still have this feeling, others will analyse the situation to see if voting for that person is the best or not (I-300), or will vote for whomever they want since the person who gave them the money cannot see who they are voting for (I-319). Feelings of *bunkhun* grew in people if they were in an extreme situation and someone loaned them money (I-303), and it is related to a difference in status and implies that the person on the receiving side is *tok yaak* (in a difficult situation) (I-328). These feelings also have to do with the size of the help given and its persistence over time. One person illustrated in this fashion: she is having financial difficulties and a person who is older but also poor has helped her with small amounts of money for food. She said that this is an expression of *namjai* (consideration, expression of goodwill) because it was not asked for, but it is not *bunkhun*. She said *bunkhun* is reserved for parents, a large amount of help rendered, or help given over a long period of time (I-319). It appears that receiver perception of motive is in part what may activate either a *bunkhun* type of grateful relationship or a transactional one. Where the receiver sees the motive as pure with no expectation of return the relationship is more likely to be *bunkhun*, whereas if the receiver sees the giver as seeking benefit from the help rendered the relationship may become transactional and put limits on the sense of obligation of the receiver. When I asked people how they know the motives of the giving person they noted that it requires time to observe how the giver acts. You watch to see if they are *sameo ton sameo blaay*, meaning that they are the same at the beginning as they are at the end. A change in the way a giving party relates to the receiver can indicate that they are expecting something in return for their giving.

The perception of motive has another dimension: it is possible for followers to misjudge giver motives (attributing to them a desire to get something in return that is not truly present) or decide that the giver is doing something for them because they deserve it in some way (I-308). In such cases it changes the sense of obligation that the person on the receiving end feels. It is also possible for givers to see the sense of obligation due them in a different light than the receivers see it. One respondent gave me the illustration of an adopted child who is made to work hard by the new parents. The child may think that she has paid back her obligation through this hard labour while the parents assume that her *bunkhun* should have no limits (I-300). This brings up another area where informants had differing views. Sometimes people indicated that there are no limits to the reciprocation in a *bunkhun* relationship (I-307), while others seemed to indicate that there are situations where limits apply (I-319).[27] One group of informants indicated that there is always space for non-cooperation with a request if the person asks you to do something morally wrong or that you do not believe in (I-319). This is one of the differences between relationships that are based in gratitude and polite deference versus those that have the *kreng klua* element of fear because of the threat of physical violence.

---

[27] One explanation for the differences in my sources here could be between *bunkhun* as an ideal concept versus the perspective of real-life, everyday interactions and relationships. Suntaree explains *bunkhun* as ongoing, a binding of good reciprocal feelings, and a lasting relationship, concluding that both time and distance do not diminish *bunkhun* (1994:46). So while in a theoretical sense there are no limitations to reciprocation, in real life, social inferiors are active agents in evaluating how they are being treated in a relationship and make adjustments in their sense of obligation and reciprocation accordingly. Suntaree notes that Thais have a phrase '*mot khwaam kreng jai*' which refers to the loss of good feelings people have for others who have in some way insulted them (1994:45). Such a loss means that they no longer feel the need to be *kreng jai* to those people, and the relationships are broken. Because of the close connection between feelings of *bunkhun* and *kreng jai* it might be possible that under altered circumstances perceived as insult, exploitation, neglect, hostility, and so on, the entire complex of reciprocal and deferential feelings is diminished or if severe enough, erased completely.

Factor # 2: Relative Size and Persistence over Time.

While the act of giving creates a bond of relationship and sense of obligation, all acts of giving are not equal. Informants make distinctions in terms of quantity as well as whether the giving is one-time or occasional, or a very frequent and long-term act. Thus small acts of kindness and goodness expressed consistently and over a long period of time can build a sense of *bunkhun*. In a similar fashion, as was illustrated above, a single larger act creates *bunkhun* in the receiver where smaller acts are considered *namjai*. It is the persistence over time (expressed as *liang brajam*) that can move the relationship between a social superior and inferior from one where there is *bunkhun* and the feeling of *kreng jai* (polite deference) on the part of the inferior to a patron-client relationship. A single, temporary expression of goodness and help establishes a relationship but without the sense of depth of obligation in the same fashion as a *luuk phii-luuk nawng* bond would (I-303). In this sense people also quantize *bunkhun* and *kreng jai* as a lot or a little (*maak* or *noi*). One person illustrated how in a decision-making situation where he was asked to help two people at the same time, he would consider which one he was the most *kreng jai* towards as the determining factor.

Factor # 3: How Close are the People in the Relationship?

The idea of *sanit* (which has to do with how close two people are in a relationship) applies to both situations where there is a large status distance between two people and where people are relatively close. In the case of a large distance, a person who is *sanit*, for instance with a *nakleng*, is part of the inner group and may have a *kreng jai* type of relationship. Those on the edges or who are in an out-group are afraid (*kreng klua*) of the *nakleng*. In a group (*phuak*) hierarchy still operates as there are people of different ages, educational status, and wealth as members. However if the atmosphere is *ben kan eng* (informal-approachable) then all members can become close and there are no limits to the kind of cooperation rendered (I-325). A person may be *kreng jai* of people in the group but if he/she is *sanit* this lessens *kreng jai*, and as one person said, 'the closer you are the less boundaries there are in rendering help to a person' (I-325). What this statement implies is that in more horizontal relations Thais are properly *kreng jai* to those who are their superiors, but there are inherent limits in terms of obligation that are lessened as relationships grow in terms of closeness (*sanit*).

Factor # 4: Motives for Cooperating Vary with the Type of Relationship.

Suntaree observes that *kreng jai* is present in all relationships; ranges from superiors to inferiors, equals, and intimates; and varies in intensity according to the degree of status discrepancy, degree of familiarity, or difference in situation (1994:45). It is expressions of goodwill, acts of kindness, and helping – primarily tangible but also possible in other non-material forms – that move a relationship to another level and can increase the degree of *kreng jai* that a person feels towards another. In my interviews I set up scenarios illustrating different status levels, degrees of intimacy, and circumstances between two people, and then asked the interviewees how they thought the person on the receiving end would feel. I also asked how this would impact a request for helping with something or joining in some endeavour that the person giving requested.

One point that emerged is that not all acts of giving result in *bunkhun*; they may only increase the degree of *kreng jai*. A second is that *kreng jai* itself has very fine-grained nuances depending on the setting. For instance, in one of the focus groups (I-325) I created the scenario of a professor and a student and asked why the student might help the professor with something. The group indicated it was *kreng jai nai thaang khaorop* (deferential response in the direction of, or on the basis of respect). Conner identified this same diversity of usage with *kreng jai* in his research among leaders in the Northeast (see 1996:253 footnote 31).

There were also indications that there are limitations to compliance. This is one way that distinctions were made between *kreng klua* and *kreng jai*. *Kreng klua* can produce a forced compliance, even to the point of a person doing something morally wrong or doing something that she really does not want to do. This can be illustrated by the situation of the *luuk nawng* of the *nakleng* who owe loyalty in return for the benefits they have received; in this case the loyalty is always informed by the potential of violence or sanctions if the receiver does not obey. However with *kreng jai* based in relationships and outside of the spheres of formal positional power (*amnaat*) and influence (*itipon*) there remains the reservation of space for non-compliance both theoretically and practically. Theoretical non-compliance comes if a request were to exceed a moral boundary for the person being asked to cooperate. This is theoretical because normally one has come to be *kreng jai* in such a relationship because the giver has exhibited good behaviour and is not expected to ask the receiver to do something wrong. Non-compliance for practical reasons comes into play if there is some obstacle that makes compliance impractical such as being sick, not having enough money, or having no time.

Finally, I have also identified types of relationships where it is possible to lie either outside or inside the sphere of *kreng jai* and *bunkhun*. These are relationships that are closer to horizontal with less status discrepancy and can be found in friendship, groups, and cliques. Informants can illustrate relations that are not characterized by *kreng jai*, *bunkhun*, *baramii*, or even respect, where people interact and cooperate (see p. 97f.).

The TLM and the Development of Interpersonal Influence

In the previous two sections I have digressed temporarily away from the *Thuukjai* Leader Model (TLM) that has been the subject of this chapter. My purpose in doing so was to set the stage for a more precise look at how this model works as a mechanism for social influence, as well as to prepare for the analysis that will follow in Chapters 5 and 6. The question under focus was to examine how this culturally preferred leader model works, with the context being the issues of patron-client relations and the nature of reciprocation and obligation.

I developed the material in those two sections in order to make three major points. The first is that the indigenous terms *amnaat* (power), *ittipon* (influence) and *baramii* (personal power) that serve as bases for interpersonal influence cannot be neatly systematized to fit either the Weberian classification of legitimate authority or classification schemes regarding power. The second is that there are other bases for influence based in more horizontal relationships that cannot be embraced by the *amnaat-ittipon-baramii* complex. Finally, the terms *kreng jai* (polite deference), *kreng klua* (fearful deference), and *bunkhun* (grateful obligation) are used across the gamut of all social relationships, all forms of legitimate authority, and all power relations. At the same time that they are used broadly and with flexibility in a variety of relationships, they are also capable of being used with very fine-grained nuances of meaning. Native speakers take into account multiple factors embedded in social relationships relating to status, motive in giving, the size and persistence over time of giving, and the type and closeness of relationship.

The plasticity inherent in these local terms argues for high levels of agency by actors in reading their circumstances and choosing their responses, and argues against a static view that would see all dyadic relations as being in the form of patron and client. The dynamism in relations involving reciprocity and obligation also argues against a static view that sees social inferiors as passive receivers of the benevolence of superiors who in turn respond with automated loyalty and deference. Patron-client relations thus become one particular form among many types of dyads that exist in a hierarchical social system.

The TLM creates the potential for influence, particularly through the private-self, inner character component coming into social expression in both the public-self behaviour configuration and the work-related relational behaviour in dyadic relations. Both of these behaviour configurations are associated with giving in some form. People who are able to act in this way can develop non-exploitative relationships characterized by positive and warm feelings of reciprocation and gratitude that are a form of personal power. This power is based not in expertise, but is closer to what is referred to as referent power (see footnote 26 above), with the emphasis on a grateful sense of obligation. One informant illustrated how this sense of obligation would stay with a person till death and how it impacted work in a very positive way. He said that the act of helping an employee during a time that he was in need of tangible assistance would build pride (*phuum jai*) on both sides of the relationship (FRL-8). Translated into a leader-follower setting this personal power can be drawn upon even where positional power and legitimate authority exist. In a setting where voluntary cooperation is necessary, as in the slum, this form of personal power will lead people to cooperate out of a warm and respectful sense of obligation or a deferential consideration that does not want to refuse a request. Both of these responses are associated with positive feelings and are not forced or compelled in any way.[28]

However, the TLM is not simply about obligation in dyadic relations; it is also about facilitating task accomplishment. Reciprocation and obligation in a relationship do not inherently make it a leader-follower relation. This is one of the problems of the patron-client rubric because it casts all relations into a frame where the social superior can wield influence and command obedience. In this prototypical model both the task and interpersonal relations dimensions are woven together and form the basis for being considered potentially influential by perceivers. Let me illustrate how the TLM enhances our understanding of influence processes in a setting outside of the slum. I noted in Chapter 2 that studies of rural leadership tend to compile lists of attributes, many of which are highly complex themselves or in their component parts (such as being respected, an elder, or wealthy) without making any connection between them or examining how they operate to create the potential for influence. In reviewing all the attributes and traits from the studies I cited in Chapter 2, I found five points reflected in the major configurations of the TLM: good manners, morality (honest, ethical), giving behaviours (benevolent, sacrificial, helping others, being one others can rely on for assistance), being informal and approachable, and industrious. What the prototypical nature of the TLM helps to clarify is the necessity of having these behavioural patterns as a part of an attribute or as the basis for building a complex attribute. It is not age, wealth, spirituality, rank, education, or social status alone or in combination that differentiates leaders from nonleaders, or those with influence and those without. People with those attributes must also have a co-occurrence of the configurations of traits found in the TLM.

I return now to a theme that I brought out at the start of this chapter from the work of Tambiah on classification systems. The TLM, developed through free-

---

[28] In Mauss' classic work on giving and reciprocation he makes the point that there really are no free gifts: that what appears to be free and disinterested is in reality constrained and self-interested (1990:4). Certainly the people that I interviewed are aware of this reality. However, what seems to energize the Thai system of reciprocation and obligation is the ideal of the giver not wanting anything in return. If the system acknowledges that all giving must be reciprocated, the ability, real or fictional, to give in a disinterested fashion is what creates a willingness to reciprocate in others. It is what makes reciprocation palatable. In situations where there is no attempt to hide self-interest, reciprocation becomes part of the proper script, but is not from the heart. Those who embody elements of the TLM draw out of people a willingness to comply because receivers see the configurations of private and public dimension behaviour as emanating from deeper level character that manifests itself in giving freely without hope of return. Receivers would also reciprocate to the giver if they saw the same complex of behaviours as being motivated by personal benefit, but not with the same sense of personal warmth and willingness.

recall listing on the domain of leadership, is a sociolinguistic map of the territory of culturally preferred conceptions of leadership. As a classificatory system it defines the traits and attributes of idealized leadership, and the entire model itself shapes one form among multiple forms of creating the potential for influence. As Tambiah notes, classificatory systems not only describe; they also make judgements and as such develop into things that are proscribed or preferred. However, Tambiah cautions that these semantic systems do not translate directly into everyday life. This serves as a reminder that the TLM as a social construction is not something slavishly reproduced, but rather provides the content for discourse and action relating to contexts where interpersonal influence is operating.

As a semantic classificatory system the TLM has some clear limitations. People use it to evaluate potential leaders, and it shapes the discourse about what leaders should be like and what they should do. But it is limited because the need for cooperation in the community exceeds the abilities of a person's dyadic relations, and as I have shown, there are other bases for cooperation that are not rooted in obligation and reciprocity. In addition to this, Tambiah has pointed out that we cannot ignore the pragmatic issues of power and prestige in social interactions, and at this point the TLM does not help us in understanding more about leadership as it is conducted in the community. In the analysis that follows in Chapters 5 and 6 I will be connecting the way in which elements of this model are drawn upon, bypassed, or ignored in the real life world of leadership both in the community and in its relations to the state. With the anthropological approach that I am taking, I will endeavour to draw a more comprehensive picture that integrates the explicit and implicit, the beliefs as well as behaviours that are a part of everyday on-the-ground leadership in LWPW.

Summary

In this chapter I began by walking through the preliminary issues and preparatory steps of determining the questions for the free-recall listing, performing the free-recall, preparing a paired similarity judgement exercise, gathering that data, and then analyzing it through a consensus analysis and correspondence analysis. I then interpreted the correspondence analysis material, bringing in additional insights from the hierarchical clustering of pile sort data and term definition interviews. I called the resulting model the *Thuukjai* Leader Model (TLM) which consists of public, private, interpersonal, and task dimensions with constellations of traits and their associated behaviours (see Figure 3). These configurations are made up of a private-self component that expresses deepest character, public-self interpersonal relations and task components, the informal-approachable trait as a connection between public-self behaviour and the work-related relations behaviour that occur in dyads, and public work behaviour that is focused on task accomplishment.

In the final section I interacted with the TLM in light of issues in the study of Thai leadership related to patron-client relations and the nature of reciprocation and obligation. I then applied the insights gained on reciprocity and obligation to answer the question as to how this model operates to create the potential for influence. I concluded by examining the limitations of the TLM in terms of helping us understand the practise of leadership in the community. In the next two chapters I will address the pragmatic issues that lie outside the boundaries of the TLM in order to bring a more comprehensive understanding of the kinds of social influence processes that are happening inside LWPW.

CHAPTER 5

Leading in LWPW: Trust, Privilege, and Suspicion

In Chapter 4 I presented data collected with methods designed to develop a map of the sociolinguistic terrain of how leadership is perceived by followers. The result was an implicit leadership theory (ILT) of a culturally preferred leader that I call the *Thuukjai* Leader Model (TLM). The TLM represents a prototypical leader who embodies characteristics that create the potential for influence with other people. As an ILT it is not automatically translated into behaviour, but is one source for material that people draw upon and manipulate in discourse in order to construct views of leadership and to negotiate their behaviour in social interactions. I pointed out that while the TLM is helpful in understanding how influence develops in dyadic relationships, it does not provide insight into how influence is built in the broader community context. Here in Chapter 5 I move from preferred conceptions of leadership to actual practise in Lang Wat Pathum Wanaram (LWPW). The focus will be on how the TLM connects to real life leadership in the community and the presence of alternative models and concepts that inform the perception and practise of leadership.

The Trustworthy Leader Model

My own observations of major events in the community and of the interactions of the committee members between themselves made it clear to me that there is no direct reproduction of the TLM in terms of the conceptualization and practise of leadership in the community. By the end of the first phase when the shape of the TLM was emerging, I felt very confused as to how that material related to everyday interaction in the community. People in LWPW confirmed the very idealistic nature of the TLM to me as I shared with them the results of the free-recall listing and talked with them about the 21 terms. I was checking to see if people felt that these terms generated in the context of an employer-employee relationship were applicable to the community committee-resident relationship. Usually people would look at the list and say all of the terms were important. There were other comments of a more general nature that made me feel the traits embraced in these 21 terms were something that resonated strongly with people and would probably be applicable to a wider range of relationships than just the employer/employee one. A couple of interviewees responded in very superlative terms to the kind of person who embodied these traits. While working on clarifying definitions for these terms one man (I-184) said:

> These 21 points are what we would call the definition of a complete *sombun* (leader) of Thai people…a person who has all of these [points] is able to manage (*borihaan*) people…if a person does not have any one of these points he will not be able to manage people or an organization successfully….There is really no one who has all of these 21 points. If you get someone who has 15 or 16 of these points you would consider them a very good person. In reality, nobody has all of these completely. Nobody has these 100 per cent; not even Buddha was like this.

In a similar vein, I showed the terms to a person who had lived in the community for eight years and was married to a woman who grew up there (I-31). When he saw them he said, 'A leader like this, if they are really like this, they would be the very best (*sut yawt*). A leader like this I would hold in my heart and die and not regret my life.'

This strong reaction to the 21 terms of the TLM contrasted sharply with the complaints and disappointment expressed concerning the committee, and the competition and manoeuvring I observed within the committee and between groups based in locality in LWPW. My first sense of the connection between the prototypical model and real life leadership came during the time frame leading up to the election of a new committee in early 2004. I began to hear that there would be the possibility of an election because there were a number of people from the Ton Pho area who were applying to be on the committee. So I went to that area and talked with some of the current Ton Pho committee members, finding that at least ten people from there had applied. I was directed to a young man (I-115) who was applying for the first time to be a committee member. He indicated that he had been invited to apply by others in Ton Pho. I asked him why he thought people would elect him to the committee, and he said it was because he was a person who could be trusted (*chuathuu*). In reflecting on our conversation I began to realize that *chuathuu* provides the conceptual link between the prototypical model and how people actually construct leadership in daily activities.

Chuathuu and the Discourse about Leadership in the Community

My conversation with I-115 started me on the path of trying to understand why *chuathuu* is critical to the understanding and practise of leadership in the community. As I interviewed people on this theme and reflected on my observations, a number of points came into sharper focus. First, it became clear that *chuathuu* shapes the discourse for the ideas of leadership emergence and practise. *Chuathuu* is related to considerations of who can lead, who should lead, who people will vote for, as well as how cooperation (*ruammuu*) is secured. Thus it is here that *chuathuu* links the preferred model and real life leadership. While the TLM is not embodied in any single person, real people can be attributed as trustworthy and there are specific identifiable behaviours that produce that attribution. Finally, as I explored *chuathuu* it became obvious that the idea of trustworthiness is used to explain only a part of what actually takes place in leadership in the community, and that there are other models and processes that are not as easily verbalized. The next two sections will go into detail as to how *chuathuu* is used in explaining leadership emergence and function. Then in a new major section I will begin to examine the evidence for another model of leadership present in the community.

Chuathuu and Leadership Emergence

I argued in Chapter 3 that a process I have termed 'officialization' has over time created the view in LWPW that only those with formal positions legally sanctioned by the state are considered legitimate. I also noted that this acceptance of the legality of the formal position did not mean that people liked, admired, or trusted those holding positions. I found that the discourse that forms the basis for a willing acceptance of the domination of others is rooted in the idea of being trustworthy (*chuathuu*).

People come to leadership positions in three different ways within the community, and in each case being *chuathuu* is credited as the reason. The first path is if there are enough people running for positions on the committee then elections are necessary; those with the most votes fill the available slots. In light of the possible election, I queried people as to what kinds of characteristics it would take to be elected, and being trustworthy (*chuathuu*) was listed as the critical factor (I-115, I-133, I-114). A second path to becoming a leader is to be chosen for the role. Once the community committee is elected or the slots are filled by applicants appointed by the District, then the task of the committee is to choose who will fulfil the required positions. Reflection on why people are chosen or not chosen is again couched in terms of *chuathuu* (I-128, I-133, I-203). A third path in emergence to a leadership role is that of invitation. With each of the last three committee presidents, they all indicated that others had invited them to run for the committee and be a part of it. When I asked L.P., a former committee president, about why he had first applied to the committee, it was because a group of his friends wanted him to join (I-128). D. also indicated that it was her friends who invited her to apply with them as a group to run for the committee to see if they could force an election (I-203). Although *chuathuu* was not mentioned directly, when probing whether or not it would be possible for a person who is not *chuathuu* to be invited to participate in a leadership role, the answer was always negative.

Chuathuu and Gaining Cooperation (ruammuu)

Being *chuathuu* is not only the key factor in leadership emergence, but also is essential to being able to carry out leadership functions in the community. I pointed out in Chapter 3 that the relationship between community leaders and residents was one of voluntary cooperation. In Chapter 4 I showed how the TLM works in dyadic relations to build the potential for influence by creating a positive sense of obligation and reciprocation on the part of followers. However, the need for cooperation in some community tasks is larger than what a single person's dyadic relations can supply. How then is influence outside of the dyad built? Again, the term used to construct this relationship is *chuathuu*. I-130 indicated that the power (*amnaat*) that brings cooperation in the community is in *chuathuu*.

When talking about community leadership, *chuathuu* and *ruammuu* (cooperation, literally 'joining hands') are often linked. Being *chuathuu* makes one capable of leading because it is the basis for getting others to *ruammuu* with leaders in activities and work. I asked L.P. how he got projects done in the community during his terms in office. He explained that others would join and help, as they were able. I asked if they would help if a person was not *chuathuu*. He said:

> They would not come, you would not have them, except if they *chuathuu* (verbal use meaning believe, have faith that) you are not crooked, not taking other people's things, that you are working with a pure heart so that your children and grandchildren can live there. Then they will be able to *chuathuu* you (I-128).

L.P. also attributed the rather low attendance at a Children's Day event to the lack of *ruammuu*, which he said was more evident in his day. Committee members' success is evaluated on the kind of cooperation that they get in large community celebrations as measured by overall attendance (PO-18, PO-327). The quality of being *chuathuu* creates the potential to draw people who are normally seeking their own interests to work for the benefit of the larger group.

Trustworthiness (chuathuu), Respect (nabthuu), and the TLM

After hearing *chuathuu* used in reference to the basis of why people would choose someone to be a community leader I began to pursue peoples' understandings of this term and to seek its relationship to the terms for respect (*khaorop*, *nabthuu*). I noted in Chapter 2 in the section on Thai social values that the literature indicated that *nabthuu* (respect) was an important factor in being a leader. On a straightforward basis from the literature, one would expect that in the community those who are respected would be the pool from which leaders are drawn. It would be a relatively simple matter of finding out who had the most prestige determinants (age, wealth, education, formal position, and so on) to see who potentially could be a leader. However, it was not nearly this simple in terms of what I observed in the composition of the committee, nor did it turn out to be the way that people chose to explain leadership emergence.

Comparing Trustworthiness (chuathuu), Respect (khaorop nabthuu), and the Good Person (khon dii)

In Table 4 and Table 5 I have summarized the results of my discussions with informants about the nature of these trust and respect terms and how they are developed in a person's life. For purposes of comparison, in Table 6 I have also added a summary about the good person (*khon dii*) since this was often mentioned as a component for being respected and considered trustworthy.

Table 4 Terms for trust

Terms and dictionary definition: *chuathuu* believe in, have faith in, *chuathuu dai* be reliable, trustworthy, *naa chuathuu* believable, trustable in the sense of being able to believe or trust in such a person.
Informant definitions and explanations
I-115 People will vote for someone they *chuathuu dai* (this is reliable, trustworthy); *chuathuu* is not the same as *nabthuu*; I-129 does not lie (*mai kohok*), speaks and does not change, follows through on what they say, not narrow in their social interaction (*mai chai wong khaeb*), those who do not help others or who have no experience are not *chuathuu*; I-134 we *chuathuu* the things that they do, things are completed according to what they have said, money is needed, *chuathuu* always has to be seen, we show it by our actions, unlike *nabthuu* which can just come from our position in society; I-117 *chuathuu* does not equal *nabthuu;* we *chuathuu* others from the things they have done, it comes from what you do and not from what you are as with *nabthuu.*
How it is developed
I-115 cooperating (*ruammuu*) with activities and work in the community, holding an honest (*sujarit*) job, helping others, not having problems with other people (*mai mii ruang kab khon*); I-129 must be *khon dii* (a good person), have education, need to have *kaan sadaeng dii* (showing goodness to others), there needs to be fruit from one's work in the community (*pon dii*) in order to maintain being considered *chuathuu* but you do not need too much to get started; I-133 they help the group/public (*chuay suanklaang*), they help every person, have an honest (*sujarit*) job, money is not needed but good character (*nisai dii*) is required, others look at the things we do (*kaankratham*); I-117 the person should know the community (in the sense of knowing the needs of the community), develop good policies, take community interests to heart, ask people how they are doing, and have a broad outlook (*mawng kwaang*), I-134 over time *chuathuu* can develop into *nabthuu.*

Table 5 Terms for respect

Terms and dictionary definition: *nabthuu* respect, revere, look up to, synonym is *khaorop* show respect, pay reverence.
Informant definitions and explanations
I-114 *nabthuu* is not necessary to be elected, but you need to be *chuajai*, *waangjai* (to trust, have confidence in), *waijai* (to trust, have faith in) and *chuathuu*; to be a leader in the community you need to be *chuathuu* and not *khaoropnabthuu*; I-23 people *nabthuu* those who are *phuu yai* (elders) and *awuso* (senior, elder) and they may pick them as community president but others do the work, sometimes people *nabthuu* those who cannot do anything, *kaankratham* (actions, the things people do) is a major component of *nabthuu*; I-134 one kind of *nabthuu* is based on *kiattiyot* (honour) that is based in position, these are people you respect but do not know them personally, the other kind of *nabthuu* happens when you observe someone's work and see their results; I-23 a person the residents *khaorop* the most may not have much to do with other people at all; I-31 residents *khaoropnabthuu* the committee, but they watch for the fruit of their work.
How it is developed
I-26 If you have a problem and a person helps you then it builds respect (*nabthuu*); I-115 you must be *dedkaat* (decisive) at work and have *namjai* (compassion, understanding, friendliness) outside of work hours; I-129 you must be *phuu yai* (a superior or elder) but you have to be *khon dii* (a good person), it can be because of position (*tamnaeng*) and the fruit of work (*pon*) plays a part; I-134 you must be *khon dii*, help society, and be the kind of person that the populace *nabthuu*, in a group if you have someone who is *chuathuu* and one who has *kiattiyot* (honour) because of position, you have to watch the *kaankratham* (works) of this person because over time he can become *chuathuu*, there is a difference between *thae* (real) *nabthuu* and that which comes from *kiattiyot* (honour), real *nabthuu* comes from people seeing you work; I-117 *nabthuu* is what comes from inside us (*pai nai*), so we *nabthuu* our aunts and uncles, or the person who has the position of being the boss (*huanaa*); I-19 (a community leader from another *chumchon*) to earn *khaorop* from residents you must do good (*tham dii*) and sacrifice for the community; I-31 the leader should take what they learn in their meetings and call a meeting to share this with the people in the community and this will build *khaorop*.

Table 6 Terms for 'good person'

Terms and dictionary definition: *khon dii* good person
Informant definitions and explanations
I-23 the residents want a leader who is *khon dii*, this means someone who passes out the things that are given to the community in a fair way, someone who sacrifices and who does not do things for their own benefit; I-129 *khwaam dii* (goodness) means not being a rogue (*keeree*), having an honest job and not causing problems for other people, while good character (*nisai dii*) means having an honest job and being generous to others (*uafua* and *obawmari*); I-133 there are many varieties of the good person, it is possible

to be a good person and not have interaction (*sungsing*) with others, a good person is one who has good human relational skills (*manutsamphan*) and a good disposition (*athayasai dii*).
How it is developed
I-34 someone who is honest (*suusat*), fair (*yutitham*), and reasonable (*mii hetpon*); I-113 someone who is pure hearted, generous (*puapae*), watches over others, and is kind (*jai dii*); I-129 you know someone is a good person if she helps others, is generous (both *uafua* and *obawm*), compassionate, understanding, and thoughtful (*namjai*), has good human relational abilities (*manutsamphan*), and is not self-centred (*mai hen kae tua*).

My conversations with people about the meaning of *chuathuu* and its relation to the idea of respect embodied in the terms *khaorop* and *nabthuu* showed that there is some ambiguity in the way that people understand and utilize these ideas. As can be seen from the summaries above, when asked directly, people in the community do not equate *chuathuu* with either *khaorop* or *nabthuu*. Informants were quite clear that one does not need to be *nabthuu* to be a community leader but must at least be *chuathuu*. Yet there are times when people use these words as synonyms, especially when explaining why people will cooperate and join in work with community leaders. How are we to understand this ambiguity and seeming plasticity in usage between these two terms? Cohen suggests one possibility when he draws upon the work of Ihde on the idea of multi-stability of images (1991:41-4). The idea is that 'any social situation presents the perceiver with a "multi-stable" image...offering different possibilities of interpretation, which will depend on his or her particular cultural, ideological, or theoretical perspective' (1991:41). The new social situation of the potential for elections in the community, and for choosing the six mandated positions on the committee within the committee itself, has resulted in a setting where *nabthuu* and *chuathuu* can be understood together in multiple ways and actors choose from these interpretations depending on the demands of the situation. The result is not a lack of clarity on the part of actors, but rather the deliberate framing of an idea for a specific purpose.

What creates this terminological flexibility is that informants see *nabthuu* as having two dimensions, one ascribed and the other achieved. In the ascribed dimension, people *nabthuu* others because of their status, such as age, wealth, educational level, or position (*tamnaeng*), which gives them *kiattiyot* (honour) or some combination of prestige determinants. Even with ascribed *nabthuu* informants were quick to point out that one needs to be a good person (*khon dii*) and must have appropriate behaviour on an ongoing basis in order to maintain the respect. In the achieved dimension, people can develop respect through their actions, what one informant referred to as 'real' respect. *Chuathuu* on the other hand is consistently understood as something that grows out of observed actions. Multi-stability means then that the emphasis can shift between either ascription or behaviour, and the similarity or difference between the two concepts.

If the focus is on similarity and the behavioural dimension, then we can use the two terms synonymously. Looking at how both *chuathuu* and *nabthuu* are developed, the core ideas that were shared included being a good person (*khon dii*), doing good actions (*kaankratham dii*), having fruit from works (*pon*), helping out society and the general public, and helping others. If the focus is on difference and the behavioural dimension, *nabthuu* or the two terms together (*khaoropnabthuu*) are clearly broader than *chuathuu* and indicate something that is much stronger and deeper. I asked I-115 to describe how one could become considered trustworthy (*chuathuu*) and, after his description, asked if those things would make others respect (*nabthuu*) him. He replied that if there was an election and he got a lot of votes, that would mean that people respected (*nabthuu*) him. The subordinate nature of *chuathuu* to *nabthuu* is evidenced in the way interviewees would explain that one does not need to be respected to be elected, just considered trustworthy. The usages show a continuum with *chuathuu* being at the lower end and graduating up to full-blown *nabthuu.*

However, if the focus is on difference and the ascribed dimension, then *chuathuu* can lie beyond the respect terms in another domain completely. I-134 indicated that a person who has respect based on *kiattiyot* (honour) may not be *chuathuu*, but if others see his actions (*kaankratham*) he can become considered trustworthy as well. My friend made a similar explanation using an illustration about a highly respected former political figure who is now older and no longer considered *chuathuu.* His conclusion was that this person would have to become *chuathuu* for people to vote for him again if he were to stand for office (M-234). So in this sense *chuathuu* becomes another concept that is very different from respect, as you can be respected and yet not *chuathuu.*

This multi-stability of images here means that if a person wants to emphasise the honour of being a leader, then she will see *chuathuu* and *nabthuu* as part of the same continuum, both developed by observed good deeds with *chuathuu* being a beginning point. However, if a person wants to show that a potential or actual leader does not fit the normative ascriptions for being considered *nabthuu*, then he can separate *chuathuu* as something built through actions and *nabthuu* as something ascribed on the basis of status determinants rather than actions.

Discussion and Analysis

In this section I will pose and discuss key questions concerning trustworthiness and its use for explaining leadership in the community, its relationship to the TLM, and its implications for understanding leadership emergence and practise.

The Choice of Chuathuu

The first question concerns why *chuathuu* is the preferred concept for talking about leadership in the community rather than *nabthuu*. One would expect *nabthuu* to carry more significance on the basis of the literature, or at least be considered an equivalent with *chuathuu* since they are often used almost synonymously and are developed by others and recognized in others in a very similar fashion.

I propose that *chuathuu*, the idea of trustworthiness, is the preferred concept for talking about community leadership in terms of emergence and securing cooperation for two reasons. First, *chuathuu* opens the door for a broader group of people to be involved in leadership, both by creating accessibility and providing a rationale for why people without traditional prestige determinants can be leaders. The people that comprise the community committee are for the most part not people who have the status determinants of age, wealth, or education, nor do they hold other formal positions that would give them social weight. Because people will naturally *nabthuu* those who have such status indicators the community needs another frame of understanding that can account for those who actually do the leading, and make leadership accessible to the people who can carry out the functions required by the government. Because of its basis in ascription *nabthuu* is a concept appropriate for situations where people are more geographically or relationally distant, where actual behaviours may not be observed on a frequent or close basis (such as with an aged person whom residents see in the community but do not know personally)[1], or where social distance keeps a relationship on a more formal basis, with the lesser party under a feeling of obligation to the superior.

Second, as I noted above, while people must gain *nabthuu* through actions and maintain it through the ongoing expression of appropriate character and behaviour, *chuathuu* is much more connected with observable behaviour and better lends itself to the complexities of daily life. The core of becoming *chuathuu* is founded on showing that one is cooperative (*ruammuu*) and helping out the community without seeking personal benefit in any way. When I asked someone (I-133) why T., the new committee president, was *chuathuu*, he said it was because T. helps the public (*chuay suan klaang*). His illustrations of this included helping at the community festivals (both financially and through labour) and taking a child to the hospital when she was bit by a dog. One of the themes for both *chuathuu* and *nabthuu* is that of having *pon ngaan*, meaning literally fruit from one's work. I-114 said that you build *pon ngaan* by helping others, such as helping when the committee asks for it and helping set up for different programmes and festivals. While you are doing these things the residents are watching you.

---

[1] I-117 said that we *nabthuu* people like aunts and uncles, and I-134 said that there are people we *nabthuu* because they have *kiattiyot* (honour), but we do not know them.

So while there are certainly contexts in which people see *nabthuu* and *chuathuu* as nearly synonymous, people in the community tend to make distinctions between the two words on the basis of both the breadth and direction of the expression of goodness. For example, residents may see leaders as good people (*khon dii*) and *nabthuu* them, but recognize that their goodness is of a private nature and often characterized by the absence of doing wrong things (I-137). Such leaders' help is narrow in scope, limited to family and those who are close by them relationally and geographically. By contrast, residents see leaders who are *chuathuu* as having a public goodness, helping in a broader sense for the good of the community and not for personal benefit. Thus the basis for becoming *chuathuu* as opposed to only *nabthuu* is doing positive deeds for others rather than just refraining from doing evil.

In general the idea of trustworthiness seems to carry more utility in the community and provides a better explanation for those who are actually involved in community leadership, and in relationships of closer contact. Respect, on the other hand, usually seems to be reserved for people of status such as the aged or those holding formal positions and is for those who are more distant, where specific behaviours are not being seen and evaluated closely.

Chuathuu as the Real-life Expression of the TLM

The second question concerns why *chuathuu* appears to be the link between the prototypical model in the community rather than *nabthuu*. When asking people to explain what they wanted from real life leaders they responded that it is the person who is trustworthy (*chuathuu*) that they want. As I mentioned above, community members seem to reserve the idea of respect (*nabthuu*) more for people whom they do not know well or have formalized interactions with, or to whom they feel obligated in some way. Focusing on ascription, people who are respected may not be the kind of people that residents want as leaders since they may have no track record of public service or proof of their ability to curb self-interest because residents do not actually know what they do.

On the other hand, people become *chuathuu* by showing observable actions for the public benefit without the expectation of getting anything in return. Over time they develop track records that show their ability to cooperate with others, which is a critical sign of being able to curb self-interest. In the messiness and complexity of everyday life lived in close contact, the *chuathuu* person is someone whom people can count on to do good for the benefit of the community; this may or may not be true of those people *nabthuu* since that could be based on an ascription only. In this way *chuathuu* becomes the primary concept for choosing leaders on the ground and explaining their ability to influence others and gain cooperation.

Residents desire a trustworthy person precisely because their experience of actual leadership in society is of leaders who cannot be trusted to act for the public good. I-184 noted in talking about the 21 terms of the preferred model that the one thing that could ruin them all in a leader is *hen kae tua* (selfishness). Conversely one of the words that appeared five times in the free-recall listing on good leaders but did not make the final list of 21 terms was *mai hen kae tua* (to be unselfish). While the rhetoric is 'for the people' and 'for the public interest', the evidence is that leaders in general act for themselves (Mulder, 1997:172). Mulder observes that the social science curriculum glosses over problems like corruption, exploitation, and social injustice (1997:61), and students must learn from reading the press that 'wider society is made up of power-hungry politicians who are given to personal greed … ' (1997: 55-56).

In the TLM the culturally preferred leader is the moral leader, and both the task and interpersonal dimensions of the model are relevant here. In the private dimension of the model, the trio of good character (*nisai dii*), compassion-understanding-friendliness (*namjai*), and kindness (*jai dii*) are expressed through non-exploitative giving behaviours, where nothing is hoped for in return (*mai wang sing tawb thaen*). On the task side of the private dimension people observe a leader's honesty, as well as the approach that she takes to the task, in terms of being responsible and industrious. The kinds of publicly observable behaviours that make a person trustworthy match those of the TLM. Helping others, serving the community, cooperation, and honesty in one's career, when observed over time causes people to believe that such a person will act for the public good. Others are willing to entrust leadership roles to those who embody these characteristics. The element of the TLM critical for the voluntary nature of community leadership is that of cooperation and service for the public good. Personalized goodness and morality may make one influential in dyadic relations, but it is socialized goodness and morality expressed for the public good that builds influence outside of dyadic relations. Thus a person does not have to directly experience the goodness of another person in order to consider that person influential, but they must 'see' the person's goodness and morality expressed in the public arena and for the public good over time.

The question could be asked as to why the terms *chuathuu* and *nabthuu* did not come out with a high frequency or salience in the free-recall listing as part of the characteristics of a preferred leader. On respect terms, *nabthuu* did not appear at all, and *khaorop* appeared only once, while terms for trust like *naa chuathuu*, *chuathuu dai*, *chuathuu*, and *waijai dai* appeared a total of seven times if taken as a cluster, which would have put them among the top 32 terms from which the final 21 were chosen. Several possible reasons suggest why these terms had small representation in the free-recalls. One certainly was the particular line of questioning that was focusing on specific working relationships. In a pilot study in May 2000 I asked a more generic question about good leadership, and there was more representation of both respect and trust terms. Since both *nabthuu* and *chuathuu* are recognized in others via a complex of behaviours, the more specific line of questioning I used would tend to elicit the specific component behaviours, while a generic line would elicit the broader terms. A second reason is that I purposely did not cluster terms on the free-recall in order to leave as much diversity as possible, and this eliminated some groupings such as trust, which would have appeared more prominently. Another possibility may be the element of choice involved in the community context (either electing the committee or within the committee choosing someone to be the president), which creates different dynamics than those in a work setting where people do not have a choice over who their boss is. In a setting where community leadership is the focus and there is freedom of choice, it may be that the idea of trust takes on increased importance.

I will make one final note to connect to a point of discussion in Chapter 5. There in the context of examining how the TLM works to create interpersonal influence I interacted with Conner's research on leadership foundations. I was critical of his use of the term *baramii* (personal power) to describe a leadership foundation because of its multiplex usage. My findings in LWPW showed that *baramii* was not used in its positive and ideal sense, but rather as prestige relating to having money, or to refer to godfather (*jao pho*) types where patron-client relations are present. Rather, it is *chuathuu* (trustworthy) that dominates the discourse of people in the community when explaining who can be considered for leadership. People in the community make a clear distinction between the terms for trustworthy (*chuathuu*), respect (*nabthuu*), and personal power (*baramii*) in its ideal sense growing out of moral goodness expressed socially. For this reason, in my opinion it brings more clarity to see the non-ascriptive uses of *chuathuu, nabthuu*, and *baramii* as representing a continuum of socialized personal power,[2] as I have represented visually in Figure 4.

Figure 4 The *chuathuu-nabthuu-baramii* continuum

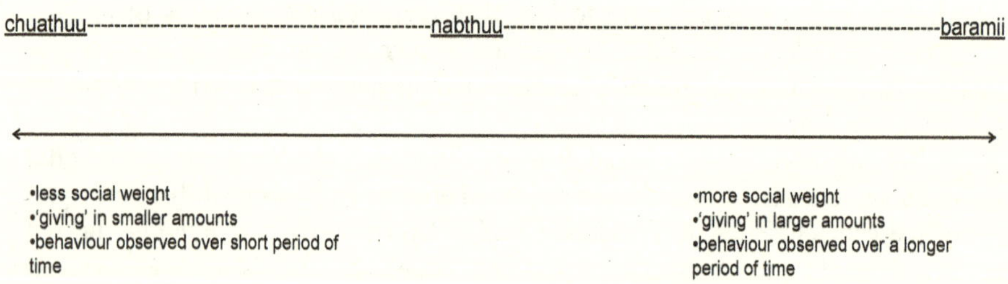

[2] This continuum is not completely precise because as I noted above there is a sense in which one could be respected but not considered *chuathuu*. However, in general the people I spoke with saw *chuathuu* as being a building block towards becoming *nabthuu*, and *nabthuu* in turn being necessary for becoming *baramii*. By using the term 'socialized' in referring to personal power I am drawing on the distinction made between a personalized power orientation where people use power for their own benefit, versus a socialized power orientation where people use power for the benefit of others (see Yukl, 2002:188-89).

The non-ascriptive uses of these terms suggest a broader category of socialized personal power (rather than linking it to a single Thai term) that recognizes the importance of trustworthiness for prototypicality for Thai leadership.

Evidence for another Model: The Acceptance of Privilege and the Reality of Suspicion

In the previous section I have shown how the idea of being trustworthy (*chuathuu*) provides the conceptual link with the TLM prototype and forms the basis for constructing situations that particularly deal with leadership emergence and gaining cooperation, which are practical issues in the life of the community. While the ideas of respect (*nabthuu*), being trustworthy (*chuathuu*), and the good person (*khon dii*) are closely linked, residents see observable action expressed in service to the community and the pursuit of community rather than personal benefit as being the critical basis for choosing a leader and link this to the idea of being trustworthy (*chuathuu*).

However, my observation and interview data not only showed that there are models of leadership that are preferred and those that are not, but also that perceptions and practises of leadership are much more complex than the kind of polar opposite good (*dii*) and not good (*mai dii*) verbalizations made by residents.[3] At the beginning of the data collection I did not have enough background and context to sort out or make any kind of distinctions among these critical comments; they just accumulated in my notes and were noticeable enough that from the free-recall listing exercise, I compiled a file of notes on critical comments about leaders in general or in the community. At first it seemed that these were simply cases of people responding subjectively to behaviours of leaders that they did not like personally. However, as time went on I realized that there was a shared perspective guiding follower perception of leaders that went far beyond subjective responses to individuals. I will argue here that while there no doubt exists a linguistically encoded ideal type of 'bad' or undesirable leader that would represent the polar opposite on a continuum from the TLM, more importantly there also exists a model of leadership that is not talked about, that is deeply embedded and implicit. This implicit model is utilized by people in general to understand, interpret, and practise leadership in daily life.

I give this implicit, top-down model the label *Sakdi* Administrative Behaviour Leadership Heuristic (SABLH), because it is neither simply a model of leadership nor a set of behaviour, but represents a complex of ideas that people draw upon in different ways depending on the particular role that they

[3] Mulder in his examination of the Thai public school sociology curriculum observes that society is seen as a moral construct and 'in a black-and-white fashion, "good" is constantly contrasted with "bad"' (Mulder, 1997:53).

are in. It can be utilized by those in formal positions to influence their values and leadership behaviour; it is also used by people who are observing formal position holders to understand and interpret their motives and actions. In the section on Thai bureaucracy in Chapter 2 I suggested that values regarding the possession of status and rank are what drive the behaviour of modern Thai administrative staff. Holding a formal position taps a set of understandings that fundamentally alters a person's self-perception as well as the perception of others towards that person to the extent that the person is assumed to have changed. My assertion here is that the values of *sakdi* administrative behaviour (SAB) are widely spread in Thai society because they grow out of the master hegemonic principle of hierarchy while taking on their own form. In LWPW, SAB values take the form of unwritten assumptions that guide both leader and follower perceptions and behaviours in actual social interactions. Thus they serve as a heuristic for understanding and interpreting what people should do or will do when holding a formal position. I will present evidence here that people in LWPW are able to shift easily from the leader perspective to the follower perspective of the SABLH, indicating that these points of view occupy different spaces so that people can do this shifting without any sense of dissonance. While *chuathuu* and related concepts shape the discourse for the emergence and selection of leaders as well as the ongoing influence of leaders, the SABLH shapes the discourse, perception, and practise of leadership for both leaders and followers particularly in the arenas of the activities and motives of leaders.

Three Lines of Evidence for the SABLH

Leadership in the Community is Understood as a Formal Position

The first line of evidence comes from the officialization process that I noted in Chapter 3, which affects people's understanding of leadership. When people think of leadership in LWPW they are thinking of formally sanctioned leaders, whether or not they like what these leaders do, and whether or not they had a hand in electing them. I also noted that a result of officialization has been the marginalization of traditional forms of leadership like the *nakleng*. Leadership in the eyes of community residents is official and formal leadership that has been legitimized by the government.

There is Widespread Suspicion of the Committee by the Residents

A second line of evidence began to accumulate regarding criticism and suspicion of the current committee. During interviews in preparation for the free-recall listing exercise there were a number of people who made comments critical towards this committee. Because I was pursuing a different line of questions for the free-recall listing at that time, I noted these comments but did not explore them. Then during the free-recall listing there were two rather strident criticisms of the committee that I noted and which left me a bit puzzled. S. introduced me to B. who had served on the committee in the past (FRL-7).

They were meeting to drink together and B. already seemed to be a bit drunk. He was quite expressive, talked freely, and was very critical of the current committee. He said that the committee members lacked knowledge, that they received 2,000 baht per month (US$ 50) and did nothing, and asserted there was no goodness (*khwaam dii*) in the community. FRL-15 was an elderly man who was also talkative and critical of the committee. One of his criticisms, which left me quite puzzled, was that the government had given LWPW a budget to build the blocks of flats after the 1973 fire, and all they had were numbers one, three, and five. (It happens that the three blocks of flats are numbered one, three, and five). He asked, 'Where is all the money for flat numbers two and four?'. The accusation seemed ludicrous since there was no committee at this time and the flats were not built by the community but by the CPB on their behalf. However, I made a note of the man's comments and asked myself if this had something to do with a general suspicion about leaders, a theme that started to coalesce with thoughts from my own experiences in Thailand.[4]

Formal Positional Leaders are Suspect of Acting for Personal Benefit

The final line of evidence that brought this material to the level of a significant theme was the realization as I started reviewing and coding interview and participant observation material with current and past committee members that virtually no person ever had anything positive to say about any of the past committees or any community leaders. During a participant observation of the King's birthday celebration in December 2004 I was spending some time with N. who was on the current committee. He was talking about how the previous committee members had been *mai brongsai* (not transparent) in their dealings, but the new committee had now eliminated that problem. At the time I merely noted his comment, but I later realized that it included the administration of L.P. who had been the president of the previous two sets of committees. From the early stages of the preparatory interviews it had become quite clear that L.P. was the most well-known and respected person in the community, so I was surprised that someone was accusing his period of leadership as being characterized by a lack of transparency.

I slowly began to understand that there was an important disjunction here between the way LWPW residents structure discourse about leaders and the criteria for becoming a leader, and the way they actually treat and perceive

---

[4] For many years I have observed that leaders in Thailand come under suspicion and criticism, but I never had any point of integration for this material. In the context of my work with a Thai organization I have observed that whoever is in current leadership is always accused of acting out of personal interest. The names of the players in the positions change but the criticism of self-interest remains the same. Similarly, in my work with urban poor I have noticed that local committee members are generally the object of criticism from others in the community, with the basis that they do not help people in general and act for their own benefit.

people in formal leadership positions. In other words, if asked to describe someone who is a leader or who was chosen to lead, people in the community use the conception of being trustworthy (*chuathuu*) to socially construct an explanation for why this person is capable of leading. One of the primary elements of building *chuathuu* is to act in the interest of the group, to sacrifice for the good of the group, to give without expectation of getting anything in return. Yet once that very same person takes on a formal position, he is immediately suspected of acting out of personal interest. You cannot be entrusted with leadership unless you are *chuathuu* and yet once you are in a position of leadership, people assume that you will act for your own benefit. Thus the suspicions about community leadership that residents expressed in various ways are not simply the subjective expressions of individuals who dislike a particular leader, but rather represent a model that structures the way that followers perceive positional leadership.

My interpretation of this disjunction is that SAB values cause people who gain the status and rank of a formal position to undergo an ontological change.[5] This activates a complex of values rooted in Buddhist notions of hierarchy grounded in merit (see Hanks, 1962:1247-9), where official status automatically accords prestige and respect (Prasan, 1975:17), and in *kin muang* culture (see the discussion of this idea on page 24) where a position holder is expected to enrich himself through those under him. Thus a person who is seen as trustworthy prior to holding a formal position becomes suspect as the ontological change indicated by official appointment means that a whole new set of ground rules enters the relationship. This change restructures the expectations for both leaders and followers. While the model of trustworthy leadership is a discursive one that people are able to talk about freely and explain, the SABLH lies outside of this discourse, being more observable in contexts of action. People do not talk about these things, nor generally show awareness that their own reactions and practises shift as they themselves

---

[5] The notion of ontological change denotes not merely a change in role or function, but a change in the being of a person, at least as assumed in the minds of the actors involved. While I was wrestling with how to encapsulate what I was seeing in a terminology, I discussed this subject with Ben Knighton of the Oxford Centre for Mission Studies (OCMS). He made the observation that from my data it appeared as if formal post-holding is assumed to bring about an ontological change just as in the Roman Catholic church justification and ordination are supposed to be ontological changes in those justified and ordained. I found this perspective very illuminating of this unconscious process that was observable in LWPW. Hanks' classic work on merit and power is supportive of this idea. He observes that a Thai is a minister or farmer only as long as he holds the station. This is found in the way people are called by title rather than name; when the King gave a rank to a person they also got a new name (1962:1252). 'By emphasis on status rather than person, the Thai equip themselves for mobility and transient position' (1962:1252). Status and rank changes a person and this change is reflected in the way the actors involved understand how they should act and how they should be treated.

change roles. In the three sections that follow I will explain the dual nature of this model, illustrate its use in leadership situations in the community, and then show how it impacts the practise of community leadership.

Elements of the SABLH

I see the idea of *chuathuu* (trustworthiness) comprising a model that is more public, 'official', and explicit. Informants could discuss *chuathuu* easily when asked direct questions about it. In contrast to this, the SABLH model that relates to leaders holding formal positions is one that is more implicit and that cannot be verbalized in the same way. SABLH consists of two sets of shared understandings that centre on people holding formal positions, and which people seem to hold independently so that conscious reflection between these notions is rare. The shared concepts act as two basic heuristics that function as interpretive keys for one's own actions and the actions of others. The model is tapped for understanding and behaviour based on the particular situation of a person, whether they are in a position of leadership and relating to followers, or whether they are in a follower role relating to a positional leader.

The First Heuristic Key: Acceptance of Privilege

The first heuristic has to do with the acceptance of privilege by those in formal leadership positions and is held by both leaders and followers. In Chapter 2 in the section on Thai social organization I discussed the pervasive nature of the principle of hierarchy. These assumptions and values about the superior-inferior relationship are manifested in the community as applied to the leader-follower relationship. One interviewee said, when talking about a boss, that leaders have special privileges, that one cannot meddle (*kaaokaai*) with them, and that it is the followers' duty to obey (L-FRL 4). He said that leaders have their own needs, they have to save themselves (*aow tua rawt*), and that is why they have to follow only their own heart (*aow tae jai*). An example of importance attached to position and the reticence to intrude can be seen in one of L.P.'s comments about when he was president; he said that during this time he would not check the treasurer's numbers because to do so was *kaaokaai* (to meddle) and it was important to *hai kiat* (give honour) to that person.

From the follower perspective there are three particular ways that leaders in the community are prone to act which are not appreciated. People accuse these leaders of not being *klaang* (literally 'in the middle') (I-150), the idea being here that they are not taking community needs into view and rather are seeking the benefit of their own group. This is manifest in both the control of information and resources. I-31 complained that the committee does not call meetings to tell the residents new information that they learn via their meetings with the various state agencies. Residents also make the constant accusation that committee members do not distribute the material items given to the community from various outside sources fairly.

An interesting insight into leader views of the formal leader role came as I was discussing with the president and main adviser the meanings of the 21 terms from the free-recall listing (I-28). I mentioned this incident in another context in Chapter 4, but I use it here to illustrate my point about the acceptance of privilege. I went through the list asking committee members to tell me which terms were relevant for the community leader-resident (*phuu nam chumchon-luukbaan*) relationship. I asked questions in the form of 'Do community leaders need to have x?' When we reached the term *namjai* (compassion, understanding, friendliness, thoughtfulness) they had a very unique interpretation; they said of course they need *namjai* because they are doing this job without any remuneration. In their thinking they were expressing *namjai* to the community by serving and this did not have to do with actually expressing *namjai* to the residents on a personal basis, which is the way most people would interpret that question. When it came to understanding residents (*khaojai luukbaan*) they said, 'No, you have to understand your team but not the residents.' Finally, in regards to loving residents (*rak luukbaan*) the president immediately said, 'No, you just love some people.' This obviously made the adviser very uncomfortable because he hastened to say that the president was *phuud len* (just joking), and explained that this was her *nisai* (character) to speak like this.

So from people in both leader and follower roles there is an understanding that leaders have certain privileges, should be treated in a certain way, and the obedience of followers is due to them. In the community it seems that this privilege is primarily manifested at the committee level in the control of information and resources. The idealized subordinate role seems to be more closely adhered to than the idealized superior role, so that both followers and leaders expect that obedience, politeness, respect, and not meddling with leader affairs are to be given (by followers) and received (by leaders).

The Second Heuristic Key: Suspicion of Leader Action for Personal and In-group Benefit

The second heuristic operates only for someone in the follower role. I make this conclusion on the basis of observing and listening to a wide range of people in the community, and from the fact that it harmonizes with my long experience in Thailand. There was no single informant that expressed propositionally 'we suspect all our leaders of acting for personal benefit,' but the cumulative weight of many encounters leads me to believe that this is an implicit and deeply held assumption that goes beyond subjective experience with individual leaders. This heuristic means that unvoiced suspicion informs all interpretations of leader actions, so that even in the face of no evidence or limited information followers assume that leaders are benefiting from their position and that they are helping their own group first.

A detailed discussion of the nature of this suspicion theme and its relationship to the preferred leader model, the trustworthy leader, and the implicit/explicit dimensions involved will take place below. Before moving to this analysis I will provide some illustrations of how the SABLH comes into play in real-life interactions. In the next section I examine the suspicion heuristic in three different illustrative contexts, and then in the section that follows I look at how the privilege heuristic in the positional model affects the practise of leadership in the community.

Three Illustrations of the SABLH as Used in Daily Life

Illustration #1: Public and Official Support with Private Criticism

At this point I will go into extended detail on three situations to illustrate how I see the ideas of trust, and the reality of the ontological change affected by the SABLH, being used to understand and explain events, and for guiding social action. L.P. served as the president of the committee for two terms covering 1998-2002, D. served for the 2002-2004 term, and T. is now the current president for the two year term starting in 2004. The first incident concerns L.P. and D. and the recall of events that happened around the time of the change of committees in 2002. In longer interviews that I taped and transcribed with each of them, they both made identical comments about each other's administrations, that neither one had accomplished a single thing. In general, on the surface level, to listen to people talk about virtually any administration of the committees that have been in existence since 1985 would bc to think that hardly anything has been done at all in terms of improving the community. From the perspective of L.P. and D., each of them had accomplished significant things during their term, and the other had accomplished nothing at all.

What does this charge of not getting anything done mean? There is a little more packed into these statements than appears on the surface. The charge of committee leadership not producing anything is one that is very common inside the community and is cited as a reason by people for wanting to run for a position on the committee. Since others are not getting anything done, they decide to be on the committee to try to accomplish somcthing. While personal feelings of jealousy or inferiority could play into criticism of other leaders and committees, my impression based on listening to people is that implicit in the criticism of not accomplishing anything is the charge of steering benefits to their own group. Whether or not this actually happens, people hold the perception that the community committee members make sure that their close friends and associates are the beneficiaries of any incoming material goods. The term used here is *phak phuak*, where *phak* is a party, particularly a political party, and *phuak* is a group or party. When used together *phak phuak* carries the idea of partisan, fellow members, close friends, or members of an intimate circle or clique. The phrase to *len phak phuak* means to show favouritism with such a group. A constant refrain from people in the community who were not born there is that the committee does not equally distribute items given to the community from various outside sources. A. used the example of 2,000 baht (US$ 50) (I am not sure if this was monthly or a one time donation) being given to help the elderly, but he said the money was taken by the committee. The point is not so much whether this happened or did not happen, as there are many such accusations in the community about the misuse of material goods that come in, but rather the perception that community members have about the use of material benefits by the committee (I-31). A. complained that people from upcountry were discriminated against in distributions, that when they went to get something the committee would say they were not on the list but the committee never told them how to get on the list. Y., a committee member who had been marginalized by poor health and alcoholism, said that this was '*ben kaan len phak phuak*' (showing favouritism to their own group).

The connection between the charge of not accomplishing anything and gaining personal benefit by being on the committee was explicitly linked in some of L.P.'s. comments as I probed some statements he made regarding the problem of not being transparent (*mai brong sai*). He spoke of how the committee raises funds for major events in the community, framing it in terms of making merit (*tham bun*). L.P. said, 'I have watched these people, sometimes when it is time to come and make merit, they do no want to. Why? They [and here this is pointing to the committee] want it, they take it and use it [*kin kan* meaning literally to eat it, and this is used for corruption]. The residents are afraid of this, very afraid.'

At this point I asked what he meant by making merit, as this was the first time I had heard of the event fund-raising being phrased in this way. He responded, 'Making merit, it's like this...if you [again this is the role of the committee] take it and really use it nobody will say anything. Sometimes you use half of it and hold on to the other half.' So I asked how these funds could be 'eaten'. He responded that it was not everyone on the committee but only some people, and that there should be a list of contributors and the amount of money left over should be announced. He concluded, 'But there is not anything left. It goes into their pocket.' He then used the relative amount of funds raised at the big celebration of the King's Birthday on 5 December 2003 as an example of the people's distrust of the current committee. In his day they would raise 80-90,000 baht (US$ 2,000-2,250), and this committee only raised around 30,000 (US$ 750), which was not enough for the budget they had set. I asked if he felt that the residents trusted (*waijai*) the committee. He said:

> They do not trust them; they are afraid of this [thing happening]. I listen to their voices....This group, they have not done anything. They will raise funds and then take them and use it for themselves (*kin kan*). They [the community residents] are very afraid of this. Take D. for instance, she drinks everyday ... How are they going to trust her? She has not yet done anything tangible (*ben chin ben an*) (I-128).

With this as background I return to my main point here, that the charge of not accomplishing anything for the benefit of the community carries with it the implication that the committee members are *len phak phuak* (showing favouritism) and seeking their own benefit by using their position as intermediaries between the government and other sources of help outside the community. This then is in line with the follower perception and expectation of positional leadership; it is done for personal benefit. In the same interview L.P. sharply criticized D. and indicated that she was not considered *chuathuu* and that her drinking was a problem in the minds of people.

From what I have described thus far L.P. seems to be operating from what is a widespread assumption that those in official positions will seek to benefit themselves. Having said all of these things about D., we also have to consider what, by his own recollection, L.P. has done in regard to D., whom he has lived in close physical proximity to the past 40 years. From the beginning I was puzzled why D. was the president of the committee. She was not the oldest, had only a second grade education, did not seem to have any evidence of being much wealthier than other committee members, was not an articulate speaker, and let others take the lead in the public meetings that I observed. It turns out that there are two accounts of how she came to be the head of the committee: D.'s account, which is very close to those of her fellow committee members, and L.P.'s account. It may be possible to conflate the two, but for the moment I want to consider his account separately.

When I asked L.P. directly how D. came to be the committee president he said that he put her there (I-256). He was at the District Office and had to fill out the forms for the positions of the new committee; he filled in her name as president and put others in the required positions as well. In public discourse L.P. gave the same construction of who can lead in the community: the person who is *chuathuu*. Yet it is quite clear that L.P. does not *chuathuu* D., and thinks that many of the residents do not either. Due to their long proximity to each other it is impossible to argue that L.P. did not know D. well, or did not know about her drinking, about the way others thought of her, and about her personal abilities. However at some level D. was a more desirable candidate for that position than the other potential candidates who made up the committee. Whether L.P. would describe it in terms of *chuathuu* or not, he was willing to put her in that position. Yet once in the position L.P. took an oppositional stance. Though public discourse is shaped around the ideas of *chuathuu* there were other factors operating in this case.

Illustration #2: The Juxtaposition of the Good Person Construct and Political Manoeuvring

The second incident concerns the appointment of the positions for the new committee. In January 2004 the term for the committee was up. One window to how decisions are made on the ground comes in the fact that it is the committee members themselves who decide who will fill what particular roles. At least the last two times there has been a change of committee it appears a kind of dual process has happened, one formal/official and the other the informal. The formal process I observed in the meeting (PO-119) where the new committee is officially appointed. This year there were only 17 people who applied for 23 slots so there was no election and all of them were officially appointed by the District. At one point in the meeting the development officer read off the list of new appointees and then told them that they needed to decide on the required six positions. In the way that he phrased it, he acted as if the people were going to have a discussion right there. This is where it became obvious that there is a parallel informal process that takes place prior to the official meeting for appointment, once it becomes clear who is going to be on the new committee. At this point L., who was the secretary of the old committee and is a member of the new one, took charge and said that they had already had a meeting and decided upon the positions, and proceeded to read them off.[6] L. was quickly reading off the positions when she was loudly interrupted by D. who asked what meeting this was. L. replied curtly that D. had not attended the meeting, and D. retorted angrily that she had not even heard about it. This led to a period of shouting and commotion until someone suggested that since D. had not been present they should go back over all the positions and vote for them now. This was done, and it simply ratified the decisions that had already been made in the unofficial meeting.

In the aftermath of the meeting, I tried to inquire about what people thought was happening in this process and why D. had been obviously excluded. I also talked with D. directly to find out her feelings. What struck me as an interesting juxtaposition of ideas was the fact that while T., the new president, and the new committee's actions were very hurtful to D. (*sia khwaam ruusuk* in the sense of hurting or wounding one's feelings), when talking about T. and his new role she said that he was '*dii chai dai mai dai ben nakleng*' (a good person, adequate, not a ruffian or gangster). So even though she was very hurt by the actions of T. and the others who did not invite her, in her discourse constructing T. he was still a good person. One might expect that a good person would not go along with something that was obviously hurtful, but D. was apparently aware of the rules of the game, and while not enjoying her treatment, she saw it as an obvious way for someone in a position of power to treat another person.

---

[6] When this happened it helped me to understand a complaint that had come from three of the committee members on the last group who were from what is called the Ton Pho area. Seven of the 11 members of the committee were from the Flats, and the Ton Pho people accused them of having a meeting *nawk rawb* (an unofficial meeting) to decide what positions would be filled. The Ton Pho members consistently expressed their dislike of the work of the rest of the committee, said that they were cut off and not consulted, and were conspicuous in their absence from helping at any of the community events. In fact the new committee for the 2004-2006 term represents a complete overthrow of the Flats leadership. Of the 17 members only D., the former president, remains on the committee. The three Ton Pho members from 2002-2004 told me that there was lots of recruiting going on to try and force an election for this changeover, as they wanted to have more voice in the committee. As it turned out there was no election because people in the Flats for the most part did not run.

Therefore, she could still construct the person in power as 'good'. Again, when people control a power base in the way the Ton Pho group controls 16 of the 17 committee slots, it seems quite natural to D. that they would act in a way that benefits their interests; yet she described T. as a 'good' leader because the public discourse demands that one cannot be a leader without being *chuathuu*, and this entails being a good person which implies having good character.

Illustration #3: Leader Ideals and the Reality of Using Position for Personal Benefit

The third incident shows most clearly the kinds of expectations that are inherent in both the TLM and the SABLH.[7] On the day of the turnover to the new committee, after the six required positions were filled, the community development officer read from a document that explained the responsibilities of each position. After this there was further discussion as to the kinds of other positions and who would fill them. The officer was again quiet during this time, and when the discussion was finished he asked if there would be any changes; the group indicated no. The final discussion concerned who would serve as advisers to the new committee, and the group indicated five people for this task.

This seemed to signal the end of the meeting, and they began the process of filling out an official form from the District entitled 'asking for a *chumchon* committee member card'. L.P. took the microphone to the sound system that can broadcast throughout the whole community and began telling how each one of the people on the new committee *yawm rap sia sala*, meaning that they accept the sacrifices that will need to be made to do their role as community leaders. When he finished, the secretary L., who was on the past committee and the new one, began to talk to the new members and exhorted them not to use the card incorrectly or improperly (*mai thuuk tawng*).[8] She then continued speaking, welcoming the new members and asking to speak on behalf of the new president. She explained that there are three principles for working on the committee: *sia sala* (sacrifice), *ruammuu* (cooperation), and *samakhii* (harmony, unity, accord). She closed the speech by thanking them for being people who are willing to sacrifice for the community and who love the community.

In this way the ideas of sacrifice and cooperation that are so critical to the construction of the trustworthy person were juxtaposed with the warning not to utilize one's position for personal benefit. The fact that these two kinds of constructions are spoken of so easily and so close together again indicates that for local people such contradictions as these are completely 'normal'.

---

[7] All of this material comes from PO-119 where I sat in on the meeting where the new committee for 2004-2006 was officially appointed.

[8] I later asked how it would be possible to use the committee membership card in an improper or incorrect fashion. I was told that a person could use the card to convince another their request to do or receive something was legitimate as a representative of the committee but then take the benefit for themselves.

Summary

In the illustrative material above I have endeavoured to show how the suspicion heuristic is deeply interwoven into people's understandings and interpretations of leadership. The reality is that interpersonal relationships between formal position holders and residents are pervaded by the suspicion that leaders are currently or will in the future use their position in order to benefit themselves or their own group (*phak phuak*). There is a constant tension between the ideals of cooperation, harmony, and sacrifice, and the pursuit of personal benefit that is not in the best interests of the community. This tension is mirrored in the way residents maintain the public rhetoric of the moral leader as the good and trustworthy person while still accepting leaders' constant manoeuvring for position and power as a matter of fact.

This kind of split between the rhetoric of morality and everyday power politics is seen all the way back to the Ayuthayan era. Chai-anan notes how Buddhism served a legitimizing function while the Hindu model of the autocratic monarchy served direct political purposes. Thus one was idealist and the other focused on pragmatic this-world concerns (see his discussion 1987b:7-10). Mulder sees the basic hierarchy within the family extended into the public world, thus the 'public world becomes personalized and privatized, subjected to the same moral rules that pertained to being a child in a hierarchically structured familial world' (1997:36). This has resulted in the conflation of the ideas of nation, state, society, nation-state, public, and populace so that it is 'possible to present society as a seamlessly integrated, structureless whole, in which differences in prestige, power, position and life chances, are nullified' (1997:53). Because society is a moral construct, ethical solutions are suggested for structural ills (1997:228, 310). Thus the rhetoric of the moral leader, one who is good and trustworthy, comes as no surprise. At the same time Mulder notes that this moral model is at complete dissonance with societal conditions, and that the source of these abuses is 'rooted in the same lifeworld construction, namely, hierarchy and the privileges inherent in inequality' (1997:310). Here is the balancing act where the TLM, ideas of trust, and the reality of the ontological change brought on by formal position holding that creates inequality are all present and being drawn upon in different settings. Ockey sees the separation of symbolic leadership as centred in the monarchy from actual leadership happening in the Sarit era (Ockey, 2004b:182-3). Thus there could be historical and more contemporary reasons for the split between rhetoric and reality in conceptions of leadership in LWPW.

How the SABLH Affects Leadership Practise in the Community

I now turn from the theme of suspicion to examine how values in the SABLH affect leadership behaviour. My assumption here is that the leader behaviours that can be observed in the community are not rigidly determined, that there is a potential range of approaches to the work of leadership in the community. What

I have observed and learned from informants reflects in part how leaders are negotiating their relationships by drawing upon values and assumptions about the leader role. At this point I am creating a partial account for why the community leaders practise leadership in the way they do rather than in other potential modes. As I noted above, the deeply embedded values of hierarchy, and particularly the corresponding acceptance of privilege by superiors, shape the understanding and practise of leadership and provide a heuristic for interpreting the leader conduct I will detail below. In working through my observational and interview data five aspects stand out as being central to both residents' perception of what leaders are doing and actual leaders' practises: the unequal distribution of things given to the community, the control of information, not requesting feedback or input, a limited scope of service, and a desire for residents to cooperate with them, particularly in their celebratory community events.

Unequal Distribution

The public rhetoric of leaders is that they are acting for the good of the community, but residents suspect them of benefiting their own group and playing favourites (*len phak phuak*). Most often this problem manifests itself in the charge that the committee does not distribute the free things that are given from outside agencies fairly. This controversy has its roots in the differing sense of identity with the community that residents hold. In Chapter 3 I pointed out the distinctions made in LWPW based on place of origin and location of residence in the community. Length of time living in the community is not necessarily related to creating an identity there. People may live there and work for the vast majority of the year, only making occasional trips back to the home village, yet never move their house registration down to the capital; for them it is a temporary residence even though this may go on for ten to 20 years. Renters do not feel they are part of the community, and they see community leadership residing with those who were born there. Interviewees who have migrated into the community expressed that outsiders are cut off from information (I-31), that community leaders are not interested in them (I-31, I-33), that they are not given things in the distributions (I-31, I-32, I-33), and that they have no rights or voice (I-201). In my interviews with three people from the Northeast (I-31-33) who live right next to the Flats, they all insisted that they were not part of the community, even though this is considered the geographic heart of the community.[9]

[9] It was interesting to observe the different stereotypes that the Bangkok born residents and the Northeasterners have of each other. Renters complain that they are discriminated against in every way, while the Bangkok locals assert that the migrants in the Rua Khiaw area are the ones with all the money, and that they work harder than the people who live in the Flats.

When I began to share with the committee members what I was hearing about the problem of inequitable distribution of materials coming into the community, they quite openly admitted that this was the case. T., the new president as of February 2004, said that they had to pass things out to the *chumchon* people first; otherwise they would complain. The problem lies in the fact that there are not enough things that come in to go around to everybody (I-150). T.'s comment here shows again the flexibility of the term *chumchon* and illustrates in this case not a difference of geography but of original residents versus those who have come in as renters from the outside.

I had a protracted conversation with M., who is a new committee member and the uncle of T., regarding this issue (I-202). He explained what is happening in this way:

> About passing things out, meaning, when things come, not everybody gets some....Things come for only a small per cent of the people who are here, the things that come, don't cover even half [the people] and what we go out and pass out we have to pass out in the local area (*phuun thii*) first, the people who are really in the *phuun thii* and then it is still not enough to pass out to everyone. If we were really going to pass things out, giving to the people who *asai* (temporarily dwell here), the people from the provinces who come and *asai* in this *phuun thii*, with what we are given, it would not cover everybody.

Just as *chumchon* has a dual use, M. changes the way he uses *phuun thii* (terrain, surface of the earth). First he refers to the local area, not in the sense of geography but as the people who are true Bangkok residents, born or raised most of their lives in the community; then in the last instance he refers to the area as a literal physical piece of space, making a distinction between true residents and those who come to dwell there temporarily.

M. was also very aware of how people perceive this situation (I-202). He commented that:

> The way it has been done in the past, for the most part they [community leaders] have given to people who were close to them (*khaang khiang*, literally those who are next to them physically). To say it simply...if lots of people are saying this it is the same as *len phuak* (to play favourites)...those who are close to you get it first, those close to you get full first.

M. constructs the problem as followers perceive it. I include this as a part of the SABLH because it appears to be a very natural part where the superior position takes the privilege of bringing benefit to one's own group first. This is the way both sides see it, although it is not appreciated by followers. In a world of hierarchy such a division seems normal and one's own group, however defined, becomes the first target for benefit. The lines of division that I noted in Chapter 3 become the boundaries for who is in and who is out, whether it is locality as in the case with Ton Pho and the Flats, or place of origin as with people born in the slum from Ton Pho and the Flats against the renters of Rua Khiaw.

Controlling Information

If inequitable distribution of goods represents the prerogative of control of physical resources for SAB leaders, the control of information represents the prerogative in the arena of non-tangible resources. Again, the values of hierarchy about not interfering with or questioning a superior are expressed here in the way that the committee is seen to hold on to information that would be of interest to other residents. This information has to do with assistance from the outside that flows into the community via the officially sanctioned leaders, which is the committee. Each month the District holds a meeting attended by the *chumchon* leaders that is informational in nature. The local leaders are given time to share needs and problems, and the district officials representing the various agencies talk about upcoming programmes, events, and budgets that are related to the poor communities (PO-88).

The perception on the part of people in the community is that the committee members do not freely share opportunities that may benefit the residents at large. Instead, they use the 'insider information' to steer benefit to themselves and their group (*phuak*). This is the view not only of those who are outsiders who rent in the community, but of those who were born there as well. I-31 and I-33 both indicated that those from the provinces who are renters are cut out from what is happening and not called for meetings that disseminate important information. In an interview with the new president T., he gave as one of his motives for applying for the committee the feeling that the committee led by D. was not *klaang* (middle, meaning neutral and fair), that she had not done things to benefit the whole community. T. insisted that his desire had been to get a group from Ton Pho together to be on the committee so they could learn about budgets and opportunities that could be accessed by the community (I-150).

My own observations of a monthly committee meeting in the community, made before my interviews with the above people, left me with the impression that sharing information and getting feedback from the community was not something that the committee regularly practised (PO-86). The main purpose of the meeting I attended was to discuss a letter that had come from the District requesting the submission of a project the community would propose for the next year's budget. In the process of their dialogue there was no reference to ideas that had been generated from discussion with community residents, nor was there any suggestion that they should poll or find a way to gain input from the residents. The committee seemed to see themselves as completely sufficient representatives of the entire community. Later on in interviewing other people and hearing their frustrations of exclusion from knowing what is happening I could understand how this perception arises from having seen in action the committee working on this one budgetary issue. There did not seem to have been any prior information gathering on potential needs at least on a formal basis, and there was certainly no inclination to get out in the community to discover what people felt should be done.

Limited Service

I have already shown in Chapter 3 how two factors cause people to feel they are not a part of the *chumchon.* They reside in the administrative unit defined by the state as the *chumchon* but they feel like the committee is not interested in them. One factor is place of residence; the farther people live from the centre of the community, the less they feel like they are a part of it. The other factor is renting; those who rent consistently feel like they are not a part of the community. The phrase I heard several times was that 'the *chumchon* does not reach here,' meaning that they were not treated in the same way as locally born residents.

My connection here to the SABLH is that the ontological change brought about by having a formal position and thus being superior and worthy of privilege is that you have your business to take care of and those under you have the role of helping you with what you are doing, but not vice versa. This manifests itself in a style of leadership in the community that sees a major part of the task as being handling the paperwork and requests of the government administrative system, while the interpersonal dimension is for the most part ignored. Outsiders do not see themselves as part of the *chumchon* because they are cut off from benefits and information and cannot become part of the in-group, while those on the geographical fringes feel they are not part of the community because the leadership has nothing to do with them. The limited scope of service provided by the committee seems to be a particular interpretation based in SAB values and not constrained by other external factors.

Cooperation and Fund-raising

Continuing the same theme as in the previous point, superiors in hierarchical relationships expect that subordinates will help them with the things they are doing. In the community this manifests itself in the attitude of the committee members that the residents should be cooperating with the various events that they put on. In a conversation that I had with some of the vendors who sell food on the edge of the community I asked them if people like themselves who rented there were part of the *chumchon* or not (I-201). They said they had no rights, no voice, 'only that [they] want us to help out'. Helping has two primary dimensions: one is participating in work days and helping with the festivals in the setting up, donating food, and other practical assistance, and the second is giving money, framed as 'making-merit', which provides the cash budget for these events.

Another point that caught my attention in the observation of the monthly meeting (PO-86), where the committee was bouncing around ideas for a project to suggest to the government, was that the rationale for one possible project was to make money for the *chumchon* and that the people were supposed to have a part (*suan ruam*) in it. The project was a centre for taking care of the small children of working parents, and apparently the income generated would be put back into the community. I was not sure of how the residents were to take part, perhaps in the sense of staffing it or paying for their children to be cared for. But at any rate the committee members saw this as a way for the residents to have a part in something that would benefit the *chumchon*. However, this benefit in terms of extra finance would be controlled by the committee so again it appears that the leaders expect the residents to help them with their work, and not the other way around.

The Potential to Use Position for Personal Gain

A final point about SABLH values has to do with the perception by leaders themselves that people holding a leadership position in the community can use it for personal gain. Early in my entry into the community I sensed a great deal of suspicion and worry that I could be in some way trying to deceive them so that residents' dwellings could be taken away. In one of my early interviews with D. who was president at that time, I was asking about issues relating to their staying on this lánd (I-153). At one point some years previously a large number of houses had been removed and the people relocated in order to make space for a memorial developed for the Queen mother. She indicated that the president then had made a lot of money by signing something allowing this driving-off to happen.[10] A few months later I was talking with a group of people on the committee and asking them why they decided to run for a position. D. said, 'I am a person from here; I did not want someone to come in and do something that is not right.' I asked her to clarify what she meant by 'not right' (*mai thuuk tawng*). She said, 'to take the position of being on the committee and use it to *maa haa kin* (make a living).' She said that people can use the position to gain personal benefit, and at this point K. said that this has happened before. A month later in a conversation with L.P. he noted that the

[10] I pieced together a possible scenario much later from dates and bits and pieces of information I collected. In L.P.'s recollection of former committee presidents, just prior to his own service as president starting in 1998 a person that he indicated was a *nakleng* was in office. The time frame for the eviction was around 1998 which means that the dealing was done prior to this. It appears that this *nakleng* was involved in some way with gaining money in this eviction. How this could be made more sense when I later heard about the school that was going to be built in the *naa wat* area. They successfully negotiated with the District to have the school built in between the funerary structure and the temple and thus spared their housing. So it appears that there is room for negotiation in such issues. It seems possible that this *nakleng* figure could take money for not pressing a negotiation or resistance to the placement of the funerary structure so as to preserve more housing. I am just speculating here, but D.'s comments now make more sense as I have seen possible mechanisms for how such a scenario could take place.

people will not like someone who uses the office for personal gain. I asked if this has ever happened and he said yes (I-144).

For a person like D. one of her motives in running for the committee was to prevent the abuse of power that has happened in the past. Using position for personal gain seems to be quite natural; it is assumed by people in follower roles. For D. the desire to prevent such abuse was a motivating factor for becoming a leader.

Summary

In this section I have looked at some of the characteristics of how community leadership is actually practised in LWPW. Formal position in the community is characterized by a control of resources expressed in inequitable distributions among the people, a tendency to favour one's own group, the control of information, a limited scope of service, a desire for residents to help them without correspondingly doing much for them, and an awareness that positions can be used for personal gain. My argument is that the SABLH provides values and assumptions that govern conceptions of holding a formal position. Having the rank and status of a position renders a person a relatively superior in the hierarchical social structure, and this means the acceptance of privilege. Acceptance of privilege then manifests itself in the kinds of behaviour on the part of the committee that I have examined in this section.

Leadership Dynamics in the Space Outside of Administrative Control

In endeavouring to create an account in cultural terms of how leadership operates in LWPW I have drawn upon Weber's three-fold typology of legitimate authority. In Chapter 3 I noted how prior to community registration in 1985 there were traditional leadership forms of respected elders and *nakleng* present in a decentralized fashion. However, with the coming of registration and the connection to the state administrative apparatus a process of 'officialization' occurred over time. In Weberian terms this was the gradual acceptance of the legal element so that eventually the same sense of traditional-legal legitimacy afforded to the state was extended to the community committee which functions as the lowest rung of the state administrative system. The result of officialization is that people now only recognize officially sanctioned positions as being legitimate in the community, which has led to the marginalizing of the purely traditional form of *nakleng* leadership. The process of officialization was facilitated by the perspectives of the *Sakdi* Administrative Behaviour Leadership Heuristic (SABLH) which causes people to see formal position holders as undergoing an ontological change. The values inherent in this model impact leaders and followers and have played a part in enhancing the sense of the legality of formal positional leadership. SABLH values are reproduced in the community on the leadership side in the acceptance of privilege, and on the follower side in the suspicion that leaders are pursuing personal benefit.

At present, the traditional *nakleng* type and traditional-legal SAB style leader are considered problematic by people in the community because those types are seen as pursuing personal and in-group interest above the interests of the entire broader community. A counterpoint to these two leadership types is the *Thuukjai* Leader Model (TLM) which operates through personal power that can be utilized with all types of legitimate authority and positional power as well. I have also argued here that the discourse of the trustworthy leader operationalizes the TLM in the community, but this has the status of being an official Thai cultural version since the SABLH for followers views all leaders with suspicion. Thus the view for public (and outsider) consumption is that community leaders must be trustworthy (*chuathuu*), and yet in actual practise it is virtually impossible for a community leader not to be under suspicion by residents of pursuing personal benefit

One might expect that the process of officialization and the use of SAB values would cause the community committee to function at a micro-level in the same way as the state administrative system. However, it must be kept in mind that I have chosen to coin terms like 'officialization' and *sakdi* administrative behaviour in order to make certain emphases and to avoid misunderstandings. The legal element, both within the traditional-legal legitimacy of the state and now in LWPW as it concerns the committee, is not rational or impersonal. SAB values mean that formal position is seen as legitimate in the complex admixture of traditional-legal understanding, but they influence people to operate on the basis of personalism, hierarchy, and patron-client style relations. In this section I will share evidence that a reproduction of these patterns in LWPW is only partial; there is an independence of the community from the views of the state. While the coming of the state administrative structure to the slum has conferred a structure and legitimacy for governing, the residents of LWPW are not passive participants in all of this. I am going to argue that under the broad umbrella of traditional-legal authority there is a small but vibrant space outside of administrative control where traditional forms of leadership are still practised. Specifically this concerns notions of the group (*phuak*), and horizontal relations that are not based in reciprocation/obligation.

Evidence of Agency in Non-administrative Space

By non-administrative space I am referring to the practise on the part of people in the community of traditional forms of leadership that find their legitimacy not in law or the regulations of the state, but through cultural values that affirm such practise. It is space where people exercise autonomy from the state, rather than simply reproducing the viewpoints reflected in state regulations or behaviour patterns. The theme that binds the two subsections here together is the independence of the community from the state in terms of the way the state conceives of the operation of the community committee.

Leadership Matters

It is my impression from time spent in the community that for people born in the community and who serve on the committee, how they conduct themselves is not a moot point or simply a matter of complying with state demands. Leadership of the community matters to those who see LWPW as their home. There are critical issues that demand someone to be vigilant on behalf of the community, the primary one being their security on the land. As I noted above in interviews about motivation for becoming a leader, one of the most important was to protect the community from the unscrupulous and to insure their continued existence. Those involved in leadership have an agenda for the community, which is to preserve it from eviction. While caught up in the larger system of state administration, the committee members still work on this agenda that brings benefit to a broader group rather than just their own personal interests.

There is a sense that residents grudgingly accept the government demands for meetings and paperwork, but between themselves they admit that outsiders representing the government actually do not do much for the community. Residents view outsiders such as members of the Bangkok City Council or the District Council as making promises during election time, but then avoiding the community after the votes are cast, except for brief visits at major festivals. Governmental activity is perceived as being more public relations oriented than based in a deep concern for the well being of the community. Residents' sense of autonomy from the government shows in the vigorous manoeuvring that goes on in order to get enough of one's own group on the committee so they can have influence in community affairs. The fact that they cannot depend on the government to keep their community from being driven off the land means that leaders play an important role that goes well beyond the administrative duties that are a part of the government system. As I noted in Chapter 3 protecting their community from eviction is definitely not part of the state agenda for the committee members. The strident criticisms that fly between factions and leaders about other factions and leaders indicate that the stakes are very real in their eyes.

Leadership and the Role of the Group

My observations and discussions with people in the community suggest that the most important factor in the dynamics of leadership in the community and the determination of the composition of the committee is the role of the group (*phuak*). In trying to understand the processes of how people become a committee member and how the committee positions are chosen I was confronted with conflicting accounts that took a while to sort out. In the end both of these processes have to do with the very different ways that people in the community practise them against the government's understanding of the situation based upon the rules and regulations.

In my initial inquiries into how the election system worked in the community I was confused because I heard two conflicting sets of information. This led me to check with another slum near where I live and they confirmed the same view as in LWPW. Informants detailed a process where you first got your group together and applied as a *chut*, meaning a set of people. However, other informants as well as the official rules in the community committee handbook indicated a process where votes were cast for individuals and the top vote getters comprised the committee. I told a community development officer at the Pathum Wan district what I was hearing about people applying as groups, and he insisted that they only apply as individuals and that votes are cast for individuals (I-23). Things became clearer during the time prior to and just after the appointment of the new committee for 2004-2006. I had already known about the fact that the committee was split eight to three, with the group of eight living for the most part in the Flats and the three coming from the Ton Pho area. As the time for the change of the committee came near I learned that the Ton Pho area was actively recruiting a large number of people to apply for the committee, with the hope of forcing an election where they would have the most candidates to choose from. Later on while interviewing D. about her time as president and how she ended up with that position she gave an explanation that also focused on the importance of the group (I-203):

> A.-Who was it who invited you to apply for the committee? Did you think of it yourself or did others invite you?
>
> D.-My group of friends, of course.
>
> A.-So it was your friends who invited you?
>
> D.-They invited me. They did not really want to be [on the committee]. We were calling around trying to create a stir (*hai wun leoy*) [in the community]. I mean that we would apply so that we could compete [against the others]. If we lose or win it is fun (*sanuk*) if we go ahead and apply to compete. Well as time went by, we all went and after we went [to apply at the District] it turned out that the only ones [who really applied] were my group (*phuak*). We went and found out that nobody else had applied to compete against us, so we lifted up our whole team, and we also had three from Ton Pho.

It is interesting to note here how D. asserts that it was her friends who invited her, but it was her group that actually became the new committee because nobody else applied. The initiative or idea to run was floated by her friends, but among those friends she was the head of that particular group.

So both views were essentially correct, and brought together they create an accurate picture of how the election and appointment process works. While the government's official position is that individuals are running for positions and voting is done by individuals for individuals, the reality is that local people are informally piecing together coalitions of small groups on the basis of friendship, as in the case of D., or on the basis of sharing similar concerns for an area in the community, such as what happened in Ton Pho with the 2004 changeover.

Group (phuak) and Horizontal Non-reciprocal Relations

I am drawing here on material that I introduced in Chapter 4 as I was examining how the TLM works to build the potential for influence in dyadic relations. There I noted that it is possible in relations that are more horizontal in nature to have cooperation that is not based in the reciprocation/obligation nexus. Withaya points out that the term *phuak* has a different sense than the English 'group', which conveys the idea of being linked together. Instead *phuak* is relationships among those that are within the circle of the *phuak*, and he summarizes the term as 'group collectivity' (1996:220).[11] Hierarchy is present in all relations in Thailand, and there are types of *phuak* where patron-client relations operate, as well as types with strong vertical connections with leaders and a sense of obligation in play (Withaya, 1996:224-6). However, my discussions as well as observations in the community lead me to believe that there are also *phuak* that are much more horizontal in nature and based on varying levels of friendship and acquaintance. In this section I will examine the operation of community leadership in and through a group collectivity at a specific point in time in LWPW, with a focus on the dynamics within the group.

Trust

I have established that in the eyes of both residents and the community committee the securing of voluntary cooperation is the critical component needed to both become a leader and practise leadership. The *phuak* is a primary mechanism for practising leadership because it is within the circle of the *phuak* that you have trusted people who will come to your aid; who will cooperate (*ruammuu*) with what you are doing; and who will help make sure that the necessary work, particularly for the large festivals, gets done. The assumption seems to be that you cannot depend on others to help you out; there are too many other intervening factors, so you need to have a group around you that will not fail. The large festivals demand a great deal of physical labour in the

---

[11] Withaya lists the following as properties of *phuak*: no formal structure, the boundaries are defined by the backgrounds of the majority of the members, being a member means to identify yourself as such, they are devoid of ideological commitments, people are looking for benefit, a small core will act in the name of the *phuak*, people can enter and leave, and there is no force to insure loyalty (1996:225-7).

preparations – putting up the staging, sound system, and lights; constructing a tent; coordinating food; hiring bands; connecting with the temple to arrange for the monks to come. Within the context of the group, this work that goes beyond the ability of a single individual, can be accomplished. In LWPW what D. called her *phuak* was an inner circle of women who were friends, but she was also part of a broader *phuak* of people in the Flats who shared a concern about the leadership of the community. L.P. as a former committee president was a part of this group (I-303), as were the men who served on the committee during the time D. was president. By contrast T., the new president, is considered to have a *phuak* because of his ability to help others with his finances and because he has rental houses that create bonds of obligation to him (I-203, I-303). It does not matter how the group is formed; what is important is having people you can count on to join you.[12]

Character

The emphasis on group also helps to explain the gist of some comments by D. on the person of good character. When I was working on term definitions I asked D. and K. about the meaning of good character, and they said, 'Someone you can get along with, that you can talk with, a person that you can talk with who will understand, whose character and personality (*nisai jai khaw*) does not go against (*mai kat kan*) your own (personality)' (I-70). When I asked how you would recognize such a person, they said that you had to be around a person (*khob kan*) for a long time and that what you were looking for was if a person would help out and be available to help. At the time of this interview I had not yet understood the role of the group, and I was still thinking in terms of the situation of choosing a leader from a group of individuals, so I asked the question, 'How do people choose a leader? Suppose you had someone with good character and one with bad character?' The answer at the time surprised me because they did not answer my question at all. They said that you choose from your *phuak*, that you would not choose someone if you did not know their *pon ngaan* in the sense of the fruit of their work, the results that have come about from their efforts.

Diffusion of Work through Mutual Help

In stark contrast to views of leadership that focus on a single person, leadership functions in the committee that served from 2002-2004 that had D. as the president were based in an advance agreement that they would all share in the work. I probed people to see if within the committee itself there was a clear hierarchy and vertical relationships. All my interactions with them led me to think that their relations were of a more horizontal nature. N. noted that people on the committee view all the positions as equal (I-72). This was not just

[12] It is the fear of not being able to garner people to help that is cited as a reason why some people do not want to lead (I-26).

rhetoric, but actually seemed to be the way this committee worked. De., N. and I met at a food shop on the night of the preparations for the King's birthday celebration in 2003. In the context of talking about the work of the committee N. noted that De. was the key person in terms of getting things done. N. and De. had done all the stage setup and the electrical wiring for this event (I-72). I asked De. if he was going to run for the new committee and he said no, he was tired. However, he said, it did not matter if he was on the committee or not as he was the one who knew how to get things done. This was not just boasting, as I observed that De. was always a main player in arranging things for the large events.

The diffusion of work throughout the group means that in practise the person who ends up as the president of the committee does not have to be the best administrator, the most knowledgeable, or the most articulate speaker. This helped to explain D. as the president of the committee, since in my observations she never appeared to be in charge of anything. At the monthly meeting in the slum (PO-86) it was De. who led the meeting and did most of the talking, and at the monthly District meeting of slum leaders (PO-88) D. sat around the main table. However, when it came time to report and make suggestions from LWPW it was the secretary L. who came up and took D.'s chair, did the speaking, and then went back to her place with D. resuming her seat around the table. At the community festivals D. was always very busy directing and working, but it was L. and L.P. who did the microphone work making announcements and acting as the emcees for the event. Although I have not watched T. yet in leading any community functions or a meeting, I-134 did say that T. was not a good speaker either.

I had the chance to talk with D. about how she was chosen to be the president of the committee, and as it was quite instructive. I will reproduce a fairly lengthy section of our dialogue here[13]:

> A.-You have told me that when you became a part of the committee they told you to be the president and you told them you had never thought to be the president.

---

[13] It was very confusing to try and understand the chronology and details from both D. and L.P.'s accounts of how she became the president. I actually went back for a clarification interview with L.P. (I-256) to try to make more sense of his statements in light of her explanations as given here. In my interview with L.P. a missing piece of information came out that helped bring the two accounts closer together. Apparently after De. said that he could not be president the group made the decision to dissolve and ask the District to hold another election. It seems like this necessitated a trip as a group or part of the group going to the actual District Office. Somewhere between the decision to dissolve and going to the District the discussion D. relates here about going down the line seeing who could be president occurred, and she agreed; thus the committee decided not to dissolve. L.P. was most likely involved in this discussion and so at the District Office inserted D.'s name as president. He likes to take credit for putting D. in office, but the actual process was based in a discussion at the group level.

> D.-That's right, I had never thought of that.
>
> A.-...I would like to know why you became the president even though you never thought to be that.
>
> D.-It's like this, before I became the president I did not think I would be [president] because I was working. We were selling things and then after a while we were not selling. So after that they applied [for the committee] and invited me to go as well, so we decided to do this and help because I could see that I was not doing anything, so if they had some work I could be able to help them. I thought that if I was on the committee, I could help here and there, this is something I like....
>
> A.-Ok, when your group came into leadership, how was the decision made for you to become the president?
>
> D.-It was like this, when they were choosing, at first they were going to have L.P. be it, but L.P. did not want it, he was not going to come into the committee again, he did not want to do it at all....He did not come in, you see he was just playing. As soon as it was clear that he was not coming in, then they wanted De. to be the president. He said, I don't want it, as he did not have time because he was working. Because you see being the president is very bothersome (*yung*), you have to go here and go there....So then they asked K. to be president, but she did not want it, then N. to be, but he did not want to. There was no one who wanted to be it. So then they asked me to do it, so I figured it might as well be me (*ben phii D. kaw laew kan*). I told them that I did not want it because I have never had experience in this area before, so if I am the president I won't know anything and then I will have to go to meetings. But they said never mind, we will help you.

In this segment the functioning of the group is seen clearly and there is a commitment on the part of the group to help out so that all of the tasks get covered. As the president D. would have lots of meetings to attend, this was part of the division of labour. D. summarizes the president role in these terms:

> ...So now that I have been [the president] I am really tired, I have no time of my own. It's like this, I can't even work for a living, next thing you know something else comes in. One moment it is a letter, the next it is one of the agencies that are coming in and I have to take them walking about to look at things. I mean that since the position dropped to me, I can do it, but it is so bothersome (*yung*).

The president role is seen as the connector between the community and the government in what are considered to be matters of lesser importance while the group itself insures that the important tasks of putting on the festivals and doing other jobs in the community are taken care of. Working as a group means that no matter whom the president is, the work can still be done.

Voice in Community Affairs

Having a group also means that you can have a voice in community affairs. The reason given for Ton Pho recruiting a large number of people to try and force an election in 2004 was that with only three people on the committee of 11 they had no voice. It was their feeling that with only three votes out of 11 they could not represent Ton Pho interests. Here is an instance that shows the double-edged nature of the idea of 'group'. Work can diffuse through the group and lighten the load, but conceptions of groupness can also divide, creating in-groups and out-groups. The clash of the value of unity with the value of group will be a point of major discussion in the next chapter.

Criteria Within the Group for Choosing the Committee Leader

On an individual basis, L.P. or De. are the people who would stand out as natural leaders of the committee. They are respected for both their character and their competence in getting tasks done in the community. When circumstances made it difficult for them to serve in this capacity, it was not simply a matter of finding the next best candidate, but rather the idea of *phuak* was activated and people thought in terms of diffusing the work through the group. However the process of choosing the president did illuminate some principles that operated within the group. As D. relates, the discussion went around the group and she was not in the first ranks of choice, but she was also above some others in the group of eight. In the end I counted four different factors that were brought out in one way or another.

The most important factor was having time. As I noted above, the position of president is considered to be bothersome and requires attendance at many district or agency meetings. After time, the second factor was that others be *kreng jai* (deferential, polite response) of the person. Interviewees noted of both D. and T. that people are *kreng jai* of them. T. said it was because he was part of the original habitants of the community. I brought this subject up with D. and asked her why people who were born in the community were more likely to be obeyed (*chuafang*) and that others would *kreng jai* them (I-203). She said:

> because some people are from here and when they say something others will believe them because some people are not from here. But if some people [who are not from here] say something that is not true then I can bawl them out….I can bawl them out and they will be afraid (*kreng*).

Thus in the circumstances where you have a locally born and bred group opposed to a migrant group, those who have the weight to be believed and respected as an authority are the ones who have been around the longest, and their knowledge must be respected. Being widely known, which was given as a reason why D. was chosen (I-114), also seems to be related to being born in the community and contributes to having others respect and obey a person.

The third factor was being widely known in and of itself. This connects with my discussion of being *chuathuu* (trustworthy), where it is not enough to be a good person in dyadic relations, but one must take an interest in the good of the community and be visible in doing good. The last factor is a contested one where there are differing opinions, which relates to whether money is necessary to be a community leader or not. Wealth makes it easier to help others without a concern for personal benefit, which is the key factor in becoming a trustworthy or respected person. What was interesting is that in asking about this, people who did not hold leadership positions insisted that having money was important, while those who were leaders were adamant in saying that it was not necessary. L.P. admitted he had resources, but said he did not use them to gain influence, while D. and T. said they did not have money. Yet all three of them insisted the others did have financial resources. Of the three, D. was known as being the person with the least money.

One day I had a conversation with Ni. who was at D.'s table where she sold food at the edge of the flat where she lives. I asked her what was most important for being a community leader and she said that you need to have money. This brought a sharp retort from D. who said that you did not need money. While this interchange between Ni. and D. was going on D. continued working and Ni. was winking at me and mouthing that D. did not have any money and that is why she was saying this (I-130). After D. left, Ni. indicated that both L.P. and T. were people who had money. On another occasion a man named O. (I-134) brought out the point that it takes money to build *baramii*, which he equated with power (he used the English word here and then said that means *amnaat* (power) in Thai). When I asked him if that meant that T. had more money than others he said, 'No, you don't have to be rich' (*ramruay*). T. himself denied that he had money saying, 'Look at your list, all these people are in the middle (*baan klaang*, meaning, in terms of finance, being in the middle range of income in the slum), anybody who had money would not be doing this' (I-133). It appears to be a matter of perspective and positioning as to whether or not money is a key factor.[14]

Analysis of Leadership on the Ground in LWPW

Trust, values that create both an SAB-style of leadership and suspicion on the part of followers, and leadership through a collective group are three key issues that relate to everyday life and leadership on the ground in the LWPW

[14] For instance, people who are not community leaders and who do not have much in available cash flow to help others, feel that they are unable to help others out even though in their heart they want to (I-113). However, from the perspective of the leaders themselves, in comparison with others in the community who have stronger financial resources, they say that they do not have money, and that it is not required to be able to lead.

community. In this final section I will examine these factors against the backdrop of a broader canvas of concepts to bring further insight to our understanding of leadership in LWPW.

The Relationship of the Factors to Other Concepts of Thai Leadership

How do the factors of trust, the SABLH model, and conceptions of 'group' relate to issues such as patron-client relationships, reciprocal relations, and status determinants? I suggest that what I have observed happening in LWPW cannot be fully explained if you take any of these three concepts as the only framework of interpretation. The public rhetoric, which is at best a 'partial transcript' is that community leaders must be *chuathuu* (trustworthy), with the implication being that this perception is held fairly broadly in the community. What one finds however is that it has more to do with a group of friends who have a common interest in helping to protect and care for their community and who informally agree to help one another out in this task. Inside of the 2002-2004 committee I could not find evidence of the type of 'lopsided friendship' that forms patron-client relations, nor was obligation the only cohesion for their groupness. The motive for cohesion was not personal benefit as in *nakleng* or money lender type relations where they have groups that surround them and will be obedient to them on the basis of fear and/or obligation. Instead, cohesion grows out of a shared concern for the benefit and protection of the community. The new context of leadership in the community consists of a formal committee sanctioned by the government, opportunity to tap government resources, and the increased threat of eviction. In these circumstances having a group of people who trust each other and who are committed to help one another in the work of caring for and protecting the community is the way leadership is conducted. Traditional social influence processes based in patron-client relations, obligation, and status determinants are modified by the group approach.

The Basis for Authority

Within the polity of the community what is happening in terms of the Weberian framework of traditional, legal, and charismatic authority? The process of officialization has brought a legal dimension to residents' understanding of legitimacy within the context of the community. Thus real leaders are those who have official positions, carry cards issued by the state, are appointed by state officers or elected in a process that is sanctioned and monitored by the state, attend meetings called by the state, and are authorized to carry on the business of the state in the community. The administrative structure that this takes is not bureaucracy in its Weberian ideal typical form (see Ritzer, 2000:234) but a bureaucratic infrastructure that runs on what I am calling *sakdi* administrative values and behaviour. Rationalized bureaucracy and constitutional democracy are the public face and veneer of a system of rank and status where formal position holding justifies the acceptance of privilege. The *Sakdi* Administrative Behaviour Leadership Heuristic (SABLH) ironically contributes to the process of officialization with its focus on the importance of legally sanctioned position, while at the same time raising resistance to those seen as legitimate under traditional-legal authority because they become suspect of acting out of personal interest.

However, to focus only upon the formal aspects of leadership in the community via the structure brought in by the state is to miss the diversity and creativity that is happening under the broader umbrella of the administrative system itself and in the non-administrative spaces now relegated to the periphery by state control of the centre. Rather than focusing on 'static wholes' the picture of 'animated in-betweens' is a more appropriate frame for focusing on social influence dynamics within LWPW.[15] The conception of *phuak* and its function for ensuring mutual assistance and diffusing the work of leadership clearly falls into the realm of a Weberian conception of traditional authority. A dynamic view of culture that sees humans as active, inventive, and social opens the door for seeing the creation of new forms in the context of new social settings (Carrithers, 1992:33). With this dynamic view of culture in mind, Cohen's rubric of 'continuity in change' (Cohen, 1991:46) seems appropriate for understanding the relationship between traditional-legal and traditional authority in the community.

In the working of the group (*phuak*) we see continuity with one of the traditional types of leadership that was in the community before it was registered with the District. Yet change is also very evident as new social relations have come into existence that create new forms of social life and of causation (Carrithers, 1992:50). I see an analogous process to what Wilson describes as happening to the thaumaturge in pre-literate societies as the social system is disrupted (Wilson, 1973:132). External forces push this role to the edge of the society and the public role is lessened even where a ceremonial role is retained (Wilson, 1973:132). Traditional forms of authority found their locus in the *nakleng* (ruffians) and those who had wealth to lend to others and create relationships of obligation. With the coming of the state administrative apparatus the more public roles that these people may have had have now diminished; they are restricted to the peripheries and are not considered leaders because they are seen as pursuing their own interests and not the good of the community. Officialization means that they no longer 'count' as community leadership because they are not official and legally sanctioned. Whereas in the

---

[15] I have taken these ideas on wholes and in-betweens from Carrithers (1992:28) who was developing them by contrasting a view of culture as a set of bounded, discrete entities with a more dynamic view argued for by Wolf, whose view of culture as a series of processes allows for seeing new social situations and relationships (Wolf, 1982; see Carrithers, 1992:25-9 for his development and application of Wolf's ideas).

past traditional authority involved patron-client relations, traditional status determinants, and *nakleng* types as potential leaders, the new social relations engendered by the entrance of the state has caused a reconfiguration of these elements creating new forms of criteria for leadership. What we are seeing is re-creation and reshaping rather than the creation of something completely new.

Dynamics between TLM, Trust, and the Reality of Suspicion

These models naturally raise questions about their origins and the interrelationships between them. In the previous chapter I looked at potential origins of the TLM as rooted in several ideal cultural values. Where *chuathuu* (trustworthy) operationalizes the prototypical leader model, it does so on the same basis by tapping critical ideal values. The socially constructed *chuathuu* leader is part of the presentational side of Thai culture that is drawn upon for official purposes and where face is involved (as with the case of the foreign researcher inquiring about community leaders).[16] This explains the discourse in the community that insists upon *chuathuu* as a basis for leadership even when in reality *chuathuu* can be used in a very nuanced fashion and as an attribute for individuals who from another perspective are suspected of not being *chuathuu*.

However, I think that the *chuathuu* model also fulfils another function besides a presentational ideal. The values of hierarchy that undergird the positional model create a reality on the ground that is not often talked about or reflected upon, but is the daily experience of people. People experience positional leadership in the community where manoeuvring, displays of self-interest, favouritism, control of information and resources, narrow scope of service, lack of creativity, and shifting allegiances are all standard fare. At higher levels in the state administrative system, exploitation and corruption are routine. This in turn fuels the suspicion theme that is part of the follower perception side of the SABLH model. Here is where the *chuathuu* model becomes desired not as an ideal but as a reality because it lends at least the potential of generating benefit for the community.

Analysts of Thai society have noted the interplay between the cultural codes of hierarchy and Thai style individualism that is anarchic and present-oriented (Cohen, 1991:11, 39, 46; Mulder, 1997:310).[17] From Cohen's perspective Thais

[16] Mulder observes that there seems to be little concern about the way Thai society is portrayed to the public; unflattering things are reported matter of factly. But image anxiety is very clear when taboos are breached internally, key institutions are questioned, Thai customs are subjected to foreign gaze, and reputation is threatened (which is pragmatically driven by the fear that a damaged international reputation will keep foreign tourists away) (Mulder, 1997:200-210).

[17] The term 'individualism' is used with reference to Thai people in a very qualified sense. On the measures of individualism and collectivism such as used by Hofstede, Thais score higher on the collective side. See Suntaree's work on Thai values and the ego orientation (1990) and Brummelhuis' interpretation of Thai individualism (1984).

value and at the same time fear their type of individualism because of its potential for leading to unbridled greed, corruption, and exploitation as people pursue their own interests. In Mulder's view the moral model of society equates the private world with the public, and thus the country is seen as a family with all that this entails in being grateful and obligated to others. The familial view of society breaks down in the everyday experiences of people with work, travel, education, and so on where they are anonymous to each other. In this anonymous social space the family conception of society in the moral construct disintegrates. Mulder says, 'anonymity also results in equality ... The experience of society individualizes, sets people free from the moral constraints of the lifeworld' (1997:310). On either account, with Thai individualism or anonymous social space created by a family construct of society, the danger is that people pursue their own interests at the expense of others.

This analysis shows the complexity of leadership in the Thai setting and the juxtaposition of trustworthiness, notions of group, the pursuit of self-interest, and suspicion. The trustworthy people are valued because of their demonstrated ability to overcome self-interest and work for the good of the community. They are in this sense 'safe' to be entrusted with leadership. But notions of 'group' that are narrow limit the applicability of the trustworthy person. Within 'our' group the familial concept holds, and it is the trustworthy person who is sought out, but when people become 'other', when the sense of groupness changes boundaries (as in Ton Pho versus the Flats rather than local born owners versus migrant renters), then they become anonymous and it is possible to pursue group and personal interests on the basis of the privileges that come from having position. This kind of behaviour then fuels suspicion on the part of those who are in the out-group, which in turn sharpens the boundaries that define who they can and cannot trust. The combination of trust, individualism, and group is inherently filled with tensions that cyclically confirm the suspicions that people have about those in formal positional leadership.

Summary

In this chapter I began by tracing the experiences that led me to see a connection between the *Thuukjai* Leader Model (TLM) and the idea of the trustworthy (*chuathuu*) person. I then developed the content of the TLM and discussed the reasons for why trust was drawn upon rather than respect as the key term for describing leadership in the community. Next I examined evidence for another model that I have called the *Sakdi* Administrative Behaviour Leadership Heuristic (SABLH). This model causes people who become formal position holders to undergo an ontological change that gives them status and prestige, and makes them worthy of privileges that common untransformed people do not experience. It has a leader dimension that influences leader behaviours and a follower dimension that influences perspectives on leaders' motives and actions. I concluded the second section by looking at how the SABLH impacts actual leadership as observed in the community.

In the third section I introduced the notion of group (*phuak*) and examined how it affects the conduct of leadership in the context of the committee. I concluded the chapter by examining these factors in light of other analytical frames to help increase understanding of what is happening in the community as well as the way in which these models relate and how they are drawn upon for social action.

In these first two analysis chapters I have developed a series of models that provide a cultural understanding of leadership broadly conceived as the social influence processes operating for community task accomplishment. I moved from the culturally preferred implicit leadership theory in Chapter 4 to look at how real-life leadership is practised in the community of LWPW in Chapter 5. In the next chapter I turn my attention to the final question of my inquiry on how the community relates to the state. In Chapter 3 I argued that the dual faces of the state towards the urban poor form the operating environment in which slum residents seek to survive. In Chapter 6 I will examine another aspect of leadership that embraces both unconscious and conscious responses growing out of the values of the community as it relates to state power.

CHAPTER 6

Relations between the Community and the State

The models and their interrelationships that I have presented in the past two chapters allow for a more nuanced analysis of social influence processes. They incorporate both culturally preferred conceptions of leadership as well as actual practises and bring insight to the ways that people in LWPW draw upon the models and the linkages between them in social action. This analysis also advances our understanding of the practise of leadership in this particular Thai social setting by relating these ideas to concepts like hierarchy and patron-client relations in a more sophisticated framework that avoids a reification of these cultural concepts. Thus far the focus has been on what is taking place inside the community itself. However, the intensive study of a single locality 'should not be seen as presuming that peoples' lives are confined to the horizons of local territories….we need to accept that localities are loci of interaction of various processes … ' (Askew, 2002:5). Slum communities are not hermetically sealed off from the rest of Bangkok; they are intimately related to the economic, religious, and political life of the city. The dimension that I will focus on in this chapter is the relationship of the state, in the form of the Bangkok Metropolitan Administration (BMA), and the community.

Durrenburger observes that local culture has been the key focus of anthropology, and that anthropologists have tended to ignore the role of the state and seen it as lacking cultural properties (1996:2). He argues that in today's world 'state power is pervasive and that, to understand local events and outlooks, we must contextualize them in terms of the machinations of states' (1996:2). In Chapter 3 I argued that the context for slum life in Bangkok was the urban poor's experience of the two faces of the state: benevolence and indifference/hostility. In keeping with my broader conception of leadership I will examine here how the community and its representatives negotiate this relationship. This discussion will diverge radically from traditional leadership studies and their focus on the leader as a locus of power and intentional activity. Instead, in keeping with my interest in leadership as social influence diffused across a social unit, I will examine processes that are decentralized, ad hoc, and driven more by deep-seated implicit values rather than explicit vision, but are nonetheless concerned with the group and task. I begin by examining potential frameworks for looking at state-community relations, then proceed to developing the relation of the LWPW community with the state in four major points. In the first I look at the disjunction between ideal, official, and local views of how community leadership is to operate and explore reasons for the particular configuration that is observed. I conclude that under the broader hegemonic view of the traditional-legal authority of the state, community leaders exercise leadership in a variety of traditional modes ranging from modifying and reapplying the key Thai cultural value of *samakhii* (unity, accord, harmony), to passive resistance against elitist hegemonic thinking, to direct resistance in the case of eviction. In the next three sections I examine each one of these forms of leadership practise in order to understand the dynamics of each of these expressions, and conclude with a section that discusses community leadership in light of relations with the state.

Community-State Relations: Frameworks for Understanding

The question could be asked, 'Why is the community-state relationship so important?' I have made the argument in Chapters 3 and 5 that when the state administrative apparatus came to LWPW through the registration process in 1985 two things occurred. The first was the process of officialization that over time increased the legal dimension of the way legitimate leadership was conceived by people in the slum. The result is that today in order to be considered a legitimate leader one must be officially sanctioned by the state. Only those holding formal positions as members of the community committee are now seen as leaders. The second was that officialization and the practise of *sakdi* administrative behaviour (SAB) by formal position holders did not eliminate agency on the part of people in LWPW or the vibrant practise of traditional forms of leadership outside of state administrative control. On one hand there appears to be nearly complete consent to the structures the state imposed (the formal committee and LWPW as an administrative unit) and a mirroring of the values of the state in practising SAB-style leading. But on the other hand the community committee exercises independence and autonomy from the views of the state in practising leadership as a 'group' (*phuak*) and in taking on the role of protecting the community from eviction. The reproduction of the dominant group is incomplete. Thus the community-state interface sheds light on the processes of leadership in LWPW as we watch the committee, operating on behalf of the community, navigate its relationship with the two faces of the state.

Before delving into specific details, it is appropriate to look at frameworks for understanding the community-state relationship. Certainly states are interested in control, and as Durrenburger suggests, it is a control designed to 'insure continuation of their privileged access to disproportionate resources' (1996:6); at the same time they do not exist by force alone (1996:6). Durrenburger's observations raise the question as to how we can understand the acceptance of the legitimacy of the state by the people in the community, which falls under the larger topic of the politics of domination and subordination.[1] Girling observed that in a country like Thailand where there has been an enduring social consensus supportive of elitist rule, the Gramscian idea of hegemony is germane (Girling, 1984:388). Turton pointed out that the state and associated institutions in Thailand have a 'monopoly of power and legitimacy rarely found to such a degree' (1987:113). The mix of factors includes a continuity of institutions, no formal colonialism, no dynastic change, and political parties that are personalistic and unstable, combined with a 'relatively high degree of linguistic, religious, and territorial homogeneity, have contributed to a close identification of nation, state, (military) government, bureaucracy, monarchy and religion' (1987:113).[2]

The question becomes whether or not the process of officialization and SAB practises seen in LWPW and the committee point to an ideological domination on the part of the state and a false consciousness on the part of the residents. On the basis of evidence I have already presented in Chapter 5, and the material that I will present here, I suggest that the Gramscian hegemony concept cannot adequately account for the kind of active agency and the forms of resistance present in the slum.[3] Durrenburger reminds us that hegemony is never complete and that it is improper to assume that hegemonic views are automatically accepted in a process of mechanical acquiescence (1996:15). If this is the case, the question then becomes what kinds of frameworks can embrace the presence of hegemonic elitist views and incomplete dominance, resident agency and apparent passivity, and resistance and compliance that are all seen in LWPW at the same time?

---

[1] Scott points out that there have been two major streams of interpretation in trying to understand the conforming behaviour of the less powerful (1990:70-2). In America the community power literature separates into pluralist and antipluralist camps. Pluralists see the absence of protest as evidence of at least a degree of satisfaction, while antipluralists see the vulnerability of subordinate groups allowing elites to control the agenda and create obstacles to participation. In Europe the trend has been towards neo-Marxian analysis referencing the ideas of hegemony and false consciousness.

[2] Girling proposes three reasons for the hegemony of the Thai élite: the dynastic modernization by King Chulalongkorn in the late nineteenth-century, late social differentiation where large disparities in income and landholding were avoided, and the ethnic division of labour with the Chinese performing labour, trade, and finance (1984:388-89).

[3] For a detailed critique and discussion of the problems of using the Gramscian hegemony concept for understanding relations of the less powerful with dominant elites see Scott (1985:314-50; 1990:70-107). For further literature on the critique of hegemony see Scott (1985:317 footnote 26). He asserts that not only does hegemony and its related concepts of false consciousness, mystification, and ideological state apparatuses 'fail to make sense of class relations' in his research setting in a Malaysian village, but they 'also are just as likely to mislead us seriously in understanding class conflict in most situations' (1985:317).

One perspective that offers fruitful insights for community-state relations comes from work on the resistance of subordinate classes. I am drawing primarily here on the work of Scott (1985 and 1990) and supplementing from other sources. There are four ideas in particular that when brought together create a lens for viewing what is happening in LWPW and render an account that explains the apparently contradictory nature of my observations in the community. The first idea concerns public versus private or hidden versions of what is happening in a given set of circumstances (1990:3-5). Scott suggests that there exist public and hidden transcripts for both dominant and subordinate parties (1990:13-14).[4] The second has to do with everyday forms of resistance employed by subordinate classes as opposed to collective defiance, what Scott calls 'the ordinary weapons of relatively powerless groups: foot dragging, dissimulation, desertion, false compliance, pilfering, feigned ignorance, slander, arson, sabotage and so on' (Scott, 1985:xvi). The third draws upon the self-interest of rational choice theory where people work the system to maximize their advantages and minimize their disadvantages (see Hobsbawm, 1973). Finally, the idea of stereotyped, ritualistic behaviours, also conceived as relationship templates on the part of subordinates in power-laden contexts, is a tool to help understand both surface behavioural conformity and ideological resistance (Bilmes, 1996:3; Scott, 1990:3).[5]

---

[4] The public transcript is the self-portrait of dominant elites as they want to be seen; it is highly partisan and a partial narrative (Scott, 1990:18). Relations between dominant and subordinate are ordinarily encounters between the public transcripts of both parties (Scott, 1990:13). The hidden transcripts of subordinates represents their thoughts when out of the gaze of dominant power (Scott, 1990:18). Scott points out that the distinctions between public and hidden transcripts and the hegemonic nature of the public transcript makes for at least four kinds of political discourse among subordinate groups: confirming the flattering self-image of elites, the hidden transcript itself, a zone between the first two that takes place in public view but is intentionally designed to have double meaning, and finally the zone where the hidden transcript goes public in open defiance and challenge (1990:18-19).

[5] As a general rule Scott observes that the greater the disparity in power between dominant and subordinate, and the more arbitrarily that power is exercised, 'the more the public transcript of subordinates will take on a stereotyped, ritualistic cast. In other words, the more menacing the power, the thicker the mask' (1990:3). Bilmes has attempted to create a model of how villagers relate to government elites using the ideas of Durkheim and Levi-Strauss where religious concepts have a counterpart in the social-political world (1996:5). He proposes an authority model where people relate to government officials in a similar fashion to the way they relate to the village spirits, and a mechanical model based on principles of impersonal justice mirrored in the way villagers relate to monks. He defines a relationship template as that which 'specifies the orientation that actors have toward each other, general expectations regarding the other's behaviour' (1996:3). He notes that social behaviour is judged in terms of conformity to the template. Thus stereotypical or 'templated' behaviour cannot be assumed to represent what people think. Basham, drawing on both Scott (1985:321-322) and Turton (1976:292) produces empirical material from his work on merit and power that is

Turton observes that the state's monopoly on power and legitimacy has limited the development of the types of institutions that are called civil society, and that the 'legitimate or claimable "space" for alternative, more democratic or participatory ideas and organizations has been severely restricted' (1987:114). In the sections that follow I will utilize these four concepts as a composite lens to examine what is happening in that limited alternative space in the social and economic margins represented by LWPW.

The State and the Role of the Committee: Rhetoric and Reality

One of the lines of questioning that I developed in the latter part of my data collection was a focus on what both leaders and residents think that community leaders should do, including the roles and duties of the committee. By this time I had become aware of issues relating to the state and planned to draw together the interview data reflecting what people think community leaders should do, what the state says they should do according to published rules and regulations, and my own observational data about what they actually do.

Public Transcript in LWPW

Throughout the process of gathering data I was aware of the fact that there were times when I was as an outsider getting an 'official answer' that represented a more ideal view but which was only part of the story.[6] This relates directly to Scott's idea of the public and official transcript utilized by subordinates in public or power-laden settings. In the interview process direct answers to my questions often came in the form of official pronouncements. By contrast, indirect speech – things I overheard, things said to others in my presence, or the use of sarcasm – represented what goes on in real life. Many times in informal interviewing situations it felt as if I was toggling between front stage and back stage, getting 'official' answers to my 'official' anthropologist role questions, and then sitting on the backstage listening and catching some of the informal banter of the hidden transcript (and no doubt missing much of it embedded in idiomatic speech).

---

consonant with their conclusions that it is in the behavioural realm that subordinates are most constrained, while they are the most radical in their beliefs, which is the opposite of what the Gramscian hegemony concept asserts (Basham, 1989:134).

[6] Part of Bechstedt's thesis research (1987) dealt with key social values like moral obligation, friendship, conflict avoidance, smooth interaction, and psychological variables like anxiety and aggression where he was particularly interested in comparing how general attitudes corresponded to actual behaviour (2002:256-57 footnote 11). He notes that in the Thai context he took the verbal responses of informants as carrying the bearing of a 'socially desired and culturally idealized behaviour according to anticipated role expectations' (2002:256-57 footnote 11).

Let me illustrate some of the public answers that people gave me about the role of the committee. At the King's birthday celebration in 2004 I was talking with N. and asked him what were the most important roles and functions of the committee. He answered in a series of terms that became very familiar as they formed a frequently repeated answer to this question. N. framed the work of the committee in terms of sacrifice (*sia sala*), placing things in three distinct categories, all of which require sacrifice on the part of leaders. In the broadest sense committee members sacrifice for the collective benefit of the community (*sia sala pheua* low tone *suan ruam* mid tone); this is the core of their work. They also work for the development (*pattana*) of the community so that it improves (*dii khun*) and so that residents will have unity, harmony, and accord (*samakhii*) (I-72). People seem to express these types of ideas when talking about what the community should be like or what they hope it would be like, as opposed to the actual activities that leaders do. As such these expressions are important in understanding how people construct the idea of community and the role of leadership in creating it.

As an example, when I asked T., who is the new president of the committee, why he wanted to be a leader he framed his answers in a way very similar to N., that the community could be improved (*dii khun*) and that people would love each other (I-133). In a similar vein, B. told me that he would like to be on the committee but he does not have time. He said that the role of the community leadership is to help the people have happiness (*khwaam suk*). He said 'you must manage work and people so that they have *samakhii* (unity, harmony, accord). Right now it is everyone for themselves (*tua khrai tua man*). Arranging activities is important in building participation (*suan ruam* falling tone)' (I-117).

These ideal views bring insights into the nature of 'groupness' in Thai society as it enters into situations where people are faced with group interests rather than only personal interests. The ideas of sacrifice, working for the public good, harmony, consensus and accord, as embraced in the word *samakhii*, participation, and cooperation are key themes that define for people the 'good' group. I have already noted above the exhortation by the secretary to the incoming committee members to sacrifice and have *samakhii* and cooperation.

Official Views of the Committee

The official view of the role and work of the *chumchon* committee is found in a small booklet entitled *Manual for the Work of Community Committees* (CDO, n.d.).[7] It is 34 pages long and includes seven major articles dealing with the

---

[7] I was given one at the Community Development Office of the Pathum Wan District when I first started the study. In my first visit there I asked for any documentation that they had about LWPW and official documents relating to the community. Later on I

definitions of *chumchon* and development, development through participation of the residents, *chumchon* development in Bangkok, the role of the *chumchon* committee, solving problems, centres for pre-school age children, the capital fund project, and an introduction to the Community Development Division of the Bangkok Metropolitan Authority. The latter part of the manual reprints the relevant part of the rules of the BMA regarding *chumchon* committees.

What is said explicitly about the role and work of the *chumchon* committee members can be summarized under the following major points. First, they are the representatives of the people in the community in two particular ways: to work on development and to coordinate with both agencies and individuals who are involved, the implication here being those involved with development (from the introduction page). In a later article (p. 6), the reason for their representative nature is explained as being a result of the fact that although development is based on the participation of the people, it is too difficult to have every single person involved. Their role is defined as being the leadership core, to coordinate, mobilize the opinions of the residents, and handle any other business for the community. They are to catalyze cooperation in development and problem solving; the examples include calling meetings, surveying problems, and setting the direction of the community. They are to propose problems (it is not stated to whom they propose these problems, but the assumption is to the government) and search for solutions. They are representatives in the implementation of the work and cooperate with both state and private agencies in ways such as attending seminars and joining with activities. They are to follow the rules laid down by the BMA, do whatever the community delegates to them, and do other things that further cooperate in developing residents' quality of life and living conditions.

The booklet also gives a list of the duties for both informal and formal leaders, which is revealing in its emphasis on relational behaviours and character traits rather than task related behaviours. This list includes building a wide base of relationships with people in the community; helping others according to one's ability; leading others in working for the public good; contacting and coordinating with individuals and agencies to work in the community and accomplish things well; being wide hearted (*jai kwaang*), which is defined as listening to the opinions of others who disagree with them; not being selfish; and behaving in a way that is not dangerous or frightening others (p. 7).

Comparing and Contrasting Dominant and Subordinate Public Transcripts

Taking a step back and viewing written, interview, and observational materials as a whole it is apparent that there is not a straightforward reproduction of the

---

asked people on the committee if they had ever seen one or if the booklets were passed out to them when a new committee came into office and they said 'No!'.

official state view in either the Community Development Office or at the community leadership level. Instead there is evidence that community leaders, while deeply influenced by the state, engage in selective collaboration and hold to themselves an agenda that falls outside of the scope of the state's interest.

When I asked informants about the role and responsibilities of the committee, their responses showed that while there is significant overlap with the official view, there are also significant differences in emphasis as well as issues that are not on the government agenda at all. The question that this material raises is how this particular configuration came about and what it says about community views of leadership and their relation to the state. The official views represented by the handbook are variously consented to, modified, ignored, and rejected, and there are roles articulated that are completely out of the purview of what the state has in mind for a community committee. In the remainder of this section my focus will be on accounting for areas where community views and state views are closest. In the final three sections I will discuss in turn the areas of disjunction between community and state views ranging from modification, to rejection, and finally in the most explicit of all, to where the community confronts the state in the issue of eviction.

From one perspective it could be said that LWPW shows a high level of consent for the stated agenda, thus reflecting ideological domination by the state in the community. In 1985 a core group of traditional elder type leaders accepted the opportunity of officially registering with the District. Over time a process of officialization has occurred; people need a formal position to be seen as legitimate; and the committee runs through all the required administrative hoops, attends meetings, does paperwork, and fills out budget requests. There are numerous physical improvements that testify to the closeness of the relationship between the community and the state.

But this is not the whole picture. My argument is that the consent seen, rather than suggesting ideological domination, can be accounted for in different terms. This includes the maximizing of the self-interests of the community,[8] the corroboration between the community and state transcripts (Durrenberger, 1996:15), and an everyday resistance strategy that takes benefit where it can be

[8] An objection could be raised here that those who initiated the registration process were not acting in the community interest but only in their own by connecting themselves with the administrative system so as to be able to draw resources to themselves. I think that those who went to the District to register were representing those who were born in the slum, who had built their own houses there, and who wanted to stay. In this sense their idea of community was much narrower than that of the District who upon registration made LWPW an administrative unit that embraced both Bangkok born/province born and owner/renter distinctions. So when I am speaking about a 'community' level here I am using more of the mindset of those born in the slum and their perception of LWPW than that of the whole administrative unit as viewed by the District.

found and practises foot dragging, non-compliance, and evasion for those things deemed unpleasant or counter to the committee members' own agenda.

In Chapter 3 I summarized my examination of both official and unofficial state policy regarding urban slums by saying that for the poor, the state has both a benevolent face and an indifferent/hostile face. Although nobody in LWPW ever verbalized it precisely in this way, people are aware of both of these faces. They are calculating in maximizing their self-interests when it comes to the benevolent face and protective of their self-interests when facing indifference or hostility. The opportunity to register as a community comes from the benevolent face; it is billed and perceived as a means of connecting state resources to the community for the purposes of development. But the underlying context is that other dimensions of the state, state power, and the interests of elites are aligned against them and the threat of eviction is always there. The stance that I see among the people in the community is a clear eyed 'playing of the game' in order to connect with state resources, while attempting to minimize the hassle associated with interfacing with the administrative system and ignoring, negotiating, or resisting when facing the indifferent or hostile face.

I will illustrate here with one example of the dual 'compliance to maximize benefit' and 'ignoring when there is no benefit' stances. At the monthly meeting I attended the big issue was developing a proposal for the next year's budget (PO-86). The letter came the day of their meeting, and the proposal was supposed to be turned in only two days later. The request for information was quite extensive, requiring a fully written out purpose statement, goal statement, details on the budget, and so on. They indicated that getting requests for information like this at the last minute was quite normal. But rather than simply ignoring the issue because it was inconvenient and confusing, they took the time to work on it because it held the potential to benefit the broader community. Connecting with potential resources both in the state and private sector is an important committee role.

Much later, after not having gone into the community for some time, I was walking through the Rua Khiaw area and noticed changes where there had been an old water control (*tod nam*) canal off the Saen Saeb with a bridge over it. Where water had once been on both sides of the bridge it was now completely filled in with garbage with new housing built on top of it. I then stopped to talk with D. and L. I asked them about the new housing, and with ironic smiles they said that the residents had helped out by filling in the water area so that it was more safe now (I-293). I asked if the District knew about this, since part of the written policy was to work through community committees to control internal expansion in the slum. They told me that the District knew but could not do anything about it. Then smiling again, they said that the people had come in to fill an empty space in order to bring public benefit. One role of the committee, as community representatives, is to serve as the window for the District to see into the community, which includes public health and safety issues as well as the overall goal of improving the physical environment rather than letting it deteriorate. However, when the local agenda does not match the state agenda, or where there is no benefit to be gained from compliance, the window can be purposely opaque.[9]

What is the meaning of the shift in the perception of legitimacy of community leadership that was brought on by the process of officialization and SAB practises by committee members? I think that these are cases where the transcripts of the community and that of the state meet. The gradual rejection of *nakleng* leadership over time is not a result of ideological domination by the state, but rather a change enabled by the state through its provision for elections or state monitored appointment in the community. These new opportunities allowed people to choose leaders, as L.P. put it, 'that we like, not that we are afraid of' (I-257).[10] Ockey's argument that more democratic and participatory forms have roots in Thai village culture is germane here (2004b:3-7). Historically, as the state became involved at the village level through instituting elections and requiring those elected to increasingly be responsible to the state, the result was that people no longer wanted to stand for election and that those elected 'were often civil servants accustomed to dealing with the state, whereas villages continued to rely on the same *nakleng* and village elders for leadership in the village' (2004b:10). This created a gap between the 'ostensibly democratic institutions initiated by the state, which were concerned with the interests of the center' (2004b:10) and the more informal and participatory forms of leadership which continued to deal with the everyday concerns of the

---

[9] Moerman writing in 1969 based on his data from the Tai-Lue village of Ban Ping in Chieng Rai province proposed what he called a 'stop-gap' conceptualization of the village headman as a synaptic leader, who by virtue of the office is the connecting point between the village and the nation and as such experiences the conflicting expectations of both sides (1969:548-49). In an urban context, Akin, writing in 1975 about data collected in the late 1960s observed a similar synaptic role among the *nakleng* of Trok Tai in both connecting and protecting residents from state power (1975b:309-10). While much has changed in the past four decades the synaptic function of leadership between the state and local communities like LWPW can still be seen. My own emphasis here in this section has been less on the details of that connection than on the way leaders in LWPW calculate, manipulate, and pose in order to maximize community benefit and minimize inconvenience or problems that would arise for them in pursuing state interests.

[10] The election system means that the potential for change always exists even when it is not used. Appointment is not automatic; there are certain criteria that the District can use to reject a person or remove them if facts come to light after the appointment. If an individual or group is in office and not liked, the election system means that in two years other people can apply and force an election by having more applicants than slots available. Thus even when elections do not happen, the system itself frees people from having to tolerate committee members that they do not think are acting in the community's best interests.

people (2004b:10).[11] The new conditions created in organized communities with a formal structure to connect with the state changed the skill set needed to get things done with the state. Thus traditional leadership forms like respected elders and 'group' (*klum*) can work the bureaucracy, while the wide (*kwaang*) connections of the *nakleng* have over time become less valuable. At the same time *nakleng* pursuit of personal benefit rather than community good and the use of influence based in obligation characterized by fear has come to be seen in a negative light. The shift is now towards the trustworthy person (*chuathuu*) who proves through observable behaviour her concern for the community.[12] Thus in LWPW rather than creating a gap between those who represent the state interests in the community (the committee) and informal types of leadership, the coming of the state to the slum has created not a bifurcation but a new style of leader who negotiates between selective collaboration with the state and the pursuit of interests that are critical for the community.

The practise of s*akdi* administrative behaviour by community leaders is not a case of locals buying into a state position; rather it reflects the master hegemonic principle of hierarchy that pervades all Thai relationships and the matching of the hidden transcripts of anyone who is 'elite' in their social setting. The hidden transcript of hierarchy affirms the kinds of Thai administrative behaviours that I have pointed out from the literature and then illustrated in Chapter 5. These represent the other side of idealized superior-subordinate relations characterized by a kind and generous paternal figure looking out for the interests of the weaker party. The reality is the acceptance of privilege and use of power to benefit both personal and in-group position. Being 'elite' is not an absolute concept but a relative one. Holding a formal position legitimated by the state, even if it is in a slum, makes one 'more elite' than those who have no position, and this taps the master principle of hierarchy and the hidden transcript of how those in power are to be treated and to treat others.

---

[11] Ockey does point out that there was always a gap between local concerns and national politics, but 'what was new was the way this gap became tied to formal institutions of leadership in the village, which in turn led to a deeper division between formal and informal leadership' (2004b:185 note 16).

[12] The *Sakdi* Administrative Behaviour Leadership Heuristic (SABLH) that I developed in Chapter 5 causes those in follower roles to be suspicious of the motives of those in formal positions. However it has to be kept in mind that people in LWPW shift back and forth very easily between explanations of leadership emergence based on being trustworthy, and the suspicion that leaders are acting in their own interests. The two positions are not at all mutually exclusive; it simply depends upon the issue that is in focus.

The Dream of Unity and the Reality of Division

The particular configuration of the way in which the community views the role of the community committee as compared to how the state views it, raises the question as to why the particular elements of that configuration have been chosen. In the previous section I developed an account for instances where state and community views seem to corroborate each other. In the next three sections I will turn to examining points where community views and state views diverge or inhabit completely different universes.

In LWPW both residents and leaders indicated that the major roles of the community committee are physical development and its closely-tied idea of coordinating with the government to draw up the budget; to watch, protect, and care for the community; and to promote and maintain *samakhii* (unity, accord, harmony) (I-34, 72, 115, 117, 128, 133, 144, 146, 203). As I compared the official version of the roles and duties with the local conception I wondered why out of numerous options were these particular roles taken and others rejected? For instance, why does *samakhii* take on such importance rather than social and economic development or building participation among the people to mobilize local resources?

As I reflected on this issue it seemed to me that these choices represent important ideas about the nature of leadership in LWPW in its most holistic and comprehensive sense, as the pursuit of the public good. At the same time this configuration serves the dual purpose of allowing the community members to match the public transcript of the state and yet retain their own hidden transcript of resistance to both ideas and practises that they reject. It is a stance that allows them to relate to both faces of the state, the benevolent and the indifferent/hostile, maximizing benefit and minimizing danger or disadvantage.

In this section I will focus upon the concept of *samakhii* as a key cultural value that is appropriated in different ways by LWPW and the state. *Samakhii* is important to understanding leadership in LWPW in three ways. First, because it is a major cultural value connected to Thai conceptions of what it means to belong to a group. The second reason is that at least for some leaders in the community *samakhii* is used in a way that resembles what Scott calls a version of the hidden transcript which is 'always present in the public discourse of subordinate groups' (1990:19). It is appropriated by the community from the official Thai cultural transcript and thus there is in general a high level of consonance with the state view of *samakhii* in order to move towards development. Yet at the same time, for some, it carries a deeper meaning that transcends the bounds of state interest and provides a basis for challenging the power of the state. For in *samakhii* lies the hope of overcoming the diverse self-interests in the community to unite in resisting the power of elite interests that would drive residents from their homes. Finally, *samakhii* is a longed-for ideal and thus pulls leaders to transcend factionalism at the same time SAB values pull in the opposite direction. At the end of the day, both the state and community invoke *samakhii* for different ends, and in both cases it remains an unrealized ideal. The forces of division in LWPW at this point in its history turn out to be too powerful for *samakhii* to overcome.

Samakhii, defined in the dictionary as unity, consent, accord, and harmony, is linked with *ruammuu* (cooperation), *suan ruam* (falling tone, participation), and the idea of being a group (*khwaam ben klum*). A typical context for these concepts appeared in a 2005 wall calendar I happened to see, which was published by the Thai Military Bank and quoted His Majesty the King concerning the importance of *samakhii*:

> *Samakhii* is an important moral virtue which groups of people who are joined together (*muu chon phuu yuu ruam kan*) must of necessity care for and protect and continuously use. If each side joins together and works with good intentions, with *samakhii*, knowledge, and ability, and with creativity, the work will be fully completed, beautiful, and according to the intended purpose.

This statement brings together key themes related to *samakhii*, its relation to 'groupness', and the accomplishment of some kind of purpose relevant to the group.

In my interview work I came upon *samakhii* from two different places. When I was asking about the most important duties and roles of the committee *samakhii* was listed. A second area was in trying to learn about the festivals and celebrations (*ngaan*). During her term as community president D. saw her most important role as putting on the community festivals (I-146). L.P.'s view of *samakhii* represents the process of officialization; he saw nothing happening prior to registration because it was not official and formally sanctioned. I reproduce here a portion of a conversation we had about festivals and the relationship of these celebrations to the notion of *samakhii* because it illustrates his official Thai cultural transcript about the nature of *samakhii*:

> A.-What is the role of the festivals? Who started them?
>
> L.P.-There was nothing before the committee…
>
> A.-Why did people start doing festivals after the ruling of 1985? [This was the ruling that encouraged the establishment of community committees.]
>
> L.P.-It was very appropriate for us to do this. We are part of the society, we should do something.
>
> A.-Why did you wait till after the formation of the committee?
>
> L.P.-Because before we were not all one group (*mai dai ben klum diaow kan*). They were all little groups, there was very little cooperation between them. After the ruling people would approve of someone [to elect, and this helped us] become

a cohesive group (*klai ben klum ben kawn*). [Then] we were able to do every kind of activity.

A.-[At this point I was trying to get a clearer understanding of what happened post-registration, so I drew out a sequential diagram and explained it in this way.] Before 1985 you were *tua khrai tua man* (everyone for themselves), then the ruling came and you became a *chumchon*, now you are a *chumchon* and you do activities in order to _____. [I indicated that I wanted him to fill in the blank in this sentence.]

L.P.-In order to have *samakhii* (unity, accord, harmony, consensus) together.

There were certainly groups (*klum*) prior to registration which put on certain festivals (such as Ton Pho doing the Civil New Year's celebration), and there was *samakhii* happening in these groups. L.P., when asked directly, does not deny all of this, but he along with others who have been on the committee think about the community in an idealized fashion based on a legal sense of a certain physical space being officially defined as the *chumchon*. In this version of history once the state legitimates physical space and the leadership structure of an elected committee, then the whole administrative unit is formally constituted a single group. When you have the conditions of groupness, then *samakhii* naturally must follow.

How *samakhii* is connected to conceptions of group has a cyclical feedback dimension. In PO-18 a discussion I had with L.P. clearly illustrates this. At the Children's Day celebration in 2004 L.P. was pointing out that not as many people came as in the past.[13] I asked why this was and he said it was because of a lack of cooperation (*ruammuu*). I then asked what caused a lack of cooperation, and he said it was because of no *samakhii*. When asked to define *samakhii* people do so in terms that require cooperation: 'it is combining together (*ruam kan* mid tone) and helping one another; it is unity (she used the English word here); it is having one voice' (I-302); 'it is helping out one another and becoming more of a group (*jat ben klum khun*)' (I-257); and when there is *samakhii* there is joining together (*ruam* falling tone *kan*) (I-257). Both cooperation and participation are evidence that there is *samakhii* within the group, and at the same time it is the sense of unity and accord that creates the grounds for people forsaking their personal interests, cooperating with each other, and participating in group activities.

In this light we see the importance of *samakhii* in securing voluntary cooperation, which is critical to task accomplishment in the community. At the King's Birthday celebration in 2003 I was talking with N. who was on the committee about all of the work it took to put on such an event. He mentioned

---

[13] Criticizing events in terms of their low participation or the work of a committee in terms of never getting anything done was the normal posture for leaders past and present. I suspect this is a case of building one's self up by putting others down.

that the community had no budget so they had to do all of the work themselves, meaning the committee members and those who joined them to help out (I-72). The implication here was that if they had money they could have hired people to set up, but since they did not have money for the event, they had to rely on those who were willing to help them out. This underscores the importance of *samakhii* to create an environment where people are willing to help (*chuay*) and cooperate (*ruammuu*).

I asked L.P. how one goes about building *samakhii*. He said that when he was a leader he would go and visit people and ask about their problems. He would also call meetings to share information (PO-18). L.P. illustrated an instance of problem solving that concerned a person not joining the group (*ruam klum*):

> Take for instance someone who does not join the group. You need to go and talk with them and ask them why, find out what happened, why they did not join the group, is there some kind of a problem? This is the most important thing. We are not forcing them because we want every person to come and join in, to talk, to find out the important things that are going on [in the community] (I-128).

Getting people to join with the group, to cooperate, to participate, and thus to have *samakhii* is not something that happens automatically. It requires effort and communication on the part of people. Leaders need to show that they are working for the common good and not their own benefit. Again, a cyclical feedback relationship between these elements is seen. Evidence of *samakhii* is people joining in activities, cooperating, and participating, and at the same time it is the sense of *samakhii* that causes people to want to join together, cooperate, and participate. The sense of groupness is not defined simply legally or organizationally; it is created and maintained through the behaviours of leaders who communicate, are involved in people's lives, listen to them, show interest in their problems, and act in a way that shows that they are putting the group above their own personal interest.

As an outsider working with a Thai organization I have over the years felt that local ideas of what it means to be a group and my ideas as an American are different in several key ways. Withaya, in his attempt to explicate the difference between the English term 'group' and the Thai *phuak*, hits on at least one of the key points of difference (see p. 140). My own sense of 'group' allows for membership based on some kind of shared criteria whether external (being a licensed member of my organization) or internal (shared convictions). My being part of the group does not necessarily compel me to cooperate or participate in every activity of the larger group. By contrast, Withaya highlights the nature of the relationship between people in the Thai *phuak* and their sense of being a group collectivity. My own observations, based on working with people in LWPW and over nearly 20 years of working with a Thai organization, is that being a 'group' is intimately tied to relationship that is manifest through cooperation and participation. To not participate and cooperate is in essence not to be a part of the group, even if you have formal 'rule based' membership.

Up to this point I have been explicating the official Thai cultural transcript of what *samakhii* means, and in this sense people in the community and the views of the state are one and the same. As I noted with the concept of hierarchy, while it is a major cultural value and widely shared, it is not a manifestation of hegemony in the Gramscian sense. I see *samakhii* in a similar way. Within the community much of the discourse about *samakhii* would completely mirror the state idea of the importance of *samakhii* for task accomplishment, specifically development of the community. However, among those who have served as community leaders and who were born on this land or who see LWPW as their home, there is another stream, an alteration of the state's utilitarian use for task accomplishment that represents a hidden transcript.

It is interesting that D. saw her key role as putting on the festivals, which are a major tool for creating *samakhii*, while her explicit motive for serving in leadership was for the protection of the community from eviction. In a conversation with L.P. about the pressure of eviction he did not use the term *samakhii* but his explanations were couched conceptually in ideas of unity. He said that he wants the people in the community to join strength (*panuk gamlang*) so that they can go and have deliberations with the government (*taw rawng*). He said that he does not want them to break apart (*taek yaek*) because if they do they will not be able to stay there, but if they join together (*ruam kan*) they will be able to continue there (I-128). In one of my clarification interviews with him on *samakhii* he made the statement, 'when we have good *samakhii* we are able to resist everything (*taw taan thuk yang*)' (I-257). Tu. and I were talking about the community and the current reduction in size and future prospects for staying on the land (I-302). She shared that in her opinion if they did not get *samakhii*, they would be off the land in four or five years. For these people *samakhii* is not just something needed to get tasks done, but has become a concept that allows them to challenge the power of the state and elite interests. This represents a modification in a quiet way where state views are upheld, but deep down they cherish *samakhii* as a hidden transcript that gives them hope for battling against the forces of eviction.

Here the rival conceptions of *samakhii* clash; the residents' view goes beyond the interests of the state to their own interests. *Samakhii* takes on its ultimate importance in the eyes of community leaders and residents because it is their one hope of challenging the power of the state and elite interests that would evict them from their land. This is why *samakhii* takes on a more salient role for community leadership and people in LWPW than it does in the official literature where it is one point among many. One potential frame of reference for understanding these differing conceptions comes in the work of Benedict Anderson on nationalism. He defines a nation as an imagined political community, which is imagined as both limited and sovereign (1991:6). Anderson argues that 'all communities larger than primordial villages of face-to-face contact (and perhaps even these) are imagined' and that 'communities are to be distinguished, not by their falseness/genuineness, but by the style in which they are imagined' (1991:6).

If Anderson is right in his assertion that virtually all communities are 'imagined', then one possible way of looking at LWPW and its relation to the state on the issue of *samakhii* is to see two forms of 'imagining' being employed. It is important to remember that the 'state' is not a monolith, and residents are very aware of the two faces that are presented to the slum. The benevolent face imagines communities where *samakhii* is an important value in order to pursue development. However, the indifferent or hostile face does not see the urban poor at all, other than as an obstacle to overcome in pursuit of economic expansion. For locals born in the community who are aware of both these faces, they reject the elitist view and imagine a community that goes beyond just developing to survive in the face of elite business interests. *Samakhii* represents a traditional form of restraint that curbs the pursuit of self-interest and focuses energy on benefit for the larger group. Anderson notes, 'regardless of the actual conditions of inequality and exploitation that may prevail in each, the nation is always conceived as a deep, horizontal comradeship' (1991:7). Imagining a community characterized by *samakhii* emphasizes horizontal bonds and creates a truly public interest to attend to. Whereas *tua khrai tua man* (everyone for themselves) is a condition dominated by the pursuit of diverse personal interests, *samakhii* that produces *khwaam ben klum* (being a group) mirrors at the local community level the disinterestedness of the 'national interests' of nation states (1991:144). Anderson develops the line of thought that things that are unchosen (thus idioms of the natural or of family), 'have about them the halo of disinterestedness...[and] for most ordinary people of whatever class the whole point of the nation is that it is interestless. Just for that reason, it can ask for sacrifices' (1991:143-44). A community of true *samakhii* is 'interestless' in the sense that it is believed to pursue no benefit for any individual or in-group at the expense of others. A community with real *samakhii* can call for sacrifices to be made precisely because those sacrifices are for the broader public interest, in this case the very survival of the community.

While *samakhii* is a longed-for ideal and is seen by some as the key to resisting the state over the issue of eviction, there are many forces in LWPW that simultaneously fight against it. Nearly all of my conversations about *samakhii* contained a part where people were complaining about the lack of *samakhii* in the community. If L.P.'s efforts at one time built *samakhii*, they have not been able to be maintained. B.'s observation is that the community is now *tua khrai tua man* (everyone for themselves) (I-117), and as I have noted, L.P. sees in reduced attendance at community functions signs that there is a lack of *samakhii*. One interviewee who is from a rural village and has lived for a number of years in the community observed that in the provinces they are much better at *ruam klum* (joining together as a group) (I-31). The reality of the numerous ways of conceiving the *chumchon* and strained relations between those who are renters and those who grew up in the community points to the fact that *samakhii* is an unrealized ideal. One's experience of *samakhii* in the community today is based on place of origin. Those born in the community or who see the community as their home can speak of *samakhii* while those who are renters nearly uniformly do not feel like they are part of the community. The legal definition of the community through registration that makes LWPW a single administrative unit on paper cannot overcome the deeply rooted divisions of territory (as between Ton Phon and the Flats) and place of origin (as between those born in the slum and those who came from the provinces as renters). In a conversation with a Thai person about *samakhii* he suggested that there is a difference between forced (*bangkhab*) *samakhii* and real *samakhii*. He pointed out that real *samakhii* is hard to build, that you need to be very close to observe one another's behaviour, and there must be a sense of family. His point was that telling people to be a group and have *samakhii* is not going to produce real unity (I-275). You can say that you have it, but it is not the real version.

The problems associated with creating and maintaining *samakhii* highlight one of the great challenges of leading in LWPW. Unity is an ideal and many people see it as the key to resisting eviction. Yet at the same time there are pressures to pursue the interests and agendas of one's own group. There is also the deep sense of mistrust and suspicion of those from other places; those not close enough relationally to people so they can observe behaviour over time. The result is that leaders are unable to overcome these pressures and suspicions in order to engage in behaviours that will build trust and the sense of *samakhii* that will lead towards greater cooperation and participation.

The State and the Concept of Development

In the previous section I suggested that local interest in the idea of *samakhii* represents a Thai value used in imagining a kind of community. With *samakhii* there is a divergence from the official view and that of the community. With the concept of development there is a multilayered complexity where both the administrative arm of the state involved in community development and the residents in LWPW practise selectivity with regard to the official position as represented by the literature. The result of this is that on the surface it appears that there is continuity between the state practise and the community view. I will argue however, that this continuity is only apparent and not real.

When I first began to learn about development it was in the context of asking about the most important work of the committee. Development (*pattana*) is considered one of the key elements that community leaders are to be involved in. As I sought to understand the meaning and nature of development, a consensus emerged among the interviewees that development consists in making things better (*dii khun*), with the illustrations of this relating to physical improvements. As I probed more into this issue I noticed a disjunction between what official policy from the Community Development Office literature said about holistic development in the physical, social, economic, and health domains, and the actual practise at the District level where the emphasis was only on infrastructure improvement. I saw that the views of residents in LWPW and the actual practise by the local community development officials and the District and Bangkok Council representatives matched.

As I looked at this in more detail I began to realize that the similarity in conceptions of development held at the District level and in the community were actually reached from two completely different routes. Rather than being an example of hegemony, this similarity of view can be understood as a form of passive resistance on the part of the community. In this resistance they reject elitist views regarding the urban poor, and practise a selective collaboration aimed at maximizing benefits for the community while minimizing the difficulties and annoyances caused by the involvement of the state administrative arm in the slum. In this section I will first examine the understanding of development on the part of people in the community, then critique various ways of accounting for what is observed, and finally argue for the view that I have set out above.

In the early days of the data collection I heard the word *pattana* used in reference to improvements being made in the slum. At that time I had no sense of how development was understood either by the residents or the state agencies that were involved. It was at the point where I started inquiring about the role of the committee that I began to encounter development as the most salient element in residents' conception about what community leaders were to do. This led me to start asking questions about what constituted development and how it was practised. The most common phrasing for defining *pattana* (development) was making things *dii khun*, which literally means to get better (I-226). A representative example of this comes from M. who said 'a place or spot that is not good (*mai dii*) or is needed to be made good – this is development' (I-202).

In an extensive interview with D. about her two years as the president of the community, we talked about what her experience had been in coordinating with the government, and the kind of things that they worked on (I-203). This included making suggestions to the District to fix problems such as cutting a tree down that was blocking a path, asking the government for cement and rock to pour a concrete walkway, and asking for budget from the Bangkok Council and District Council representatives in projects such as building concrete walkways and getting children's playground equipment. She pointed out that the committee has the right to ask for help from the various agencies that are involved with the slum, but it does not mean that they are always going to get what they ask for. The physical orientation of the definition of development was confirmed as I asked people for examples. All they could give me were examples of tangible things: tables, chairs, the children's playground equipment, the health clinic building, the concrete covered central meeting area, concrete walkways, garbage areas, the bridge across the canal, the fire fighting equipment, brooms, and drainage pipes (I-226, I-128, I-202, I-203).

So what appeared to be happening was a perfect correspondence between the way that development was practised by the community development arm and politicians, and the understanding of the people in the community. The idea on both sides was to improve physical space, but do nothing to address the issues that create situations that cause people to live in such physical space. From my middle class perspective I imagined that the poor themselves would be extremely interested in finding ways to improve both their educational and economic situations. The seemingly passive acceptance of the status quo and the passivity engendered by waiting for the government to provide budget for projects, looked like the false consciousness of the Gramscian concept of hegemony. I wondered if the involvement of the state in providing things was not a means of pacification, buying off the cooperation of the poor in exchange for what amounts to band-aid solutions to the complex problems of poverty.

My line of thinking changed when at a later point I began to read official development literature and learn about policy as well as practise. Here I discovered the holistic emphasis that I have noted in Chapter 3, beginning in the mid-1970s. The *Manual for the Work of Community Committees* (CDO, n.d.:1) defines community development (*pattana*) as:

> changing the components of the community from its current conditions to meet the goals that have been set, namely to be intentional so that community change happens in order to change the conditions of the various components in the community from a condition of not being what people want to a condition of being what people desire according to the goals that the community has set.

Seeing this dual rejection of the official policy by both the community and the local administrative arm charged with development raised the question of how to explain this particular configuration. The continuity between the state's practise of development and the community's understanding was now problematized because the official ideology could have been taken up by the community and used as a tool in working with or against the government. There is a great deal of space even within the official rules concerning the rights and duties of the committee to be involved in creative problem solving. But as I have noted both in Chapter 5 and here, community leaders have not taken up these types of functions.

One possible interpretation of this configuration is to account for it in terms of hierarchy and a strong view of the importance of patron-client relations. This is the approach that Demaine takes in his analysis of Thai views of development. He points out that *kaan pattana* (development) is a relatively new term, emerging only after 1957 during the leadership of Field Marshal Sarit Thanarat. The word *burana*, meaning to reconstruct, rehabilitate, repair, or restore was related to a narrow view of development as public works. This was 'consistent with the historical traditions of Thai society in which the monarchy promoted and supervised public construction, while the public supplied the necessary labour' (Demaine, 1986:95). Post 1932 during the period of Field Marshal Plaek Phibunsongkram the term *wattana* had been used. Both *pattana* and *wattana* have dictionary definitions of 'progress, advancement' which is the kind of terminology 'used for human development by those colonial economic historians for whom development itself is seen mainly in the terms of resource exploitation' (Demaine, 1986:95).

The thrust of Demaine's argument is that despite the vocabulary change after 1932, there has not really been movement away from the traditional idea until very recently. Phibun's *wattana* focused mainly on the outward appearances of modernity, while Sarit drew upon the Sukhothai tradition of the *phokhun* paternal ruler, a model which 'assumed that the government was able to interpret and understand the wishes of the people, relying on a flow of information from the bureaucracy which in turn served the population by carrying out necessary (benevolent) policies' (Demaine, 1986:96). Writing in the mid-1980s, Demaine traces the changes in formal policy of the National Economic and Social Development Board, showing that even with new sensitivities towards social development among the planning elite, expressed in ideas such as participation and the belief that people can help themselves, the context is the continuation of the patrimonial framework.[14] Demaine admits that his analysis is a pessimistic one, saying that:

> for all the apparent change of emphasis contained in the Fifth Plan, the views of development adhered to by the main actors in the process, government officials on the one hand and the rural population on the other, have yet to undergo any basic transformation (1986:112).

He sees the old patrimonial framework as remaining intact despite the shifts in terminology represented by *burana*, *wattana*, and *pattana*. 'Development continues to be seen in terms of patrons (the government or its officials) offering services to clients (the population) in return for loyal support' (1986:112).

Demaine's analysis has much to commend it, and even though 20 years have passed from his writing, and over 30 from the time of Jacob's work, his description of what I am calling *sakdi* administrative values and behaviour can still be seen in the administrative apparatus of the government. However, I

[14] Demaine, following Jacobs' work, uses the term patrimonial to express the kinds of values and practises that are observable inside of the Thai administrative system. I have chosen to express this idea as Sakdi Administrative Behaviour for specific reasons that I have spelled out in Chapter 2 in the section on Thai bureaucracy.

want to introduce another possible explanation that allows for more agency on the part of the people in the community as they relate to the state. In Chapter 5 I have argued that while patron-client is an important part of Thai relations, that framework is unable to account for many of the types of relations that were observed in the community. A state-as-patron and community-as-client view falls into the trap of seeing everything as patron-client, and cannot be supported by what is observed in LWPW.

I suggest that what appears to be passivity is actually a more active form of resistance to certain elitist views that underlie the conceptualization and practise of development. Theoretically, I am drawing upon the work of Scott (1985; 1990) who sees many kinds of everyday resistance being utilized by the poor. These are not open forms of resistance and are often mistaken for passivity. However, thinking of passivity as a form of resistance helps foreground other dimensions and brings more explanatory power to the observed material.

The first set of observations has to do with observed passivity in some dimensions, with observed activity and initiative in other dimensions. Over my time in the community I observed a great deal of activity where people were pursuing lines of interest for their own benefit. According to conversations I had with people, the elaborate set of community festivals that mark the calendar year are completely the work and initiative of the community. These events require time, fund raising for money, and a lot of cooperative labour to put together. There is abundant evidence of business related activity such as refurbishing buildings, building new housing, cutting down branches, and adding new business opportunities like public washing machines and a video game parlour. There is involvement in putting on sporting events, a public exercise time, and participating in ceremonies at the Sra Pathum temple, and there has been collaboration with other communities in protest against eviction. My point here is that it is possible to use a lens of active agency on the part of many segments of the community. People are involved in advancing their own interests and also community interests, and in many dimensions they are not simply waiting for outsiders such as the state to help them out. When people talk about waiting for state budget to do things, it represents only one dimension of the situation.

So how then can the passivity in regards to initiating development, and the rejection of both a more holistic viewpoint and the role of the committee as community mobilizers for participatory development be understood? Here I will introduce two more sets of observations to bring a more nuanced perspective on the attitudes and practises of the community committee. The first is the comments I have already noted from people who expressed the idea that the coming of the state administrative arm increased hassle and annoyance for people in the community, particularly the leaders, while yielding relatively few benefits. Cooperation is often given grudgingly or not at all in some matters. I observed that when committee members did not want to go to a meeting or some required activity, they did not go. Rather than seeing straight passivity, an alternate view is to see selective collaboration designed to maximize benefits, with the passivity being a form of resistance.

But what precisely is being resisted? The second set of observations addresses this issue, which has to do with elitist attitudes about the poor that underlie state views of development. The benevolent patron attitude noted by Demaine is based on the explicit understanding that the poor are somehow deficient and therefore are in need of development. The *Manual for the Work of Community Committees* states that community development intends to develop people to have opinions and abilities in order to be able to help themselves, and then states that community development 'is a process of giving education to the people of any gender and age on a continuing basis for their whole life with the ultimate purpose of improving the quality of the people' (CDO, n.d.:2). In the history of the community development document, the unnamed writers critique the first two national plans where the emphasis was on building housing for the poor saying, 'it is not only finding places to live or building new places to live, people who live in the community should also receive development as well' (CDO, 1996:6). This became explicit in the fifth national plan with the philosophic turn to emphasizing the development of people rather than only improving physical and economic conditions (CDO, 1996:69). But why do people need to be developed? In a description of problems found by community development workers with local committees, the locals are said to lack strength and have limited potential in doing their work, which includes areas of knowledge, understanding responsibilities and roles, and the ability to mobilize people to cooperate in problem-solving and coordinating (CDO, 1996:226-7).

I have already noted Demaine's observation that it is the bureaucracy that identifies needs, not the locals. He adds:

> the truth is that there is a continued perception by many officials that they are "the developers" and the rural population "the developed," a segmentation which at its worst leads many local officials, however junior, to perceive themselves as infinitely superior to the "uneducated," and therefore "ignorant," villagers (1986:110).

Commenting on the change of thinking that moved into the third national development plan, Demaine points out that the problem of groups being cut out of development 'was conceived by the planners largely as the inability of large sections of society to take advantage of offered opportunities because of their lack of educational attainments' (1986:100), low level of understanding, and analytical skills (1986:110-11). In addition to being pessimistic about state efforts to change deeply rooted attitudes, he sees poor communities becoming more dependent on state help and thus less capable of solving their own problems and working in a participatory manner (1986:111-12).

An alternative reading to a straightforward patron-client interpretation is to see the observed configuration by community leaders as a form of resistance that rejects the elitist view of the poor as ignorant and needing to be developed. Presenting needs to the state and waiting for budget is not a difficult task, and it brings tangible benefits to the physical status of the community. In not picking up the more participatory emphases that form the rhetoric of state development, community leaders are actively rejecting the elitist notion that the poor have problems. As I will demonstrate in the next section, the state basically ignores the most pressing need of the urban poor, which is for housing security. For leadership in LWPW their first priority is to protect their status on the land; after that they would like to be left alone to pursue their own interests and goals with as little interference from the state as possible. The observed lack of mobilization and the participatory work of seeking local solutions is not because of ignorance or lack of ability but is based in slum people's counter-belief that they can manage on their own.[15] People's apparent buy-in to the state practise of development that I noted in the beginning of this section is more of a playing along with the state to get what benefits are possible, while minimizing disruption to the community and their personal lives, and with vigilance against the threat of eviction that is always in the background. In this sense it is a rejection of the social values upon which the social deprivation that the urban poor experience is based. They are not accorded prestige, power, or status, but in pursuing their own agenda against that of the official agenda of holistic development based in its negative view of the poor, in a small and indirect way they show their rejection and disdain for those who perpetuate such values.

The view that I have proposed here sees community residents in a much more active light than as passive recipients of state help. Passivity can be construed as a form of resistance to the elitist view of the deficiency of the poor. This kind of diffuse and decentralized resistance is not strategized out and intentionally implemented, but represents an unconscious value held by the powerless in the face of state power. In postulating resistance I am not asserting a single dimension explanation for the observed pattern.[16] Another major factor

---

[15] Two other issues are often raised by committee members for why they do not do more. They say that a lack of time and money limits them. While certainly there is an element of truth to these claims, the general impression that one gets from being in the community is that people do what they want to do with their time and seem to be able to access finances for all kinds of ventures where there is the hope of some profit.

[16] There are two other factors that I think play a part in the way that people approach development from the infrastructure side rather than the social, physical, and economic sides. I have often observed a general pessimism among people, who are afraid of putting out effort on something uncertain or that may fail. Another concerns the SAB model for leadership with its acceptance of privilege. The participatory model that dominates the development rhetoric cuts against SAB values. Demaine noticed this in the attitudes that keep lower level development officials from working with poor

is the rational choice calculation of benefits versus costs. I have observed repeatedly how people from outside the slum, whether in the public or private sector, approach the urban poor with the idea that they have the solution to urban poverty. The underlying message that comes across to slum dwellers is that people think they are poor because they are lazy and lack knowledge. The reality is that residents of places like LWPW are highly skilled at survival and are very street smart about what it will take to make an enterprise work in their setting. Thus when the state or elite outsiders offer answers for questions their community never asked, and propose solutions that the poor know will never work, they quite rationally weigh benefits versus costs, do what will maximize their gains, and simply ignore the rest.

In my analysis here I have tried to show community leaders as active agents rather than passive clients. They are constantly manoeuvring in their relations with the state to maximize their benefits, and practise a form of passive resistance through rejecting the elitist view that they are ignorant and in need of being developed socially. In the next section I will show how this active agency takes its strongest and most explicit expression in the struggle against eviction.

The State and Eviction

Thus far I have developed two themes that are part of the hidden transcript in which the urban poor of LWPW have created alternatives to elitist views under the broader umbrella of the traditional-legal legitimacy accorded the state and its administrative staff. The concepts of unity and development illustrate the use of the hidden transcript on the part of LWPW in an implicit fashion. I now turn to a conscious and active form of resistance, where community members use direct means to confront the powers of the state and business interests regarding eviction from their homes. The perception that community leaders are to protect the community from eviction is an area where there is no analogue in the official descriptions of duties. In the remainder of this section I will examine how LWPW has responded to the problem of eviction, and then suggest a framework for placing the community among other forms of resistance and the development of civil society.

When I first began data collection the subject of eviction came up early, but it was not a part of my original focal questions at that time so I did not follow up on it. It was as I started working on the role of the committee and studying state policy regarding slums that I realized that residents' interest in protecting their homes was not shared by the state. As I noted in Chapter 3, the shadow of eviction stands over the community and constantly weighs on residents' thinking and planning. In L.P.'s opinion the land has been red-lined (I-128),

---

communities in a participatory fashion, and this model is taken up by community leaders who also make decisions on what residents need without consultation.

and this has had a limiting effect on their ability to develop. He indicated that the District did not want to help them with anything because of this:

> If this place had not been red-lined we could have gone a lot farther. I could have gone much further by now. I have talked with all the big people and major players, especially the head officer of the District and the Minister of Parliament. We have talked and if this [place] was clear (*brong sai*) they would have let us continue renting it. But now that is impossible because over there (*thaang noon*) they have not given us permission. You see the Flats, they are not even collecting rent anymore (I-128).

Both L.P. and D. connect the taking of the land to money. Here is a segment of a discussion that I had with D. on eviction problems:

> A.-Here they are going to evict everyone, isn't that right? I mean completely.
>
> D.-There won't be anything left, they are going to run us off so that it is all open.
>
> A.-So how is the *chumchon* going to fight against this…the monks at the temple can't help can they?
>
> D.-No way.
>
> A.-Can the Minister of Parliament help?
>
> D.-There is no way, they are not part of this at all.
>
> A.-So who is part of this? Who has the right to come in here and do this?
>
> D.-The government of course! They just take the land that they want to take. Those rich bastards, you know what I mean? Because if they take the land, this group, it will be nothing but money for them.
>
> A.-You're right, look over here where they are building [a new building was being built behind the current World Trade Plaza].
>
> D.-No matter what they build, it will be all money because it is right in the heart of the city. Anybody would want this. But here, the King built this for us [speaking of the flats that were built by the King after the 1973 fire], these three buildings. He sent his secretary to look at the situation, and he ordered that they be built, back when the fire happened (I-203).

D. blames things on the 'government' (*raatchakaan*) and the wealthy. The government in this case is the Expressway Authority, as the context of our conversation was about the freeway exit that threatens the community. The wealthy are those who run the large businesses in the area who have a vested interest in getting the freeway to bring cars right down to their shopping malls.

The issue of eviction reveals something about the relationship of the state and the powerful with those who live at the margins, as well as the complexity of compartmentalization within the state itself where one part can assert itself while other segments have no power to intervene at all. The overall result is a sense of resignation in the people in LWPW that someday they will be driven off the land even when others are not in favour. For people like D. and her group, helping to preserve the community (*raksa baan rao*) was a major reason for becoming a part of the committee. She felt that bad leadership could harm the community (I-146, I-153). Eviction also illustrates dynamics internal to LWPW. I will begin with the protest in connection with Bankhrua against the Expressway Authority[17] because it is the most overt form of resistance displayed by LWPW, and then look at other instances both past and present.

The reason for eviction was due to the planned construction of an exit ramp off a new spur of freeway that would bring cars right down onto Ratchadamri Road in the Bratuu Nam area. The land was being expropriated by the Expressway and Rapid Transit Authority (ETA) (Ockey, 2004b:135) and the exit ramp involved five different communities. Ockey's analysis, focusing on the different forms of resistance manifested in different slums over time, shows that Bankhrua developed a special working committee to deal with the eviction threat; organized a 24-hour patrol to watch for fires; sought help outside the community with academicians, Muslim politicians, and NGOs; pursued technical information to use in the debate; utilized the media and petitions; enlisted the support of politicians; and used demonstrations and protests (Ockey, 2004b:136-140).

The fate of LWPW was tied with that of Bankhrua in that if they lost the battle against eviction, the exit ramp would go through and since they are the last community in line before Ratchadamri Road they would also be eliminated. However, the response inside of LWPW contrasted sharply with the activity and level of organization in Bankhrua. From what I gathered in my discussions with L.P. and D. their resistance took two major forms: it was connected by relationships one of their committee members had with Bankhrua leaders, and it was based in participating in demonstrations when they were called upon to do so. L., who serves as the committee secretary, had some kind of relationship with people in Bankhrua, and it was through her that Bankhrua would contact people when they needed more participants in protests. D. explained it like this:

> Generally, we went to Bankhrua a lot. It was like this – whenever Bankhrua had something, they would coordinate with L. because she knows everyone in the community, because she has been doing this for a long time. They would coordinate with L. and then she would come back and tell us everything (I-203).

[17] See Ockey's chapter on slum leadership and eviction (2004b) and Askew (2002:295-99) for details.

From what I could gather the committee did not mobilize large numbers of people to join the protests. The threat did not galvanize LWPW in the same way that it did Bankhrua, which was the starting point for the eviction and the focal point of the action of the government against them. L. and L.P. went and probably some others accompanied, but it was more of a representative nature. To this point the protests of Bankhrua and the other four communities have been successful in the sense that the exit ramp has not been built. However, for both D. and L.P. it is not a dead issue, but rather one that is temporarily on hold; it is not a situation that is completely safe for them (I-257, I-203), and they feel a continuing sense of need to protect the community.

Photograph 7 Eviction area in Rua Khiaw

It is interesting that unity (*samakhii*) is seen as a key element in resisting eviction because it is in previous evictions that the lack of unity and the forces of division are revealed. Eviction is the generic ever-present threat, but the response to specific instances of eviction varies. The eviction of the land behind the temple to move in the funerary structure did not elicit any kind of protest or resistance. This was an instance bringing together both religion and the monarchy, and the CPB prepared land in advance for people at two locations. People were willing to fight the state over the matter of the freeway exit which is seen as being motivated by money, but they were not willing to protest being moved from their homes when land was needed for religious purposes and connected with the monarchy.

The division between owners who have house registration numbers and the majority of Rua Khiaw who do not is seen in the ease with which the cement company was able to move into the Rua Khiaw area. The community committee says they can do nothing and residents agree with this assessment. This situation however highlights the place of origin divisions by revealing the limited nature of the conception of community. The core of Ton Pho and the Flats are fought for, but Rua Khiaw has no advocates at all in terms of the committee. Even people with house registration numbers on the periphery lie outside the scope of the concern of the committee. The people who are closest to the temple (*naa wat*) had their own representatives go to the District and work out a compromise on the building of a new school. From the perspective of the person I spoke with, the community committee was not involved because they were not interested in helping them (I-341).

Community-State Relations and the Nature of Leadership in LWPW

Watching LWPW relate to the two faces of the state opens windows on the nature of leadership processes in the community. In this section I will summarize some key insights that grow out of my analysis in this chapter.

The Ambiguity of 'Community' and 'Leadership'

The review of evictions and the varying responses of the committee shows the complexity of bringing the words 'community' and 'leadership' together. If community involves social cohesion, being a collectivity, and social interaction; and leadership as influence has its locus in formal positions; then the idea of 'community leadership' is fictional. The government's formalization of LWPW as an administrative unit and installation of a committee system to relate to its administrative arm is a veneer over deep fractures along place of origin and renting/owning. The formal committee does not speak for, and is not even interested in, the entire administrative unit. Its members' inability to mobilize very many people at what was their most critical moment in terms of the possibility of eviction reveals their relative lack of influence.

Leading as Caretaking

By pointing out the contested nature of the ideas of leadership and community in LWPW I do not mean to imply that nothing ever gets done or that formal position holders do not play a part in facilitating task accomplishment. The process of officialization means that leadership processes are now associated as happening primarily through formal position holders. As the representatives of the community to the community development administrative arm of the state the committee facilitates infrastructural development, watches over the administrative unit to insure its orderly functioning, and maintains its symbolic life through the production of festivals and celebrations. At the same time when the formal system fails people, within the context of their group, ad hoc traditional leaders will arise to represent the group, as was the case with the *naa wat* people who fended off a potential eviction.

I see the committee members acting in the role of caretakers for LWPW. If the committee lacks the ability to influence in the sense of rallying the voluntary cooperation of large segments of LWPW, they wield an indirect and less powerful form of influence through their caretaking. The influence of caretaking is limited, but is nonetheless influential because it flows from values, and encompasses both what is done and what is not done. The committee as caretaker does the work that nobody else wants to do, the myriad of small things that keep the system operating such as filling out forms to obtain the development budget, making sure the fire equipment is in working order, organizing cleaning days in preparation for celebrations, writing reports, mediating conflicts, representing the community to the state, and even resisting the state in the issue of eviction. Caretaking flows out of values, and the way that things are done and not done, and who it is done with and to, are as important as the actions themselves. This is the locus of influence in caretaking, the ethos that sets the atmosphere for the community, because choices are not determined. The work of the committee in LWPW shows that values constrain the kinds of choices made. Whether it is choosing the SAB-style of leadership, notions of group that carve up the community, or views about participation and problem-solving, the practise or non-practise of these things is a decision that influences how life is lived in LWPW. The influence of caretaking is implicit and not explicit. That is why I see the committee's rejection of holistic development as a form of unconscious, value-driven leading; it is a choice of direction for LWPW as caretakers that influences the quality of life in the community.

Caretaking and Civil Society in LWPW

This micro-study of LWPW has shown that the community defies description in terms of common representations of slums as assertive bargainers with the state, collectivities of the poor advocating for their rights, unconnected individual opportunists, or a tightly bonded face-to-face society (Askew, 2002:140). While LWPW has much in common with slum communities in general throughout Bangkok, its configurations in terms of leadership processes have developed out of its particular history and material circumstances. LWPW illustrates the difficulty in taking a single conceptual framework and using it as a rubric to capture all of what is happening in social life in that setting. Some have argued that the experience of resisting eviction has led to a transformation in slum communities so that there is a more participatory environment and an increase in democratic values. I will argue here that the caretaking form of leading carried on by the committee members shows that their experiences to this point have not led them to a more democratic environment.

In Ockey's study on leadership and eviction in slum communities he argues that over time there have been changes in leadership patterns that have emerged with changes in national politics (2004b:124-150). In the period of authoritarian rule in the 1960s it was male *nakleng* with their personal contacts who led the struggle against eviction. Over the last two decades, as the structure of leadership has become more complex and patron-client ties have eroded, there are more younger and female leaders, and new tactics being developed (2004b:144-147). Ockey points out that the democratic movement has affected the attitudes of slum dwellers, promoting the idea of the equality of individuals and the ability of people to be heard not through their patrons but as citizens (2004b:148). In his eviction examples from more recent years, and in the work of the Assembly of the Poor he sees democratic structures leading to democratic values (2004b:150). No matter what the results are, 'those who witness struggles, learn a great deal about the way democracy works, and the way it should work. Especially among the poor, democracy, rather than development, leads to democratic knowledge and participation' (2004b:150). Ockey sees the spread of these new attitudes among the poor as a positive sign for the development of a more democratic society (2004b:149).

Missingham, who studied the Assembly of the Poor, reaches a similar conclusion (2003:21:215). He argues that it is precisely in the practises of meeting, networking, and protesting that people gain new consciousness and ways of being in the world (2003:21). Missingham found local grievances and material problems as the motivating principle for mobilization and participation and the starting point for developing political consciousness (2003:218-219). It is local problems that 'provide the concrete experiences from which to develop a political consciousness of the causes of poverty and inequality, and challenge the hegemony of development as an ideology' (2003:219). He argues that:

> Participation in campaigns, rallies, and protests provide experiences that dialectically transform identity, solidarity, and political consciousness. Participants literally learn through experience that "Solidarity is strength" and see their own political agency in action (2003:219).

Missingham shows how NGOs have been one mechanism to bring people together at the local level and beyond into regional networks and national level networks where connections between local problems and national level problems can be made (2003:118-20).

Certainly one can see in the community many of the new directions that Ockey documents in other slums happening in LWPW: the decline of the influence of *nakleng*, the expanded participation of women, and the participation in protest over eviction through connection with broader networks as evidenced in the five communities that joined with Bankhrua. If what Ockey describes is a trend, the move towards more democratic and participatory structures that lead to valuing those ideas can be seen as key indicators or markers that define the leading edge of the trend. However, societal change does not move through all social segments or even within a social segment at the same pace. A community like LWPW lies on the periphery rather than the leading edge of democratic and participatory trends. LWPW's participation with Bankhrua on the issue of eviction was both literally and metaphorically peripheral. They were at the end point of where the exit ramp would come down to the road; Bankhrua was at the beginning of the ramp. Bankhrua was the centre of focus for the protests and was assisted by outside activists and academics; LWPW only sent people to join in without it being a community wide mobilization. LWPW's experience of protest was only a foray into the world of explicit resistance. The exposure was not long or deep enough to transform values and practises and thus never challenged the *sakdi* administrative values and behaviours that actually inhibit participation in LWPW.

Missingham notes that the concept of 'civil society' has become a tool in the analysis of social domains and the impacts of social movements; although it is an ambiguous and contested term (2003:7). On the basis of his research he shows that two major conceptions of civil society have been drawn upon by academics and NGO activists (2003:10, 215): 'political space'[18] and the Gramscian view that it is 'a terrain of struggle over hegemony' (2003:9).[19]

Is LWPW's relations with the state, such as the emphasis on *samakhii*, the perspective on development, and the practise of protest over eviction, all in the context of s*akdi* administrative behaviour style, evidence of the growth of civil society under either of these conceptions? I think that both the 'political space' view and the Gramscian perspective on civil society cannot account for the observed combination of the officialization framework, practise of SAB

[18] The spatial metaphor of 'political space' sees people forming independent and autonomous associations outside of the domain of the state so that they can mediate with and contest state power (Missingham, 2003:7). In this view the social networks of the Assembly of the Poor represent 'relatively new and powerful forms of organization and activism that are changing the nature of rural politics' (Missingham, 2003:215).

[19] In the Gramscian perspective civil society as 'a terrain of struggle over hegemony' is not 'a privileged domain of freedom and democratization' but is the social domain where 'ideological and cultural processes operate to organize social life and create consent to the dominant elite and existing social order' and encompasses 'the whole range of nonstate institutions and organizations that structure social life and may either reproduce or challenge hegemony' (Missingham, 2003:200). In the Assembly of the Poor, Missingham sees new forms of struggle emerging around oppositional consciousness, collective identity, and the deployment of culture (2003:215). The educated leadership of the movement thus sees civil society in Thailand 'in terms of an ongoing cultural and ideological struggle over the political consciousness of the poor' (2003:10).

leadership, traditional leadership relating to the 'group', and the forms of resistance seen inside the community. I think a case can be made for seeing a community like LWPW and others in similar material and social conditions as representing a third alternative to 'political space' and Gramscian views of civil society. This alternative rests on the periphery of burgeoning civil society as observed by both Ockey and Missingham. It is characterized by officialization and *sakdi* administrative values and practises, while at the same time evincing forms of resistance that are decentralized and represent the hidden transcript of the marginalized. Overt forms of resistance are driven by local issues but result in mere forays into the realm of civil society without actually embracing the values that bring a greater level of transformation in the direction of democracy and participation.

Seeing a third alternative in the configuration of LWPW as it relates to, negotiates with, manipulates, and resists state power points out the need for caution in basing analysis upon a single conceptual framework like 'civil society' or patron-client relations. A micro-level analysis like this study reveals both *more* agency and space for alternatives than patron-client can accommodate and *less* transformation than studies focusing on the growth of civil society would indicate. The committee members as caretakers do not so much challenge the existing order as ignore it and put up with it. Caretaking values are conservative; preservation is the order of the day rather than the change and struggle inherent in ideas of civil society. *Sakdi* administrative values and behaviour maintain hierarchy, but caretakers have something to take care of, and when preservation means they have to resist the state, they will do so. This resistance however is more likely to be conducted through traditional means rather than the new activist forms that are part of notions of civil society.

Perhaps as a third alternative to the two views of civil society, LWPW reveals something about Thai social relations under the conditions of an absence of crisis. The evictions I have documented have been piecemeal, working the margins, and done over time. Except in the initial rumours of 1973 and the issue of the freeway ramp, there has never been a challenge to the core zones of the Bangkok born residents in Ton Pho and the Flats. There has never been a crisis of the proportion that hit Bankhrua where violence and arson were part of the stakes. No NGOs entered the community to create awareness or organize the people around local concerns. Both before and after registration the traditional and now official forms of community leadership were involved in caretaking, not mobilizing around a vision. In such conditions, LWPW illustrates how conceptions of 'group' take on a fracturing power that resists other forces that attempt to unify.

In leading, 'group' facilitates task accomplishment; you rely on your group for cooperation, you trust your group, and it is the source of ready labour in time of need. Work can be diffused through the group, lightening the load of individuals. At the same time however the narrow notions of 'group' divide; the interests of different groups are pitted against each other. The differences between groups reveal the presence of another dominant/hidden transcript pair. Those who have the power and dominate the formal committee structure are the ones who get to define the parameters of the community, the result being that people can live physically in the *chumchon* and yet not feel that they are a part of it.

Conceptions of 'group' are deeply rooted; even when the state formally recognizes a certain geographic configuration as a community and sanctions a community to represent that administrative unit, it is nothing more than a veneer over the fault lines of groupness. At the end of the day the notion of group is more powerful than the concept of unity (*samakhii*). The dominant group defines when and where *samakhii* should happen; it becomes formalized and scripted out for use with festivals and community celebrations. In reality in-group concerns and s*akdi* administrative behaviour ensures that true *samakhii* cannot be built.

Summary

In this chapter I have moved the level of analysis out from leadership on the ground within the community itself, to focus on the relationship of the community to the state. At the same time I have used the state-community relationship to shine further light on the conduct of leadership within the community. I developed this material in four major sections and used a combination of perspectives primarily based on Scott's theory of public and hidden transcripts as a frame for understanding how the community moves in resistance to state and elitist power. I began by examining areas of apparent overlap in state and community conceptions about leadership in the community and created an account based in the idea of the corroboration of the public transcript by the hidden transcript of the community by the hegemonic principle of hierarchy in Thai society. I then looked at how the concept of *samakhii* (unity, accord, consensus) is drawn upon in different ways by both the state and the community.

Next I examined state and community conceptions of development, and suggested that the continuity in views between the two is not evidence of hegemony, but rather a form of resistance in which urban poor reject the elitist view that they need to be developed socially. I then moved to a more open form of resistance in the struggle against eviction. In the final section I discussed issues relating to community leadership that are highlighted by relations with the state. This includes the problematic nature of the ideas of 'community' and 'leadership', the suggestion that the community committee functions in a caretaker role, and a consideration of whether or not LWPW has developed space for civil society and thus become more participatory and democratic in its leadership practises. I suggested a third alternative to views of growing civil society in Thailand, one that is transitional and on the periphery rather than the leading edge of democratic change. Finally, I looked at how the concept of 'group' operates in this alternative form in both positive ways that help the community and as a force of division that separates and hinders the development of participatory practises. Micro-studies like this one show the complexity of relationships operating in a locality and suggest caution in utilizing single concept frameworks like patron-client and civil society that totalize and do not allow for the kind of practise of agency within the context of the dominant social order seen in the community.

CHAPTER 7

Application for Leadership Practise and Training

My interest in understanding Thai leadership grew out of my experiences working in a Thai organization. As Geertz points out, we quickly learn that people do things differently around the world (1995:45); as I watched and participated in various events, crises, and meetings, I was very aware of how different my own approach would have been to what I was seeing among my Thai co-workers. This created in me a desire to try and understand what distinguishes 'Thai' leadership from that of other sociocultural settings. My investigations in the literature revealed the need for exploratory, mid–range theory generation work rooted in the sociocultural and linguistic terrain of local actors. In addition to this I chose as a target population the urban poor because most leadership research in Thailand has been done with people of higher socioeconomic status and education levels. These convictions led me to design a study to develop a cultural account of leading in a Thai social setting in the anthropological tradition, conducting an investigation in the small-scale environment of a single urban slum. Committed to an exploratory approach, I followed various trails and lines of thought that came to me in the process of the data collection, and at the end of the day I raised more questions than answers. Predictably, I found that my original conceptions were too narrow to embrace the findings and I struggled with how to make sense of what my informants were telling me and what I was observing in the community. Chapters 4 through 6 trace this path that led me past my first plans to find a single model of "Thai" leadership in the slum into areas that I had not considered before beginning the inquiry.

In this chapter I want to continue in the anthropological tradition and use the particulars gained from my work in Lang Wat Pathum Wanaram (LWPW) to say something about the general (Tambiah, 1970:1), working out theoretical ideas 'with reference to insight that can be gained only through intensive fieldwork' (Keyes, 1978:2). Although this study ended up going beyond leading and social influence processes, in keeping with my interests in a cultural account of Thai leadership I am going to examine here insights from the fieldwork that relate to leadership in the Thai setting and leadership research in general.

The material falls into three major sections. I begin by reviewing the results of my inquiry as this serves as the base for my remarks in the second section dealing with applications and implications for leadership practise and training that grow out of this study. In that section I seek to serve three distinct audiences throughout the four headings, dealing with a totalization approach to leadership, the idea of creating leadership maps, the explicit and implicit, and the role of trust and group in Thai leadership. The audiences are Thai leaders working in the Thai social context, leaders in other contexts, and those who work in the arena of training leaders. The final section focuses specifically on the issues of leadership training and suggests methodologies that are informed by the anthropological approach I used.

Solving the Puzzle: Answers to the Focal Questions

The first two keys questions dealt with community perception of the qualities and performances of leaders, and the meanings, components, and interrelationships of the terms that represent those perceptions. The first finding developed to answer those questions was the *Thuukjai* Leader Model (TLM) which represents an implicit leadership theory of culturally preferred leadership in the community. The TLM serves as a representation of the prototypical leader and works in two ways. In dyadic relations the behaviour of the TLM builds relations characterized by a positive and non-exploitative sense of reciprocity and obligation. It represents a form of socialized personal power that leaders are able to draw upon to gain compliance and cooperation in voluntary settings or without resorting to positional power in settings of formal authority. While no single person embodies the TLM, there are people who operationalize the traits and associated behaviour enough so that others see them as being desirable to work with, effective, and people capable of influencing others.

The focus of the third question was on how these perceptions and concepts are drawn upon and enacted in social interactions between leaders and followers. In answering this I developed a set of three interrelated models and concepts. In the second major finding I connected how everyday leadership in the community draws upon the TLM and, at the same time, showed how the TLM operates outside the bounds of dyadic relations to serve as a prototype of interpersonal influence. In the community the discourse used to describe those considered capable of wielding influence to lead is found in the idea of being trustworthy (*chuathuu*). Becoming a trustworthy person is based in a constellation of behaviours closely tied to giving in both tangible and intangible forms and which are found in the interpersonal relations dimension of the TLM. At the same time trust is built through observable behaviours for the public benefit that are connected to the task dimension of the TLM as well. While the TLM serves as a prototype, becoming a trustworthy person is seen as something attainable by people in the community.

A third finding grows out of the disjunction between the attribution of being trustworthy and the suspicion that is endemic to all leader-follower relations in the community. This led me to formulate a third model which acts as a heuristic for formal position holders (like the community committee) and those observing and relating to formal position holders. I call it the *Sakdi* Administrative Behaviour Leadership Heuristic (SABLH) because it functions to help people understand what to do (if holding a formal position) or to interpret what is being done (if observing someone in a formal position). The *sakdi* administrative behaviour (SAB) heuristic causes people to see formal position holding as affecting an ontological change in a person. For those in formal positions the SABLH justifies the acceptance of privilege and the practise of seeking personal and in-group benefit. For those observing people in formal positions, SAB is not only accepted as normal, it is assumed even when there is no or only slight evidence of such behaviour. Thus suspicion that personal and in-group benefit is being pursued provides the lens through which people view leaders in the community.

The model of the trustworthy person forms the basis for leadership emergence, while SABLH shapes the perspective of nonleaders about the motives and actions of leaders. People in LWPW do not see these two perspectives as mutually exclusive. An inquiry as to why a person is a community committee member, or the president of the committee, or why a person would be elected is likely to be answered in terms of the trustworthy leader model. However, at the same time it is also likely that the same person will be under suspicion for acting for his own benefit. It is helpful to think of the TLM, trustworthy person, and SAB style leader each with its own continuum and with an interaction between the two. Stronger TLM/trust behaviour weakens SAB-style leadership and the element of suspicion. Conversely, the stronger SAB leadership is, the weaker the attribution of the TLM and trustworthiness will be, and this will lead to a higher element of suspicion.

A fourth key finding concerns the distribution of leadership through a group consisting primarily of horizontal relations. This is contrary to views that emphasize vertical relations and specifically assert that groups are created around and bound by patron-client relations. In LWPW there is evidence that people bind together on the basis of friendship and a common interest in the protection and development of the community. As a group they distribute leadership functions through the group and operate on motives other than reciprocity and obligation. In LWPW this means that the formal positional leader within the group may not be the most capable, while those who are capable remain in the background due to time issues. Those in formal positions have the time, while those with the capability do not have the time, but work to ensure that critical functions are covered. Those who have time carry on the task of relating to state demands for meetings and information, while issues of greater substance to the community such as putting on festivals and celebrations is carried out by those with the requisite skills. Rather than leadership resting in a single person it is distributed throughout the group with different people playing different roles in order to accomplish tasks that are of importance to them as a community. The community committee can consist of more than one group, with a group being larger than just those on the committee. Groups built on horizontal relations are based on trust and provide a ready source of assistance for tasks that are larger than an individual or set of dyadic relations can handle.

The final key finding answers the question I posed about community-state relations. It has to do with the practise of community leadership in the shadow of state and elite power and with the threat of eviction hanging over their heads. Committee members carry out the complex task of relating to both the benevolent and indifferent/hostile faces of the state as it confronts the urban poor. They negotiate a course whereby they consume state resources, maximizing benefit for the community as a whole, while at the same time positioning themselves to resist state power. They do so primarily through everyday forms of resistance but they are ready to move into the open in the case of eviction, which would touch the core of the Bangkok-born community. Under the broader umbrella of the legitimacy accorded to the state, the committee members operate along traditional lines, carving out non-administrative space where they pursue their agenda that modifies, ignores, or rejects state views. I have also shown that LWPW occupies a kind of middle ground that is neither hegemonic domination nor full blown civil society. Participation in protest movements has been limited to threats to the community, and has remained at primarily a symbolic level. It has not resulted, as has been observed in some networks associated with the Assembly of the Poor, in more participatory and democratic practices in the everyday life of the community. I suggest that seeing the committee members as caretakers is one way of understanding the kind of 'leading' that they do. As caretakers they do the routine administration and labour that helps the community as an administrative unit to function. They also lead via the values that they bring to caretaking, creating an atmosphere that shapes what is seen as possible in LWPW. Finally, as caretakers they are willing to contend against the state if necessary to protect what is under their care.

Applications and Implications from this Investigation for the Practise of Real Life Leadership

The findings summarized in the section above are embedded in the broader setting of Thailand and the specific micro-world of Lang Wat Pathum Wanaram. In this section I will look at points of application where this material can be used to clarify our understanding and practise of leadership in other contexts and social settings. The work of application is grounded in the belief that leadership does indeed make a difference. As Wright points out, the study of leadership is different from other fields in that the aim of leadership research is to help leaders lead more effectively (1996:228). In everyday life people find themselves in situations where they have to get along and accomplish a task, with varying degrees of emphasis on those two dimensions. It is here that 'leadership', 'leadership and management' (if you choose to separate the two), or 'managerial leadership' (if you want to find a way of bringing them together) is required in its task, social, participative, and charismatic roles (Kanungo & Mendonca, 1996:268). Our shared experience of everyday life also shows us that there are better and worse forms of practise in these four roles, and that the human and social consequences of leader behaviour are immense.

One could conceivably argue that people, societies, and the world in general have gotten along quite well for the vast majority of human history without the formal study of leadership. As Wright says, leadership researchers find themselves in the position of 'attempting to improve something which people have, for the most part, been reasonably good at over the centuries' (1996:231). However, as Dasgupta points out, we must resist the temptation to regard observed practises as socially optimal (2000:327). It is not enough to perform the descriptive task and assume that 'the way it is done' means that it is the best social fit and most productive for that sociocultural setting. What this means is that the answers to the questions I posed, set in the context of LWPW, are not of interest merely for academic and theoretical reasons, but have real life implications. Mintzberg's (1982) now famous essay entitled 'If You're Not Serving Bill and Barbara, Then You're Not Serving Leadership' reminds us that leadership research should meet the needs of actual leaders working in the real world of limited time and work pressures. In the four sections that follow I will attempt to serve the needs of three specific audiences. The first are the Wirachais and Watcharis who serve in Thai social settings. The second group are the Bills and Barbaras who lead outside of Thailand; for them I endeavour to show here how the broader approach reveals key principles for improving leadership practise. The final group is represented by those involved in training current and future leaders.

Thinking of Leadership as a Totality

What has always struck me as a weakness in the leadership literature that aims at improving leadership practise is the way that it tends to atomize its subject into a multitude of principles or axioms that are disembodied from real social life. It has never seemed to me reasonable to expect that people in the midst of real life complexities can pull out of their memory the proper principle out of the multitude that are proposed. Then there is the whole problem of applying supposedly generic principles in specific contexts, for often the underlying cultural basis of such principles is ignored and universality assumed.[1]

---

[1] See Wildavsky (2005) for his idea that leadership is a function of regime. He identifies four types of political regimes and notes how leadership practise is constrained by each particular context. From another angle Schon's work on professional work and

However, it turns out that these principles, generated in specific contexts, are not as easily applied outside of their original setting.[2] With some research streams seeking to assert the universal nature of certain forms of leadership,[3] Weber's comment is still germane:

> The more comprehensive the validity – or scope – of a term, the more it leads us away from the richness of reality since in order to include the common elements of the largest possible number of phenomena, it must necessarily be as abstract as possible and hence devoid of content. In the cultural sciences, the knowledge of the universal or general is never valuable in itself (1949:80).[4]

The challenge then is to find a way of looking holistically at leadership as perceived and practised in real-life settings. Universalist schemes and macro-theories have their place, and are necessary for developing the abstract conceptual grids that make comparison possible, but at the same time they leave an unexplained gap in the micro-processes that happen between people in sociocultural settings. If Carrither's observation is correct, that the most important universal is the plasticity of humankind, the 'capacity to be formed by the life of the society into which one is born' (1992:6), then it is the study of leadership embedded in social context that will prove most important for improving it.

---

reflection in action details the limitations of the technical rationality model on which the professions are based and shows how real life complexity and uncertainty leads professionals to reflect in action rather than simply problem solve based on existing theory. He points out that 'in order to solve a problem by the application of existing theory or technique, a practitioner must be able to map those categories onto features of the practise situation' (1982:41). This is precisely the problem of taking generic leadership principles from one 'practise situation' and trying to apply them in the practise situation of another social context. The practitioners in the new social context lack the ability to map the principles they are learning onto the new context in part because the whole exercise is based on the assumption of the universality of the principles.

[2] I sat through a leadership training seminar where an American-based organization was providing training to Asian leaders. One of the principles was to evaluate one's life and see where your biggest contribution and greatest effectiveness lay and then spend the majority of your time on those things. After the session I was visiting with a group of leaders and they were complaining about how overwhelmed they were in their work and that they could never get at really important things. So I brought up the point made in the seminar and they responded that they 'knew all of that already' but that they cannot say no or turn down requests to help in their social setting. It turns out that this 'rule' of leadership effectiveness presupposes the ability to say no and create space in one's personal schedule that is extremely difficult to achieve in some social settings.

[3] Bass, Kanungo and Mendonca, and the GLOBE Project all argue for the universality of the charismatic/transformational leadership paradigm (Bass, 1997; Den Hartog, House, Henges, Ruiz-Qintanilla, & *et al.*, 1999; Kanungo & Mendonca, 1996).

[4] Geertz makes a similar point, arguing that the grand strategy of searching for human universals fails to move towards the essentials of the human situation (1973:37-43).

An alternative approach to dissecting leadership into component parts came to me as I read Tambiah's essay on the galactic polity (1985:252-86). His notion of 'totalization' and the explanation of 'extant actualities' in terms of the elucidation of indigenous concepts gave me a tool for thinking about leadership in a way that counters the atomizing and abstracting tendencies in leadership studies (1985:258). In trying to understand the design of traditional Southeast Asian kingdoms, he notes that any explanation that draws on a single mode of explanation—whether cosmological (the traditional one in this case), religious, political, or economic—ultimately falls short. What the Western analytic tradition separates, Tambiah points out, more likely 'constituted a single interpenetrating reality' (1985:257).

What does leadership as a 'single interpenetrating reality' look like? The simplest analogy is to think in terms of the difference between practicing the distinct skills of a sport versus integrating them into an actual game being played. It is one thing to practise the skills of dribbling and shooting a basketball and another to perform them in a game against real live opponents. A totalization approach to leadership means that you are trying to capture some of the 'flow' in the sense of the dynamic action of a live game being played, and the 'feeling' in that some actions intuitively feel right. Staying with my sports analogy, it seems to me that the way we try to help people lead better is to tell them about a specific skill like dribbling (such as the task dimension, or having vision) and then assume that they will be able to integrate this into the 'game' unproblematically. In a game you do not have the luxury of picking out a response from a range of choices and implementing it, because you are constantly responding to the changing configurations presented by your opponent. Similarly, in real life leadership settings you rarely have time to serially go through lists of options on how to act drawn from a host of leadership principles; the configurations are constantly changing as people are responding and reacting to the current circumstances.

The interpenetrating reality of leadership in real life settings which makes up the 'flow' of the 'game' is found in the cultural resources that both constrain and form the material from which people creatively craft their responses. Improving leadership in a local setting does not ultimately lie with abstract and generic principles stripped of the flesh and bones of their sociocultural context, but in the disassembling and reassembling, the untangling of the explicit and implicit, and the challenging of conventional wisdom of leadership on the ground so that practitioners can see themselves and their setting with increased clarity. Then they can draw upon their unique pool of shared cultural resources for new, revised, or revived strategies of action.

I want to illustrate here how the account I have developed follows a 'totalization' ethos and examine how it is potentially helpful to Thai practitioners. First, I have tried to develop an account that is based in indigenous concepts or practises. The 21 terms of the *Thuukjai* Leader Model represent key ideas that shape the discourse of prototypical and preferred leadership attributes and behaviours. What came to me while I was mulling over the results of the correspondence analysis was that in general the further left a term placed on the diagram, from the task toward the relational side, the more difficult it became to translate that term with a single word or short phrase. This led to the next observation, that in general the more difficult it was to render a term in English (see the term list in Chapter 4, for instance *namjai, jai dii, nisai dii, ben kan eng*), the more likely it was that the term was part of a Thai cultural conception. Such terms also tend to serve as demarcation lines that highlight Thai cultural components in leadership. Connecting and indicating some of the relations between ideas of trust (*chuathuu*), respect (*nabthuu*), and personal power (*baramii*) along with terms dealing with deference (*kreng jai* and *kreng klua*) and grateful obligation (*bunkhun*), as well as the functioning of groups or cliques (*phuak*) and the role of unity (*samakhii*) for leaders and group life, moves towards a holistic configuration.

However, it is not enough to simply re-describe things in local terms; there has to be a reconnection as to how the elements described interrelate so as to draw together both ideal conceptions and actual practise. In this case I have attempted to elucidate both the 'official' Thai cultural transcript and actual leadership practises in the community by showing how concepts are utilized, transformed, clash, or seem to inhabit separate cognitive worlds. At this point I draw upon concepts that go beyond local terminology and emic structures to describe what is happening in a way that local actors would not be able to articulate in the same way. As Tambiah moved from local concepts of *mandala* (Thai *monthon*) to describe the structure of Southeast Asian kingdoms as a galactic polity, I have moved from local terms and practises to another level of abstraction to describe the *Thuukjai* Leader Model and *Sakdi* Administrative Behaviour-style leadership. Finally, I have sought to achieve 'totalization' by consciously seeking out what is explicit that people can articulate and talk about, and that which is implicit and out of verbal reach. In the case of LWPW it happens that people can discourse freely about the culturally preferred model, the trustworthy leader, and their suspicions of those with leadership positions as well. However, people have much more difficulty in talking about *akdi* administrative behaviour; they can describe this behaviour of others, but generally do not consciously recognise it in themselves when practising leadership. Thus the phenomena I observed in LWPW is that people are suspicious of leaders, yet practise the very things they are suspicious of when leaders themselves.

The perspectives brought by this material is of value to Thai leaders at several levels. Of immediate use is the explication of the discourse of preferred leadership behaviour. To intentionally find ways of integrating these major concepts into one's own actions would result in attributions of trustworthiness and would create a climate for voluntary cooperation on the part of others. It also suggests that leaders need to confront the issues of suspicion by examining their own behaviours as well as seeking out creative ways to do the opposite of people's expectations and thus build trust rather than suspicion. Finally, there is the whole area of things we do not talk about. If leaders could move things that remain implicit into the realm of dialogue it creates the climate for personal change by taking what 'feels' right and subjecting it to public critique. We cannot change what we do naturally until we are first aware that we are doing it, and that is in part the value of the development of a cultural account with a totalization perspective. It makes us aware of some of the 'flow' and 'feeling' issues that are normally going by so fast that we are unaware of them. A 'totalization' approach is not *the* answer, but it points in a hopeful direction because it can highlight areas of disjunction, clashing, and disconnection between ideal values and other values that drive the behaviour of real politics on the ground.

Mapping Leadership

In the point above I argued that leadership studies that study micro-processes, and are embedded in a particular sociocultural setting, are more valuable in terms of helping people in those contexts improve their practise of leadership than world-level studies. The latter have their place as they form the abstract grid upon which cross-cultural comparisons can be made, and their results provoke questions for further lines of inquiry. However, in matters of improving leadership practise, studies like the GLOBE project, which shows that Thais score higher on the culturally endorsed leadership theories of the humane orientation and the self-protective orientation (House *et al.*, 2004:684), shed little light on where to start for practitioners. We need the abstract grid to orient us to the bigger picture, but something different to help people function successfully in their own local setting.

These two approaches to the study of leadership are comparable to the differences between modern navigational maps and those of antiquity. During the Middle Ages ships followed the coastlines and used charts called portolans (harbour guides) that told them all the facts about the coastlines such as depth of the water, rocks and shoals, special landmarks, and so on (Barnett, 1998:97). Later, after the problem of calculating longitude was solved, latitude and longitude served as an abstract grid that navigators could apply to all maps thus bringing them into conformity. Barnett notes, 'Despite their virtue of an empirical approach, the portolans told local, piecemeal stories – not only did each tell the tale of a tiny part of the world, but no two portolans of the same place were identical' (1998:101). Each kind of map tells you where you are in a different fashion. A modern map with longitude and latitude provides one perspective, while a harbour guide of a particular spot would provide another completely different perspective. The different information can be used for different purposes.

If we are thinking about leading in a specific social setting, then an anthropological approach with a totalization ethos can produce what amounts to a leadership 'harbour guide' for that particular place and time. There are two specific ways that this kind of a map can help practitioners and trainers. The first is that in helping you get to where you want to go, it points out the obstacles and danger zones that are present. Studies that deal with ideal modes of explanation, whether via implicit leadership theories, cultural models, or some other method reveal how things should be done but they miss half the reality of everyday on the ground leadership practise. This is the fact that leaders often ignore the very behaviour patterns, attributes, and practises that they themselves articulate as being capable of producing interpersonal influence. Inherent in any prototypical model is a dark side; the things that are valued are valued precisely because they are not practised. The reasons that ideal and culturally preferred models are not actualized flows from other values and practises that exist within the sociocultural system in a much more implicit form. The leadership portolan from LWPW shows the hindrances, obstacles, barriers, and blind spots that derail good leadership practises located within their setting.

The second value of a leadership harbour guide is that it provides insights on improving leadership practise that are right within the sociocultural system at hand. A person can not only learn about what behaviours and attitudes to avoid, such a map also spells out specific strategies for developing interpersonal influence. This is a key difference and benefit brought by an anthropological approach versus a cross-cultural comparative approach generating abstract concepts. For instance, it is one thing to assert that leaders must have credibility, it is completely another to know the specific constellation of behaviours within a social setting that will make that happen.

Taken as a whole a leadership map can be used by leaders and those who train leaders as a tool to help measure their practises in light of both preferred and non-preferred models and stimulate analysis as to why preferred behaviours are difficult to enact and why problematic ones so easily serve as the default position. It takes vast amounts of courage and reflexivity to examine one's assumptions and cherished values to see where they may need to be changed in order to be more effective as a leader. However, it is precisely at this point that the leverage for improving leadership lies; leadership behaviours will not change until underlying values and assumptions are brought to the surface and challenged. It is noteworthy that in a study of school principals in Thailand, who were able to bring documented reform to their institutions, the researcher found it was precisely because they did not act in the normal and expected fashion that they were successful. They relinquished some of the authority that their position would normally assume, using a more participatory style, and thus were able to negotiate changes that were resisted and subverted in other schools (Hallinger & Pornkasem, 2000). In LWPW my interviews showed that Uncle P. was the most respected person. He did two things which were very appreciated by people and differed from usual leader behaviour. When serving as committee president he walked around the community inquiring how people were doing; also, one interviewee noted how he called frequent meetings to share information, which made people respect him even more. While reflection on the differing cultural materials available for leadership behaviour may be rare, there are people that do this, and discussing such examples can open the door for seeing new and culturally relevant options for leadership practise. A pedagogy for improving leadership should not simply focus on passing on facts and principles, but should work at sensitizing and providing skills in mining the implicit in one's cultural setting and leadership practise to bring them into conscious thought. An anthropological approach to leadership that produces a leadership map serves as a tool to enhance this process of bringing the implicit to the surface.

Finding Disjunction: the Explicit and Implicit

In my previous point I noted the dark side of leadership and argued for the role of 'leadership harbour guides' that can help practitioners and those training leaders to work on strategies for avoiding these problem areas. It turns out that the process of confronting issues that derail preferred modes of leadership is not only complex but painful; the insight and willingness to examine what is normally unexamined and unnoticed is gained only at a price. In this section I will expand upon the issue of the explicitly and implicitly held models in LWPW and examine some concepts that help to frame this issue, then make a general observation about the enterprise of improving leadership practise.

As the study progressed I was fascinated that people seemed to be able to verbalize about the TLM and the trustworthy (*chuathuu*) leader model, yet would act contrary to the ideals of these models when they occupied a formal leadership position themselves, even criticising other leaders who did so as well. Seeking an explanation for this cleavage between thought and action illustrates the dilemma and complexity of trying to bring change in positive directions for leadership in communities such as LWPW. It also helps to suggest the lines of a possible pedagogy to improve leadership skills in different contexts.

Giddens points out that our discourse, what we are able to put into words 'about our actions, and our reasons for them, only touches on certain aspects of what we do in our day-to-day lives' (1987:7). He asserts that there is a highly complex non-discursive side to our activities (1987:7). Hierarchy, as a master concept deeply embedded and implicit in Thai people's worldview, lies in part in this non-discursive zone. I have spelled out some of the implications of the hierarchy cultural code for leadership in my discussion of the *sakdi* administrative behaviour complex. It seems to me that much of what constitutes leadership behaviour in LWPW flows from this implicit and non-discursive side. The concept of cultural models is helpful here because it provides an account from a cognitive perspective of the different types of processing used with explicit and implicit knowledge. Cognitive anthropology asserts that the most basic models of culture are learned through a form of cognitive processing that handles implicit knowledge, and as such, it is difficult to critique or modify.[5] Much of what people do in the interactions of leadership stems from this implicit knowledge; in this sense it is not 'thought out' in advance, but is intuitively 'felt' to be the right thing to do. Both official views like *chuathuu* and the much more messy realities like follower experiences of daily leadership (such as observing inequitable distribution, the pursuit of personal and in-group benefit, and not sharing information) are out in the open, the subject of discourse, and thus explicit. Yet when a person becomes a leader it is deeply embedded, implicit values like hierarchy that shape much leader behaviour, and these values are rarely brought into the level of discourse. In this way leaders continue to manifest behaviours that they themselves would be suspicious of in the follower role, and this creates a self-reinforcing cycle of behaviour that feeds the suspicion heuristic of the SABLH.

While a cultural models perspective can offer some insight into the compartmentalization observed in those who play dual roles as leaders and followers, Carrithers goes a step further in arguing his mutualist perspective against those who hold to an independent reality of culture as mental models (see Carrithers, 1992, particularly Chapters 5 and 6 where he develops these ideas in detail). Drawing on the work of Bruner (1986), he makes a distinction between paradigmatic and narrative thought. Narrative thought is a 'capacity to cognize not merely immediate relations between oneself and another, but many-sided human interactions carried out over a considerable period' (Carrithers, 1992:82). Carrithers explains that narrative thought is not just telling stories but 'understanding complex nets of deeds and attitudes' (1992:82), and he illustrates from his work in a Jain community in India how people's knowledge of Jainism was local, particular, and narrative (1992:109-10). By way of contrast, paradigmatic thought is the abstracted, schematic, and systematic thought which is pulled out of its social nexus (1992:76, 109-14).

Bringing both the cultural models and mutualist perspectives together, I make the following three assertions. First, the TLM and ideas of the trustworthy leader represent the paradigmatic, a vision of the ideal based on the moral model of society and by extension leadership that is abstracted from real social life. Second, people in the follower role experience others' practise of leadership through the narrative mode of thinking and learning. Through constant involvement in the stories of leaders' lives and through both watching and interacting in leader-follower relations, people in LWPW have a localized a particularistic 'story' of which the acknowledgment of privilege and the suspicion of its abuse is central. Finally, when people become leaders, their practise follows more from the non-discursive and implicit forms of knowledge

[5] See D'Andrade (1995:178) for insight into this non-discursive side of human behaviour from the viewpoint of cognitive anthropology and Shore for an example of explicit and tacit models in Samoan conceptions of village space (1996:272-73).

than it does from thought-out strategies based in paradigmatic reasoning. Although Carrithers does not make this point I would also suggest that it is in the constant process of negotiating relationships in order to make meaning (Carrithers, 1992:106), and involvement in the lived 'story' of watching and experiencing others lead, where people participate in meaning creation. Over time a shared interpretation develops that is deeply implicit about the nature of leadership practises. It is narrative thought through which much of culture is acquired, and which forms the implicit knowledge that is primarily outside of conscious. This kind of thought forms the backdrop and interpretive schemes whereby we draw on more public sources of cultural materials to utilize in social interaction.

Taken as a whole the combined notions of discursive and non-discursive knowledge, cultural models, and the distinction between paradigmatic and narrative thought suggest a methodology for helping leaders improve their practise. In general when we talk about leadership we do so in paradigmatic terms that are the most abstract and farthest from real life. However, the implicit, non-discursive, and narrative thought all point to much of leadership flowing out of a side that we do not verbalize easily; thus you cannot simply fax leadership principles into the heads of people and expect them to convert them into action. What we 'think' about leading is merely the tip of the iceberg while the bulk lies beneath the surface in implicit knowledge. Methods of inquiry that produce only paradigmatic knowledge have only done half the work that needs to be done. Those who are interested in improving leadership practise in a given setting need to utilize methods that will allow them to capture the non-discursive side embedded in leader-follower behaviour and interactions. The next step is to bring this material into public dialogue with leaders to look for local solutions to problem points. This discussion again highlights the importance of a 'totalization' ethos rooted in an anthropological approach where participant observation brings one close to issues on the ground with a sensitivity to their formulation in indigenous concepts.

Trust and Group: Dilemmas of Thai Leadership

Weber's observation still stands: at the end of the day legitimation is something that the people grant to leaders. Whether it is traditional, legal-rational, or charismatic authority, the glue that holds legitimation in place is trust. In LWPW trust has to do with leadership emergence and the ability to secure cooperation. Yet distrust is manifestly everywhere throughout the slum. This illustrates for me the dilemma and complexity of Thai leadership from urban slums to national politics. The suspicion heuristic of the follower dimension of the *Sakdi* Administrative Behaviour model forms the operational context for leadership. It is precisely ongoing repetitions of blatant pursuit of personal gain on the part of elite levels in Thai society that feeds and makes plausible the suspicion heuristic as it concerns leaders.

Trust is not something unique to the Thai leadership setting. There is a growing literature about the role of trust in and between organizations,[6] and in the notion of social capital where trust is a critical component of social organization, particularly of horizontal networks that make up the informal institutions between the individual and the state and commonly understood as civil society (Dasgupta, 2000:327-8).[7] There are some points in the literature that sharpen the material I have developed from LWPW and will set the stage for my discussion that follows. There are several theoretical perspectives on trust[8] but they all usually assume three major elements: that there is a degree of interdependence between the two parties, that trust provides a way to cope with uncertainty in exchange relationships, and finally that the party made vulnerable through the assumption of risk will not be taken advantage of by the other party (Lane, 1998:3). What is particularly relevant for the discussion here is that trust can be analysed across distinct levels, moving from the micro-level between individuals and organizations, to institutional based, system based, and societal trust.[9] The important point here is that different kinds and levels of

---

[6] For background on trust in organizations and bibliographic leads see Dirks and Skarlicki (2004), Fukuyama (1995), Kramer and Cook (2004), Lane (1998), Six (2005), and Kanter (1979). Trust carries with it the notion of consistency and predictability in the behaviour of others. Dasgupta defines trust 'in the context of an individual forming expectations about actions of others that have a bearing on this individual's choice of action, when that action must be chosen before he or she can observe the actions of those others' (2000:330). According to Fukuyama, 'Trust is the expectation that arises within a community of regular, honest, and cooperative behaviour, based on commonly shared norms, on the part of other members of that community' (1995:26).

[7] For background on social capital see World Bank (2006); Bordieu (1992); Coleman (1988); Dasgupta and Serageldin (2000); Putnam (1993); and Putnam, Leonard, & Nanetti, (1993).

[8] Trust is viewed as having different bases. There is relationship-based trust rooted in how the follower sees the relationship. It is not based in economic contract but trust in the goodwill of the other and the perception of moral obligation (Dirks & Skarlicki, 2004:22). Character-based trust is based on the perception of the leaders' character (Dirks & Skarlicki, 2004:22). Dirks and Skarlicki also see two dimensions of trust: cognitive, which is based in the perception of integrity and capability, and affective which is a special relationship with a person so that the leader demonstrates a concern for the follower's welfare (2004:28). From what I have observed in LWPW it seems to me both bases and both dimensions of trust are manifest. This seems inherent in the ideal model that includes both character issues as well as relational issues.

[9] In her theoretical overview Lane sees four major types of trust: calculative, based on weighing cost-benefits; value or norm based trust that develops around common values; common cognition trust where expectations held in common structure behaviour in predictable ways and create trust; and institutional based trust, which is on the opposite pole of trust based in interpersonal familiarity, and is trust in what is impersonal (1998:5-12). Fukuyama looks at trust on a societal level and notes that some societies have bridges to forms of sociability that lie outside the family, while others do not (1995:63).

trust require different methods to build it (Lane, 1998:21). Lane points out that researchers split on whether trust can be built intentionally or whether it is emergent (1998:21). Here it becomes apparent that trust, as with leadership, is culturally constrained and socially constructed. This is in and of itself a topic of interest for comparison, and one of value to leaders because it is helpful to be aware of how trust is built and lost within the sociocultural setting one is working in.[10]

The subject of building trust naturally implies that trust can be broken.[11] The literature refers to this as opportunism, defined as self-interest seeking with guile (Lane, 1998:22). This brings us back to LWPW and the dilemma of Thai leadership, and by extension to a problematic in broader Thai society. Trust is critical in the slum for leadership emergence and cooperation precisely because of the deeply rooted suspicion of the practise of opportunism. The fact that in the literature there exists discussion about opportunism, distrust, and the need for social controls indicates that trust is inherently exploitable. The element of guile is the second edge to the two-edged sword; the social appearances of trust can be maintained and cultivated for the express purpose of taking advantage. Thus trust is not only critical to the success of organizations; it is the tool of the deceitful that makes manipulation possible.

One of the theoretical perspectives on trust is that of common cognition, where expectations held in common by people structure behaviour in certain predictable ways (Lane, 1998:10). I want to suggest that there exist in Thai society common cognitions for both trust and mistrust, and these are what structure the ideas behind the TLM and the suspicion of the SABLH. Whatever the source of opportunism in Thai society it has been prevalent enough to create the common expectation of predictable behaviour on the part of those who are in leadership positions.[12]

The problematic then, in my opinion, is that the preferred leader and trustworthy leader models, based in giving behaviours, and notions of

---

[10] Kouzes and Posner, in a United States based setting surveyed people on the attributes they most admired in leaders and found the four top ranked attributes as: honest, forward-looking, inspiring, and competent (1993:14-5). Literature from the field of communication lists being honest, inspiring, and competent as the key components for source credibility (1993:21-2). Three of the four overlap with their list of most admired attributes; thus they argue that credibility (in the sense of belief, faith, confidence, and trust in their integrity, knowledge, and skill of leaders) is the foundation for good leadership (1993:22).

[11] Dirks and Skarlicki introduce the idea of 'trust dilemmas' where there are tradeoffs necessitated in multiple relationships. Meeting the expectations of one party means violating the expectations of another (2004:34). They also observe that trust is more easily broken than built (2004:35).

[12] See Chapter 5, p. 149 for Mulder's idea of how people outside of family become anonymous to each other where it is thus normal to pursue self-interest at the expense of others.

deference, reciprocity, and obligation, are by their very nature symbol systems easily manipulated by people who can thus maintain a public face of benevolence, concern, and generosity while pursuing personal advantage.[13] Ease of manipulation leading to common cognitions of mistrust vastly complicates the practise of leadership.

The issue of trust raised here can be used by Thai leaders, whether in slums or beyond those environs, to improve the practise of leadership in two ways. The first way is to utilize the models produced here to intentionally shape their practise to avoid problem areas. The problematic of suspicion that I have identified and the common cognition of mistrust means that leadership in any Thai setting is very complicated. Because trust is low and suspicion high, leaders tend to rely on their group (*phuak*), who they do trust.[14] The more that information stays in the group and the more the group demands benefits to the exclusion of others, the greater the sense of distrust and suspicion on the part of those outside the group. It seems to me necessary to intentionally bring into conscious thought the suspicion heuristic and work precisely in the opposite direction of what suspicion expects. This is part of the trust dilemma of meeting the needs of some and violating the trust of others, but from my observations too many local leaders tolerate behaviour in themselves that they do not tolerate in others.

The issue of trust can also be used to ask questions that probe social relations in Thai society and may open the door to finding new leadership patterns that have the potential to improve the quality of life for people. I believe that in strengthening horizontal networks lies the hope for bettering life for people in slums and growing civil society. As it appears to me, inside of *phuak* (group) it is possible to work in terms of horizontal relations because there is a level of trust between parties, but outside of *phuak*, s*akdi* administrative behaviour is activated. This research has generated some insight into how a single group works, but there are other key questions that need to be

[13] Lord reminds us that when you leave face-to-face dyadic relations and move to higher or aggregate levels in leadership you are dealing with power, symbolic management, and organizational culture (see 1991:10-12). Suntaree notes it is possible for people to manipulate the grateful relationship value. Those who are power oriented can utilize the *kreng jai* value which causes people to refuse kindnesses offered and give tangible benefits that mask the appearance of *bunkhun*. Since the motivation of *bunkhun* lies inside the person rendering it, it is only in the relationship over time that the reason for gifts, favours, and kindness can become apparent. This giving thus creates gratitude on the part of the receiver, which can be used to build power connections and an entourage through the manipulation of the *bunkhun-katanyuu* value system (1990: 141-42).

[14] Kanter talks about how uncertainty abounds even in bureaucratic systems and how this uncertainty in human institutions means that there is a degree for a need to rely on human persons (1979:25). What she calls the 'uncertainty quotient' causes people in leadership positions to create tight inner circles with homogeneous relations and loyalty (1979:26).

asked. How can different *phuak* connect with each other? How is a *phuak* built and how can it be enlarged?

Birner and Wittmer's concepts of devolution and decentralization seem relevant here (2003:292-93). In devolution there is the transfer of authority, rights, and responsibility from the state to non-governmental bodies, local communities, and user groups. In decentralization, decision-making authority is pushed to lower levels of government. Slum leaders in LWPW are quite adept at shifting between their roles. They slip between being low-level administrators to working outside of administrative bounds in their own horizontal *phuak*, or to carrying on their own agenda of resistance and maximizing community benefit while maintaining the front of cooperation with the state. The problem, as I see it, is that devolution gets circumvented by the limitations of *phuak* and the limitations on trust outside of one's *phuak*. Rather than expanding and strengthening informal institutions and civil society in the community, the inability of *phuak* to connect means that such institutions are curtailed. Lack of trust and low spontaneous sociability mean that one has to rely on administrative methods to get things done because horizontal relations are weak.[15] This in turn is problematic because in administrative mode s*akdi* administrative behaviour arises and feeds the negative feedback cycle of distrust.

Issues of trust and distrust and the nature of groups illustrate both the complexity of leadership in the Thai setting and the benefits of a methodology that is able to probe beyond the ideal and paradigmatic. Breaking the cycle of distrust is a key to improving leadership in Thai settings, and the conceptualization of s*akdi* administrative behaviour values serves as a tool to bring into dialogue what is normally just assumed. This also illustrates that while issues of trust exist in different cultural settings, the ways in which trust is gained and broken vary. Thus leadership research that is going to hold promise for helping practitioners needs to unpack the issues relating to trust within that local setting as I have tried to do here for the Thai setting.

Leadership Training

In this final section I will now draw upon the various insights gained from this investigation to suggest a pedagogy to work on improving the practise of leadership in general. The contrast I am making here is between conventional approaches epitomized by the seminar style of leadership training and what I

[15] Fukuyama gives an example of a town in Italy in the 1950s with wealthy citizens who could not come together to found either a school or hospital because they believed it was the obligation of the state (1995:9). He summarizes by saying 'the absence of a proclivity for community…inhibits people from exploiting economic opportunities that are available to them' (1995:10). There are resources inside of LWPW that remain untapped because of the lack of spontaneous sociability.

have advocated here as an anthropological approach that seeks a 'totalization' perspective on leadership within a sociocultural setting. The seminar style focuses on the unidirectional telling of participants about universal, globalized, and timeless 'leadership principles' and assumes the ability of those in the training to be able to apply these concepts in their local setting. The approach emphasizes the cognitive component of leading, ignores local culture, draws upon research primarily generated in Western settings, and is by design a short term event. The advantages of such an approach are obvious because it only requires trainers to be familiar with the database of Western based empirical research. This makes it possible to train anywhere with only a minimum of inconvenience, which generally consists of having written materials translated into the local language.

An anthropological approach, by way of contrast, is much more demanding on the trainer because it requires familiarity both with the Western based literature and the expenditure of time and effort to understand local concepts, the explicit and paradigmatic as well as the non-discursive in what works and does not work, and in inequities and power relations. Thus by definition an anthropological approach cannot be a one-time training event, but has to be viewed as a process over time. This training pedagogy flows into a natural three step sequence where each part builds on the other.

Seek Understanding of the Local Leadership Context First

This is where I see the role of intentionality in the work of training leaders. Seeking holistic understanding does not happen by accident, nor is it the work of a moment. It demands that we intentionally insert ourselves *as learners and listeners* into the flow of social life in order to at least grasp some things that will enable us as trainers to raise the right questions with those we seek to train. The leadership 'map' that I developed for LWPW shows that within the sociocultural system itself are both the conception of the practises for successful leadership and the hindrances, obstacles, barriers, and blind spots that derail good leadership practises. We cannot teach someone how to be a good leader if we have no clue as to what good leadership looks and functions like in that particular sociocultural setting. Good leadership training is either going to work at mining this material out in advance, or at least helping trainees learn how to ask the kinds of questions that will lead to this information.

Bring the Implicit to the Surface

Learning the terrain requires a great deal of effort and commitment on the part of trainers to understand what is happening, but it is only the first half of the work. Simply sharing these results as paradigmatic knowledge is to miss the whole point of the implicit nature of much leadership knowledge. The second step in the pedagogical process for leadership training is to utilize the insights from the study of leadership in that setting to bring to the surface what is normally unexamined and unnoticed. The critical leverage for helping to improve leadership in a given sociocultural setting is to find a way to help people talk about what is usually implicit. This involves facilitating people to dialogue about how and why they default to unproductive leadership patterns and why culturally preferred behaviours remain for the most part ideals. This is not only an exercise in awareness, but it requires participants to find cultural resources that will help them to value and integrate into practise their own culturally preferred forms of leadership.

For instance, in the Thai setting, leaders need to recognize and intentionally bring into conscious thought the suspicion heuristic and work precisely in the opposite direction of what suspicion expects. To do this will require behaviour that runs counter to some of the privileges that leaders have come to expect, but the results of enhanced influence by being considered trustworthy will result in increased cooperation. The issue of trust could also be used to ask questions that probe social relations in Thai society and may open the door to finding new leadership patterns that have the potential to improve group cohesion and task accomplishment.

Look for Local Answers to Cultural Problems

The final step in the pedagogical process builds upon the insights that grow out of the empirical work of step one and the dialogue of step two. It involves searching for and discussing answers to leadership problems that are already found within the sociocultural system. This includes ideal and preferred models as well as real life examples of people who are seen as practicing such ideals. While nobody in LWPW completely embodied the culturally preferred TLM some were considered more desirable leaders than others. I have already noted above a study that showed principals who went against expected behaviours were more effective in implementing long-term change in their schools. It may very well be that it is precisely those people who are able to step outside of themselves and reflect on leadership behaviour in the light of idealized cultural preferences, the implicit, and the assumed, who are able to devise strategies of action that are fruitful for task accomplishment. Such people are valuable sources for learning not only what they do, but the conditions and circumstances that are involved in their practise. Positive and successful examples can be probed as to how and why they were able to tap one source of culturally preferred material over another.

Summary

In this last chapter I have delved into the potential relevance of this study for the Wirachais and Watcharis of Thailand who lead in a variety of different settings. It is my sincere hope that they will find something of value here for their practise of leadership. For the Bills and Barbaras of the leadership world, I suspect that any value they gain from this work will be that which reading ethnographic accounts of different places does for all of us: shines light on our own social settings by reflecting it off another society.

For those involved in training leaders, I argue for thinking much more in terms of a process with an emphasis on the local and context bound. The three sequential steps I have delineated here, understanding leadership in its context, surfacing the implicit, and seeking local answers, both imply and are rooted in several assumptions that grow out of the insights that come from an anthropological approach to understanding leadership. While conventional practice emphasizes training events and cognitive learning, the steps I advocate here are processes; thus training viewed in this frame requires time. The time spent includes both development of an empirical base of observations about leadership in the local setting as well as the trust building that enables dialogue so participants can talk about what is normally invisible to them. It is an intentional process as well that requires a commitment on the part of trainers to listen, learn, and facilitate rather than simply tell.

Epilogue

In 1978 Akin wrote about the rise and fall of the Bangkok slum that he had studied. Walking through the constantly changing landscape of Lang Wat Pathum Wanaram makes me wonder if I will one day have to do the same. I know that residents are not optimistic about their future on the land. However, these people are survivors, and I know that whatever happens they will continue to find their way along on the periphery of Thai society. I conclude this book with a hope and a wish. My hope is that in some small way I will be able over time to return the kindness the residents there have shown to me as an outsider, allowing me to take so much from their lives and community. As for my wish, I wish for the community of Lang Wat Pathum Wanaram true *samakhii* so that, in the words of L.P., they can truly 'do everything'.

Glossary of Thai Terms

amnaat	power
baan	house, village, dwellings on land
bang	locality along a waterway
baramii	prestige, influence, generally used in the text as personal power
bunkhun	indebted goodness
chuathuu	trustworthy
chumchon	an assemblage of people, a technical term for a slum community
farang	Westerner, white person
ittipon	influence
jao pho	used now to refer to 'godfather' types
katanyuu	gratitude
khlong	canal, watercourse
klum	group
kreng jai	to have consideration for, reluctant to impose on, polite deference
kreng klua	fear
brong sai	transparent, *mai brong sai* means not transparent
muang	city
naa wat	in front of the temple, used as a geographic designation in LWPW
nabthuu	respect
nakleng	ruffian, rogue, bold person
pattana	development
phuak	group, party, *phak phuak* as a clique
phuu nam	leader
phuu noi	inferior
phuu yai	superior, adult
Rua Khiaw	literally Green Fence, a geographic designation in LWPW
sakdi	rank, authority, status
sakdina	literally authority over rice fields, later used as dignity marks
samakhii	unity, consensus, accord
thuukjai	pleased, satisfied
Ton Pho	Pipal tree, a geographic designation in LWPW
trok	lane, alley

Appendix: Methodology

The contested nature of social science research and the fact that there are no definitive answers to the methodological debates means that it is incumbent upon researchers to trace out in some detail the stance taken on critical issues.[1] This includes what kind of knowledge is produced, the line of approach, and the specific methods used to produce that knowledge. Consideration of the various possible ways of answering a research question moves us into the realm of examining research methodology.[2] This appendix provides an overview of the philosophical positions I take as well as the actual methods used in the collection of the data. Taken together these constitute what can be called a research or inquiry paradigm.[3] I begin with my choice of an interpretivist approach and the goal of developing a factor theory and then look at the status of anthropological knowledge. I review my philosophical commitments to the 'militant middle ground' and 'reflexive methodology' and then look at myself as the biographically situation researcher. I conclude by overviewing the specific methods used and mode of analysis for working with the data.

The focal question for the study was 'What are the shared understandings that Thais in the target community have about the leader-follower relationship, and how are these understandings utilized and enacted in social contexts?' I chose to answer this question primarily in terms of an interpretive

---

[1] The 'paradigm wars' (Punch, 1998:2) and the increased sensitivity to the metaphysical issues they represent require that researchers locate their work clearly within a paradigm and acknowledge how this position affects the types of claims that they will make. The task of choosing an inquiry paradigm from among what are often thought of in social science circles as competing views, some of which are considered incommensurable, is no easy task. The complexity is seen in attempts at charting out or diagramming ontological and epistemological positions so as to show the linkages between various metaphysical commitments and particular research techniques (Guba & Lincoln, 1998:202-218; Knight, 2002:26-33; Lincoln & Guba, 2000:165-74).

[2] I follow Bryman in his use of methodology to refer to an epistemological position, with 'method' or 'technique' used as synonyms to refer to particular ways of gathering empirical materials (1984:76).

[3] An *inquiry paradigm* answers the three fundamental questions of ontology, epistemology, and particular method (Guba & Lincoln, 1998:201). The broader methodological concerns of ontology (what exists) and epistemology (how we may know about it) in research are important because they influence the claims that researchers are able to make, and because of the interrelationships between metaphysical concerns and specific methods where some inquiry methods 'are more congenial to some epistemological and ontological views than others' (Knight, 2002:23, 33). See Knight (2002:33) for a list of six implications for research that grow out of epistemological and ontological positions.

understanding, with certain qualifications.[4] There are several variations within the interpretivist approach (see Schwandt, 1998; 2000 for distinctions drawn between interpretivist, constructivist, and hermeneutic positions), but they share in common the search for understanding 'the processes by which…meanings are created, negotiated, sustained, and modified within a specific context of human action' (Schwandt, 1998:225).

What is the status of the knowledge produced by an interpretive understanding? Social scientists, like their counterparts in the natural sciences, produce theory.[5] My goal is to develop theory based in interpretive understanding. There is lively debate in the social sciences as to what precisely is meant by the word theory.[6] In this study I use 'theory' in the broader sense identified by Calhoun as theoretical orientations or perspectives which provide the background for understanding and evaluating both facts and explanations (1996:432-33). The type of theory I am aiming to produce is what Kaplan and Manners refer to as factor theory rather than law type theory such as universal laws or statistical generalizations (1972:15-16). Factor theory seeks to identify networks of relations and configurations or patterns (1972:16). In this sense, I am using a theory generation approach or, as Punch calls it, a theory-after versus a theory-first approach (1998:16).[7]

If I produce a theory of the factor type, the question that follows is what is the status of this form of knowledge? Is there anything about anthropological knowledge that is different from everyday knowledge? Carrithers proposes a framework for breaking down the barrier between interpretive understanding and scientific knowledge. He summarizes the argument against ethnographic knowledge in this way:

---

[4] Knight defines understanding in terms of knowledge as a creation of minds at work. In this sense it includes explanation and understanding, involves the making sense of information and not just amassing it, and includes connecting information with existing understandings either through assimilating new understandings with the old or accommodating the old understandings with the new (2002:20). Schwandt points out that in all postempiricist philosophies of the human sciences understanding is bound up with interpretation because 'knowledge of what others are doing or saying always depends upon some background or context of other meanings, beliefs, values, practices and so forth' (2000:201).

[5] Hammersley and Atkinson see social science as having the distinctive purpose of producing social theory. Even though its methods are refinements and developments of those that people use in everyday life, theory production is what sets social science off from journalism and literature (1995:15).

[6] See Thomas & James, 2005.

[7] Theory-first work has been precisely the way most research on Thai leadership has been conducted: starting with a particular pre-existing theory, deducing hypotheses from it, and then testing those hypotheses. I am proposing to do theory-after work, but I am qualifying 'theory' in the very specific sense of a factor/pattern theory as defined by Kaplan and Manners.

> [It] begins as personal knowledge about particular people in a particular place at a particular time ... [and] if the knowledge is only personal, then it is only your knowledge, and therefore is not necessarily valid knowledge for others ... this opens ethnography to the objection that its plausibility is not factual but merely literary (1992:148).

While acknowledging that anthropological knowledge is based on personal experience and the personal capacities that allow us to engage social life beginning as children, immigrants, converts (or anthropologists), and learn to find our way around new social settings and institutions; he argues that it is also more complex than this (1992:149-50). Anthropological knowledge moves from the base of everyday knowledge such as narrative and mind-reading to build a structure of paradigmatic knowledge (1992:150). Practical knowledge used in social life is verified and corrected on a continuing basis in everyday life. Paradigmatic knowledge is 'knowledge [that] is transformed from knowing how to knowing that, from a performer to a critic's consciousness, from narrative to paradigmatic thought' (1992:175). There is a move from consensible[8] patterns gained through everyday life experience to consensus in this larger community – a move which is rooted in understanding based in real life social interaction (1992:175-76). In Carrither's view ethnographic product and the patterns produced are a:

> synthesis, an artefact, but one produced under a particular constraint: it had to set out in a perspicuous order those events and attributions adequate to produce an account of what made participants act, and what the consequences of those acts were (1992:169).

There is no way to guarantee that all relevant details are included in a constructed account, but its authority in a modified sociological realist view does not rest in it being true in a one-to-one correspondence sense, but rather pragmatically in its ability to be used (1992:153, 173). Carrithers notes that the requirements of this new paradigmatic knowledge 'are quite foreign to its original matrix' in that it is abstracted to fit views of human societies and must be falsifiable (1992:176). The factor theory that I produced is a constructed account in the form of paradigmatic knowledge based in the consensibility of the narrative and the patterns that I will set forth.

In terms of the basic philosophical commitments that form the foundation of the inquiry, I have been influenced by the 'militant middle ground' approach to anthropology of Herzfeld (2001) and the 'reflexive methodology' approach of Alvesson and Sköldberg (2000). Herzfeld takes a critical position that seeks to avoid the problems at either end of the poles represented by dogmatic positions on positivism at one end and postmodernism on the other. The 'militant middle

---

[8] Carrithers defines consensibility as 'the ability of people to perceive things in common, to agree upon and to share perceptions' (1992:156).

ground' is thus 'a space that at once is strongly resistant to closure and that is truly grounded in an open-ended appreciation of the empirical' (2001:x).[9] The 'reflexive methodology' of Alvesson and Sköldberg seeks to problematize research without succumbing to the problems of what they call 'methodological textbook wisdom' with its uncritical handling of empirical data, and that of postmodernism/poststructuralism where empirical reality is ignored altogether (2000:2-3). In seeking the middle ground, I use a critical realism combined with a weak constructionism or 'contextual empiricism' (Longino 1993a cited in Schwandt, 2000) where the real world constrains knowledge construction. I am following Parker who asserts that there is a reality that exists outside of discourse and which provides the materials by which we structure the world through discourse (Parker 1992 cited in Burr, 1995:88). In this framework the empirical material and research process do not capture reality but rather provide a reconstruction of social reality. There is openness to further insight and increased understanding so that conclusions and evaluations are always held lightly and are subject to revision as better interpretations come along (Bohman 1991a:146 cited by Schwandt, 2000:202).[10]

A final issue concerns 'the biographically situated researcher' (Denzin & Lincoln, 1998:24). The socially situated researcher lies behind all of the phases that define the research process and all observations are made through the lenses of language, gender, social class, race, ethnicity, theory, and political and cultural circumstances (Alvesson & Skoldberg, 2000:6; Denzin & Lincoln, 1998:24). I come to this study as a white, middle class, North American male who has lived in Thailand for nearly 20 years. I am fluent in reading, writing, and speaking central Thai and work closely with Thais in my professional career serving in a Thai Christian foundation. While nobody can be entirely aware of their own biases, there are three areas in particular that I consider to be in the realm of leanings, tendencies, or values that I have brought to this study.

I do not come to this study as a neutral observer. One of the main focuses of my job the past seven to eight years has been working with urban poor. My friends who live in slums have opened my eyes to the kinds of issues faced by

---

[9] 'Where is that middle ground – between what poles does it provide a space for reflection? It lies between the sometimes crass extremes of positivism and deconstruction, with their deliciously similar panoplies of self-justifying and self-referential rhetoric; between the disembodied abstractions of grand theory and the ingrown self-absorption of local interests and "national" studies; between self-satisfied rationalism and equally self-satisfied nihilism' (2001:xi).

[10] My position is consonant with what Kilduff and Mehra call an affirmative (rather than sceptical) postmodernism (1997:455). In this view it is possible to make discriminations among competing positions (1997:455); it sees contexts as relatively stable, which allows for coherent interpretation; and it believes that 'the material world imposes constraints on the multiplicity of meanings that can be attributed to signifiers' (1997:461).

the urban poor. Listening to their stories – catching their perspective on life and poverty – has shown me that the playing field is not level. The 'system' in its broadest sense is weighted against them. A second area has to do with my interest in local cultural factors rather than a focus on universals. My work experience in a Thai organization has been a long-term laboratory allowing me to watch Thai and Western leadership patterns meet and on occasion clash. This has created in me a deep sense that understanding 'the imaginative universe within which their acts are signs' is the critical task (Geertz, 1973:13) rather than the codification of laws or viewing local people through an imported theoretical lens.

A third area that can bring bias to the results of this study is my tendency as a Westerner to be much too direct and blunt in my question asking. Even after knowing that indirect communication and face-saving are important in relationships, I am certain that I asked and phrased questions that a Thai researcher would never have asked. This means that the answers given in these cases reflect my breach of a proper approach. Throughout the analysis I have tried to reflect on these instances and avoid a reporting style that acts as if the interview materials are straightforward depictions of what is happening. However, there are no doubt points in my data that reflect this problem and where I have not adequately interrogated my sources.

I have specifically chosen methods within the broader qualitative research approach in order to tap actor viewpoints and gain insight into how intersubjectively shared meanings are utilized and negotiated in real life settings.[11] Two styles in Clammer's typology cover the most ground in identifying my orientation to fieldwork. The first is what he calls the theory and description style where descriptive work sets the backdrop for interpretive understanding and theory building growing from the empirical material (1984:71-2). My primary tools for this were observation, informal interviews, formal interviews that were taped and transcribed, and working with written sources. The second is a formal emic approach. Using systematic data collection I employ the techniques of free-recall listing, saliency analysis, and correspondence analysis of paired similarity data to examine the sociolinguistic terrain of the domain of leadership (for further overviews of these methods see Bernard, 1988; Bernard, 1995; Bernard, 1998; Weller, 1998; Weller & Romney, 1988, 1990). The approach is emic in that local actors provide the material, but the product as a cultural model is etic in nature because local actors do not carry around in their heads such a model in that form. Cultural models are a co-creation between the researcher and the informants (Keesing,

---

[11] Bryman *et al.* point out a number of problems associated with quantitative approaches to the study of leadership and suggest that a qualitative approach in the interpretive line may be beneficial because it takes the actor's viewpoint as the central focus and also has the potential to bring to the surface topics and issues relevant to the actors rather than the researcher (1988:14, 16-17).

1987:382), and as culturally constructed common sense they do not represent cognitive organization but rather operating strategies for using cultural knowledge in the world (1987:380).

In terms of the mode of analysis I worked with two perspectives. The first is grounded in the empirical material and actors' viewpoints. The second moves from the data to more abstract conceptions that represent ideas that are distanced from local and everyday viewpoints. Alvesson and Sköldberg describe this difference in styles as based in the dimension of 'distance to that which is studied' (2000:33). The approach that I have used for working closely with the empirical material is most closely related to grounded theory.[12] However, I did not strictly follow that method from beginning to end. What did influence me throughout the entire project was the emphasis on induction and asking questions that look for distinctions, comparisons, and relationships from the very beginning. After completing the systematic data collection I began to interview people, following up on questions and leads from the material that were of interest to me. With a growing amount of interview and observational material I reorganized everything into a database and then used the coding paradigm suggested by Strauss in *Qualitative Analysis for Social Scientists* (1987) to do an initial round of coding and memo writing. This work clarified several key categories that then became the basis for further interviewing to expand and clarify, and more memoing on these subjects.

---

[12] Grounded theory was developed by Barney Glaser and Anselm Strauss in the 1967 book *The Discovery of Grounded Theory* (Glaser & Strauss, 1967). It has become the most widely used qualitative interpretive framework (Alvesson & Skoldberg, 2000:12) and is considered the major contributor to helping qualitative methods gain legitimacy in the social sciences (Thomas & James, 2005:1). Charmaz notes some of the critique that has been generated both within and without the grounded theory camp (2000:509-10). There is a clear literary trail that can be traced which shows the later developments where Glaser and Strauss (along with his new coauthor Juliet Corbin) part ways (Charmaz, 2000:509-10; Stern, 1994:212-13). Stern notes the Glaserian school can still be called grounded theory, while the Straussian school is better labeled 'conceptual description' (Stern, 1994:213).

Bibliography

ABBREVIATIONS

CUSRI	The Chulalongkorn University Social Research Institute
BMA	Bangkok Metropolitan Authority
CDO	Community Development Office
CODI	Community of Organizations Development Institute
MOB	Municipality of Bangkok
NSO	National Statistical Office
NHA	National Housing Authority
TPRD	The Public Relations Department, Office of the Prime Minister
OPM	Office of the Prime Minister
TDRI	Thailand Development Research Institute
PWDO	Pathum Wan District Office
PWCDO	Pathum Wan Community Development Office

PRIMARY SOURCES

Government Publications

BMA. (1999). *Jaak thetsabaal suu krung thep mahanakorn* [From municipality to the city of angels, the great city]. Bangkok: Chuan Pim Publishing.

BMA. (2006). Bangkok: General information. Available at: http://www.bma.go.th/bmaeng/body_general.html [2006, 5 June].

BMA. (n.d.). *Krung thep maha nakorn: Nangsuu naenam krung thep mahanakorn* [Krung Thep Mahanakorn: A book introducing Krung Thep Mahanakorn]. Bangkok: Media Active Ltd.

CDO. (1994). *Khawmun chumchon krung thep mahanakorn* [Chumchon statistics for Bangkok]. Bangkok: Community Development Office.

CDO. (1996). *Aekasaan gaan pattana chumchon khong krun thep mahanakorn* [Documents on community development of the Bangkok Metropolitan Authority]. Bangkok: Community Development Office, Bangkok Metropolitan Administration.

CDO. (Ed.). (2001). *Khawmun chumchon krung thep mahanakon* [Chumchon statistics for Bangkok]. Bangkok: Wiranin Publishing.

CDO. (2001). *Khawmun chumchon krung thep mahanakorn* [Chumchon statistics for Bangkok]. Bangkok: Department of Research and Planning, Community Development Office, Bangkok Metropolitan Administration.

CDO. (2002). *10 bii samnakngaan pattana chumchon* [10 years of the Community Development Office]. Bangkok: Community Development Office, Bangkok Metropolitan Administration.

CDO. (n.d.). *Khumuu batibat ngaan gamagaan chumchon* [Manual for the work of community committees]. Bangkok: Community Development Office, Bangkok Metropolitan Administration.

NESDB. (1999). Country paper on poverty measurement in Thailand. Available at: http://www.unescap.org/Stat/meet/povstat/pov7_thi.pdf [2006, 13 June].

NESDB. (2006). Thailand's official poverty lines. Available at: http://www.nscb.gov.ph/poverty/conference/papers/7_Thai%20official%20poverty.pdf [2006, 13 June].

NHA. (1997). *Raay ngaan phol gaansamruat crowded communities in krung thep mahanakorn* [Report on the survey of crowded slum communities in Bangkok]. Bangkok: National Housing Administration.

NSO. (2000). *Phaen thii lae khawmun phuunthaan khong krung thep mahanakorn 2543* [Map and basic data of Bangkok 2000]. Bangkok: National Statistical Office, Office of the Prime Minister.

PWCDO. (2002). *Chumchon lang wat pathum wanaram* [Lang Wat Pathum Wanaram Community]. Bangkok: Pathum Wan Community Development Office.

PWDO. (2002). *Khawmun: Gan batibat naa thii khong fai pattana chumchon lae sawatigan sangkom* [Data: The work of the community development and social welfare divisions]. Bangkok: Pathum Wan District Office, Bangkok Metropolitan Administration.

Interviews

6 Jan. 2004	#16 *Nakleng*
13 Jan. 2004	#19 Somchai on slum leadership
14 Jan. 2004	#23 Election process and slum leadership history of *Fai Pat*
7 Dec. 2003	#26 Interview at hospital
28 Jan. 2004	#28 Interview on relation of 21 terms to slum leaders
21 Jan. 2004	#31 Interview on the work of the leaders in the community
21 Jan. 2004	#32 Interview on work of the committee
21 Jan. 2004	#33 Interview on working of the committee
21 Jan. 2004	#34 Interview on working of the committee
19 Dec. 2002	#64 Workings of the slum committee
1 Jan. 2003	#65 History of the slum
3 Jan. 2003	#66 On slum committee
31 Jan. 2003	#67 On slum life in general
30 Jan. 2003	#68 *Nakleng*
28 Mar. 2003	#69 Work as leaders
24 Jun. 2003	#70 Good character definition and expansion of key concepts
24 Jun. 2003	#71 Motivations for leadership
5 Dec. 2003	#72 On work in slum, King's birthday
4 Jul. 2003	#84 Kai at District Office on questions
28 Jan. 2004	#113 Interview on term definition-*khon dii, nisai dii, jai dii*
28 Jan. 2004	#114 Talking about the role of the committee
28 Jan. 2004	#115 Talk with person running for new committee
4 Feb. 2004	#117 Pairs definitions and clarification
11 Feb. 2003	#120 On meanings of key terms

29 Feb. 2004 #129 Talking about term definitions
29 Feb. 2004 #130 Interview with Ni. on terms, *temroi*
16 Mar. 2004 #132 Interview with new committee on situation with new construction
16 Mar. 2004 #133 Questions for the new president, some term definitions
16 Mar. 2004 #134 Defining words, term discussions
17 Mar. 2004 #137 Defining the 'good person'
15 Jan. 2003 #140 Interview on how the festivals are planned
15 Jan. 2003 #141 Notes on elections/appointment for the slum committee
11 Jul. 2003 #144 The work of the committee
1 Dec. 2003 #146 On becoming president, role of committee
31 Mar. 2003 #148 Talk with Lek
4 Feb. 2004 #150 Talk with a person running for the committee
7 Apr. 2003 #153 On work in committee, running again, problems in being a leader
17 Feb. 2004 #177 New committee and old committee members
28 Jan. 2004 #178 Meaning of *khon dii*
26 May 2004 #185 Clarification on Community Development Office
24 Jun. 2004 #199 Questions on what constitutes development
24 Jun. 2004 #200 On development, groups, eviction
24 Jun. 2004 #201 On moving house registration, *pattana*, what do leaders do?
10 Aug. 2004 #226 Miscellaneous questions filling in the gaps
22 Sep. 2004 #229 Community Development Department on history
22 Sep. 2004 #231 On leadership prior to current committee system
24 Feb. 2005 #254 Questions on governance and slum communities
23 Feb. 2005 #256 Clarifications with L.P. and D.
23 Feb. 2005 #257 History interview on the community and governance
16 Mar. 2005 #261 Clarification on founding of committee and *samakhii*
17 Mar. 2005 #262 Discussion with Namchai on relationship of state to *chumchon*
18 Mar. 2005 #264 Questions about formation of committees in *chumchons*
13 Apr. 2005 #265 Discussion on formation of committee
23 Apr. 2005 #273 Definition of *tua khrai tua man*
7 Aug. 2005 #274 Discussion with Phut in Khlong Beng
28 Aug. 2005 #275 Talk about *samakhii*
7 Aug. 2005 #279 Conversation with Ut at Khlong Beng
7 Aug. 2005 #280 Conversation with Supapon the head of *Fai Pat* Wattana
14 Jan. 2004 #281 21 terms definitions interviews
18 Oct. 2005 #289 Comments on leadership, Na Ali on forming leadership
27 Oct. 2005 #293 Filling in gaps questions
27 Oct. 2005 #294 Clarification on *luuk phii* and *luuk nong* and *nakleng*
27 Oct. 2005 #295 On *chuathuu*, *nakleng*, and patron-client
27 Oct. 2005 #296 History interview and work on *nakleng* and people who are *dang*
12 Nov. 2005 #302 Interview at centre on work day for cleaning landing at khlong
12 Nov. 2005 #303 History interview with M.
12 Nov. 2005 #304 Map of the *chumchon*
11 Nov. 2005 #305 Talk on *samakhii* in *chumchon*
14 Nov. 2005 #307 On bonds of relation influence and power

20 Nov. 2005	#308 Conversation on *kreng jai* and patron-client
1 Dec. 2005	#320 On *kreng jai* and *kreng glua*
21 Nov. 2005	#321 On *kreng jai* and *kreng glua*
3 Dec. 2005	#323 Interview on early committee history
5 Dec. 2005	#328 Looking at how bonds are created across social distance
10 Dec. 2005	#329 Conversation on *nakleng*, comments on the TLM
14 Feb. 2006	#336 On *bunkhun* and its limitations with T.
9 Feb. 2006	#337 Conversation with irrigation engineer on train from Chiang Mai
16 Mar. 2006	#338 On how *win motorcy* were changed under Thaksin
4 Mar. 2006	#339 On ideal culture versus actual behaviour and the tensions
28 Feb. 2004	#128 Interview with L.P. on his work on the committee and president
16 Mar. 2004	#184 On the key terms
12 May 2004	#202 On projects inside the *chumchon*
30 May 2004	#203 D. Parts 1 and 2 general interview
18 Apr. 2006	#341 Final interviews in LWPW
18 Apr. 2006	#342 Final interviews on slum conditions

Focus groups

30 Oct. 2005	#300 Focus group interview on *nakleng*, relationships
23 Nov. 2005	#319 Focus group on *kreng jai* and *kreng klua bunkhun* clarifications
4 Dec. 2005	#325 Focus group on relational bonds

Participant observations

10 Jan. 2004	#18 Children's Day 2004
11 Jan. 2003	#85 Children's Day 2003
27 Jan. 2003	#86 Monthly slum committee meeting
19 Dec. 2002	#87 Anti-drug day
28 Mar. 2003	#88 Monthly meeting at the District Office for *chumchon* leaders
13 Apr. 2003	#89 Thai New Year 2003
5 Dec. 2003	#90 The King's birthday celebration 2003
16 Feb. 2004	#119 The official appointment of the new slum committee
12 Nov. 2005	#306 Participant observation on cleaning landing day
20 Nov. 2005	#309 Observing a community meeting at Lang Saw Naw
3 Dec. 2005	#324 Cleaning the flats day
5 Dec. 2005	#327 Participant observation of the King's birthday celebration 2005
1 Jul. 2003	#335 Khao Pansaa

SECONDARY SOURCES

2Bangkok.com. (2006). *Bangkok's crucible of construction.* Available at: http://2Bangkok. com/ 2bangkok/ MassTransit/crucible.shtml [2006, 14 June].

Akimoto, T. (1998). When and how do slums disappear? In T. Akimoto (Ed.), *Shrinkage of urban slums in Asia and their employment aspects* (pp. 1-64). Bangkok: ILO Regional Office for Asia and the Pacific.

Akin Rabibhadana. (1975a). Clientship and class structure in the early Bangkok period. In G.W. Skinner & A.T. Kirsch (Eds.), *Change and persistence in Thai society* (pp. 93-124). Ithaca, New York: Cornell University Press.

Akin Rabibhadana. (1975b). *Bangkok slum: Aspects of social organization*. Unpublished Ph.D. dissertation, Cornell University.

Alvesson, M., & Skoldberg, K. (2000). *Reflexive methodology: New vistas of qualitative research*. London: Sage.

Anderson, B. (1978). Studies of the Thai state: The state of Thai studies. In E.B. Ayal (Ed.), *The study of Thailand: Analyses of knowledge, approaches, and prospects in anthropology, art history, economics, history and political science*. (Vol. 54, pp. 193-247). Athens, Ohio: Ohio University, Center for International Studies, Southeast Asia Program.

Anderson, B. (1991). *Imagined communities: Reflections on the origin and spread of nationalism* (Revised ed.). London: Verso.

Arghiros, D. (2001). *Democracy, development and decentralization in provincial Thailand* (Vol. 8). Richmond, Surrey: Curzon Press.

Askew, M. (1994). Bangkok: Transformation of the Thai city. In M. Askew & W.S. Logan (Eds.), *Cultural identity and urban change in Southeast Asia: Interpretive essays* (pp. 85-116). Geelong, Victoria, Australia: Deakin University Press.

Askew, M. (2002). *Bangkok: Place, practice and representation*. London: Routledge.

AUA Language Center Library. (1971). *The history and culture of Thailand: A bibliography*. Bangkok: AUA Language Center.

Ayal, E.B. (1978). Introduction. In E.B. Ayal (Ed.), *The study of Thailand: Analyses of knowledge, approaches, and prospects in anthropology, art history, economics, history and political science*. (Vol. 54, pp. vii-xi). Athens, Ohio. Ohio University, Center for International Studies, Southeast Asia Program.

Aymot, J., & Suthep Soontornpashuch. (1965). *Provisional paper on changing patterns of social structure in Thailand, 1851-1965: An annotated bibliography with comments*. Delhi, India: UNESCO Research Centre.

Baker, C., & Phongpaichit, P. (2005). *A history of Thailand*. Cambridge: Cambridge University Press.

Barnett, J.E. (1998). *Time's pendulum: From sundials to atomic clocks, the fascinating history of timekeeping and how our discoveries changed the world*. San Diego, California: Harvest.

Basham, R. (1989). 'False consciousness' and the problem of merit and power in Thailand. *Mankind*, 126-37.

Bass, B. (1990). *Bass and Stodgill's handbook of leadership: Theory, research and managerial applications* (3rd ed.). New York: The Free Press.

Bass, B.M. (1997). Does the transactional-transformational leadership paradigm transcend organizational and national boundaries? *American Psychologist*, 52, 130-39.

Bechstedt, H.-D. (1987). *Change and persistence in Thai rural society: An empirical study of hierarchical relations and their psychological manifestation*. Unpublished Ph.D., University of Bielefeld.

Behe, M.J. (1996). *Darwin's black box*. New York: The Free Press.

Bello, W., Cunningham, S., & Pho, L.K. (1998). *A Siamese tragedy: Development and disintegration in modern Thailand.* London: Zed Books.

Bernard, H.R. (1988). *Research methods in cultural anthropology.* Newbury Park, California: Sage.

Bernard, H.R. (1995). *Research methods in anthropology: Qualitative and quantitative approaches* (2nd ed.). London: AltaMira Press.

Bilmes, J. (1996). Villages and officials: Toward a model of Northern Thai village social organization, *Proceeding of the 6th international conference on Thai studies theme VII toward a new frontier of Thai studies* (pp. 1-12). Chiang Mai, Thailand.

Birner, R., & Wittmer, H. (2003). Using social capital to create political capital: How do local communities gain political influence? A theoretical approach and empirical evidence from Thailand. In N. Dolsak & E. Ostrom (Eds.), *The commons in the new millennium: Challenges and adaptation* (pp. 291-334). Cambridge, Massachusetts: MIT Press.

Blanc Szanton, M.C. (1982). *People in movement: Mobility and leadership in a central Thai town.* Unpublished Ph.D. dissertation, Columbia University.

Bordieu, P. (1992). Okonomisches kapital-kulturelles kapital-soziales kapital [Economic capital-cultural capital-social capital], *Die verborgenen mechanismen der mach [The hidden mechanisms of power]* (Vol. 1). Hamburg: VSA-Verlag.

Borgatti, S.P. (1990). ANTHROPAC 4.0 methods guide. Natrick, MA: Analytic Technologies.

Brummelhuis, H. ten. (1984). Abundance and avoidance: An interpretation of Thai individualism. In H. ten Brummelhuis & J.H. Kemp (Eds.), *Strategies and structures in Thai society* (Vol. 31, pp. 39-54). Amsterdam: Anthropological-Sociological Centre, University of Amsterdam.

Brummelhuis, H. ten., & Kemp, J.H. (1984). Introduction: Issues in the development of the study of Thai society. In H. ten Brummelhuis & J.H. Kemp (Eds.), *Strategies and structures in Thai society* (Vol. 31, pp. 9-18). Amsterdam: Anthropological-Sociological Centre, University of Amsterdam.

Bruner, J. (1986). *Actual minds, possible worlds.* Cambridge, Massachusetts: Harvard University Press.

Bryman, A. (1984). The debate above quantitative and qualitative research: A question of method or epistemology. *British Journal of Sociology*, 35(1), 75-92.

Bryman, A., Bresnen, M.J., Beardsworth, A., & Keil, T. (1988). Qualitative research and the study of leadership. *Human Relations*, 41(1), 13-30.

Burr, V. (1995). *An introduction to social constructionism.* London: Routledge.

Calhoun, C. (1996). Social theory and the public sphere. In B.S. Turner (Ed.), *The Blackwell companion to social theory* (pp. 429-70). Oxford, U.K.: Blackwell Publishers.

Carrithers, M. (1992). *Why humans have cultures: Explaining anthropology and social diversity.* Oxford: Oxford University Press.

Cattell, R. (1968). Traits. In D.L. Sills (Ed.), *International encyclopedia of the social sciences* (Vol. 16, pp. 123-28): The Macmillan Company and the Free Press.

Central Library of Chulalongkorn University. (1960). *Bibliography of material about Thailand in western languages.* Bangkok: Chulalongkorn University.

Chai-anan Samudavanija. (1987a). The bureaucracy. In S. Xuto (Ed.), *Government and politics in Thailand* (pp. 75-109). Singapore: Oxford University Press.

Chai-anan Samudavanija. (1987b). Political history. In S. Xuto (Ed.), *Government and politics in Thailand* (pp. 1-40). Singapore: Oxford University Press.

Chakrit Noranitipadungkarn. (1981). *Elites, power structure and politics in Thai communities*. Bangkok, Thailand: The National Institute of Development Administration.

Charmaz, K. (2000). Grounded theory: Objectivist and constructivist methods. In N.K. Denzin & Y.S. Lincoln (Eds.), *The handbook of qualitative research* (2nd ed., pp. 509-35). Thousand Oaks, CA: Sage.

Chuanpis Chaimuenvong. (2004). *National Housing Authority*. The Post Publishing Company. Available at: http://www.bangkokpost.net/58years/nati.html [2006, 7 June].

Chulalongkorn University. (1999). *Pathum wana*. Bangkok: Chulalongkorn University Press.

CIA World Factbook. (2006). *Thailand*. Central Intelligence Agency. Available at: http://www.cia.gov/cia/publications/factbook/geos/th.html#Issues [2006, 16 May 2006].

Cimatu, F. (2003). *Shades of Manila slums in Bangkok*. Available at: http://www.inq7.net/brk/2003/oct/20/brkpol_3-1.htm [2005, 14 April].

Clammer, J. (1984). Approaches to ethnographic research. In R.F. Ellen (Ed.), *Ethnographic research: A guide to general conduct* (Vol. 1, pp. 63-85). London: Academic Press.

CODI. (2005). *Problems of the poor and the role of CODI*. Community of Organizations Development Institute. Available at: http://www.codi.or.th/index.php?option=displaypage&Itemid=108&op=page&SubMenu= [2005, 14 July].

Cohen, E. (Ed.). (1991). *Thai society in comparative perspective: Collected essays*. Bangkok: White Lotus.

Coleman, J. (1988). Social capital in the creation of human capital. *American Journal of Sociology*, 94, S95-S120.

Conner, D. (1996). *Personal power, authority, and influence: Cultural foundations for leadership and leadership formation in Northeast Thailand and implications for adult leadership training*. Unpublished Ph.D. dissertation, Northern Illinois University, Dekalb, Illinois.

Dahl, R.A. (1968). Power. In D.L. Sills (Ed.), *International encyclopedia of the social sciences* (Vol. 12, pp. 405-15): The Macmillan Company.

D'Andrade, R. (1995). *The development of cognitive anthropology*. Cambridge: Cambridge University Press.

Daniere, A.G., & Takahashi, L.M. (1999). Environmental behavior in Bangkok, Thailand: A portrait of attitudes, values, and behavior. *Economic Development and Cultural Change*, 47(3), 525-57.

Dansereau, F., & Yammarino, F.J. (1998a). Introduction and overview, *Leadership: The multiple-level approaches classical and new wave* (Vol. 24A, pp. xxv-xliii). Stamford, CT: JAI Press.

Dasgupta, P. (2000). Economic progress and the idea of social capital. In P. Dasgupta & I. Serageldin (Eds.), *Social capital: A multifaceted perspective* (pp. 325-424). Washington, D.C.: World Bank.

Dasgupta, P., & Serageldin, I. (Eds.). (2000). *Social capital: A multifaceted perspective*. Washington, D.C.: World Bank.

Demaine, H. (1986). Kanpatthana: Thai views of development. In M. Hobart & R.H. Taylor (Eds.), *Context, meaning and power in Southeast Asia* (pp. 93-114). Ithaca, NY: Cornell University Southeast Asia Program.

Den Hartog, D.N., House, R.J., Henges, P.J., Ruiz-Qintanilla, S.S., & *et al.* (1999). Emics and etics of culturally endorsed implicit leadership theories: Are attributes of charismatic/transformational leadership universally endorsed? *Leadership Quarterly*, 10(2), 219-56.

Denzin, N.K., & Lincoln, Y.S. (1998). Introduction: Entering the field of qualitative research. In N.K. Denzin & Y.S. Lincoln (Eds.), *The landscape of qualitative research: Theories and issues* (pp. 1-34). London: Sage.

Dirks, K.T., & Skarlicki, D.P. (2004). Trust in leaders: Existing research and emerging issues. In R. Kramer, M. & K.S. Cook (Eds.), *Trust and distrust in organizations: Dilemmas and approaches* (Vol. VII, pp. 21-40). New York: Russell Sage Foundation.

Dixon, C. (1999). *The Thai economy: Uneven development and internationalisation.* London: Routledge.

Dubrin, A.J. (1998). *Leadership: Research, findings, practice and skills* (2nd ed.). Boston: Houghton Mifflin.

Duncan, H.S. (1980). *The social organization of irrigation: A study of the Channasut land consolidation project in Thailand.* Unpublished Ph.D. dissertation, University of California, Los Angeles.

Durrenberger, E.P. (1996). The power of culture and the culture of states. In E.P. Durrenberger (Ed.), *State power and culture in Thailand* (Vol. Monograph 44, pp. 1-21). New Haven, CT: Yale University Southeast Asia Studies.

Evers, H.-D., & Korff, R. (2000). *Southeast Asian urbanism: The meaning and power of social space.* Singapore: Institute of Southeast Asian Studies.

Fukuyama, F. (1995). *Trust: The social virtues and creation of prosperity.* London: Hamish Hamilton.

Geertz, C. (1973). *The interpretation of cultures.* Basic Books.

Geertz, C. (1995). *After the fact: Two countries, four decades, one anthropologist.* Cambridge, Massachusetts: Harvard University Press.

Giddens, A. (1987). *Social theory and modern sociology.* Stanford, CA: Stanford University Press.

Girling, J. (1996). *Interpreting development: Capitalism, democracy, and the middle class in Thailand.* Ithaca, New York: Cornell University, Southeast Asia Program,.

Girling, J.L.S. (1981). *Thailand: Society and politics.* Ithaca, NY: Cornell University Press.

Girling, J.L.S. (1984). Thailand in Gramscian perspective. *Pacific Affairs*, 57(3), 385-403.

Glaser, B.G., & Strauss, A.L. (1967). *The discovery of grounded theory: Strategies for qualitative research.* New York: Aldine Publishing.

Glock, C., & Stark, R. (1965). *Religion and society in tension.* Chicago: Rand McNally.

Guba, E.G., & Lincoln, Y.S. (1998). Competing paradigms in qualitative research. In N. K. Denzin & Y.S. Lincoln (Eds.), *The landscape of qualitative research: Theories and issues* (pp. 195-220). London: Sage.

Haas, M.R. (1964). *Thai-English student's dictionary.* London: Oxford University Press.

Hallinger, P., & Pornkasem Kantamara. (2000). Educational change in Thailand: Opening a window onto leadership as a cultural process. *School Leadership & Management*, 20(2), 189-205.

Hammersley, M., & Atkinson, P. (1995). *Ethnography: Principles in practice* (2nd ed.). London: Routledge.

Handwerker, W.P., & Borgatti, S.P. (1998). Reasoning with numbers. In H.R. Bernard (Ed.), *Handbook of methods in cultural anthropology* (pp. 549-93). Walnut Creek, California: Altamira Press.

Hanks, L.M.J. (1962). Merit and power in the Thai social order. *American Anthropologist*, 64, 1247-261.

Hanks, L.M.J. (1975). The Thai social order as entourage and social circle. In G.W. Skinner & A.T. Kirsch (Eds.), *Change and persistence in Thai society* (pp. 197-218). Ithaca, NY: Cornell University Press.

Henderson, J.W., Barth, H.A., Heimann, J.M., Moeller, P.W., Shinn, R.-S., Soriano, F.S., Weaver, J.O., & White, E.T. (1971). *Area handbook for Thailand.* Washington, D.C.: U.S. Government Printing Office.

Herzfeld, M. (2001). *Anthropology: Theoretical practice in culture and society*. Malden, MA: Blackwell.

Hobsbawm, E. (1973). Peasants and politics. *Journal of Peasant Studies*, 1(1), 3-22.

House, R.J., Hanges, P.J., Javidan, M., Dorfman, P.W., & Gupta, V. (Eds.). (2004). *Culture, leadership and organizations: The globe study of 62 societies*. Thousand Oaks, CA: Sage.

Iliffe, J. (1987). *The African poor: A history*. Cambridge: Cambridge University Press.

Institute of Developing Economies, (1972). *Union catalogue of Thai materials I.* Tokyo, Japan: Institute of Developing Economies.

Jareonrat Saranuwat. (2005). *Brab pang...Lae muang hai yang yuun [Adjust the plan and the city will endure]*. Thailand Environment Institute. Available at: http://www.tel.or.th/PliBai/th_plibai55_2.htm [2005, 5 May 2005].

Johnson, A.R. (2002). *The language of leadership in Thailand.* Unpublished M.A. thesis, Azusa Pacific University, Azusa, CA.

Johnson, T.E. (1979). *Urban social structure: A case study of slums in Bangkok, Thailand.*

Kanter, R.M. (1979). How the top is different. In R.M. Kanter & B. Stein (Eds.), *Life in organizations: Workplaces as people experience them* (pp. 20-35). New York: Bantam Books.

Kanungo, R.N., & Mendonca, M. (1996). Cultural contingencies and leadership in developing countries. In P.A. Bamberger & M. Erez & S.B. Bacharach (Eds.), *Cross-cultural analysis of organizations* (Vol. 14, pp. 263-96). Greenwich, CT: JAI.

Kaplan, D., & Manners, R. (1972). *Culture theory*. Englewood Cliffs, NJ: Prentice-Hall.

Kaufman, H.K. (1960). *Bangkhuad: A community study in Thailand.* Locust Valley, NY: J.J. Augustin.

Keesing, R. (1987). Models "folk" and "cultural": Paradigms regained? In D.C. Holland & N. Quinn (Eds.), *Cultural models in language and thought* (pp. 369-393). Cambridge: Cambridge University Press.

Kemp, J.H. (1982). A tail wagging the dog: The patron-client model in Thai studies. In C. Clapham (Ed.), *Private patronage and public power* (pp. 142-61). London: Frances Pinter.

Kemp, J.H. (1984). The manipulation of personal relations: From kinship to patron-clientage. In H. ten Brummelhuis & J.H. Kemp (Eds.), *Strategies and structures in Thai society* (pp. 55-69). Amsterdam: Anthropological-Sociological Centre, University of Amsterdam.

Keyes, C. (1978). Ethnography and anthropological interpretation in the study of Thailand. In E.B. Ayal (Ed.), *The study of Thailand: Analyses of knowledge, approaches, and prospects in anthropology, art history, economics, history and political science.* (Vol. 54, pp. 1-60). Athens, Ohio: Ohio University, Center for International Studies, Southeast Asia Program.

Keyes, C. (1979a). Local leadership in rural Thailand. In C.D. Neher (Ed.), *Modern Thai politics: From village to nation* (pp. 219-49). Cambridge, MA: Schenkman Publishing.

Keyes, C. (1979b). *Southeast Asian research tools* (Vol. Southeast Asia Paper No. 16, Part VI). Honolulu, Hawaii: University of Hawaii.

Keyes, C. (1987). *Thailand: Buddhist kingdom as modern nation-state*. Boulder, CO: Westview Press.

Keyes, C. (2006). *Thailand bibliography*. Available at:http://www.lib.washington.edu/southeastasia/bthaiab.html [2006, 25 May].

Kilduff, M., & Mehra, A. (1997). Postmodernism and organizational research. *Academy of Management Review*, 22(2), 453-81.

Klausner, W. (1966). The "cool heart": Social relationship in a northeastern Thai village. *Warasan Sangkomsat [The Journal of the Social Sciences]*, 4(2), 117-24.

Klausner, W.J. (1997). *Thai culture in transition: Collected writings of William J. Klausner*. Bangkok: Siam Society.

Knight, P.T. (2002). *Small-scale research: Pragmatic inquiry in social science and the caring professions*. London: Sage.

Kouzes, J.M., & Posner, B.Z. (1993). *Credibility: How leaders gain and lose it, why people demand it*. San Francisco, CA: Jossey-Bass.

Kramer, R., M., & Cook, K.S. (2004). Trust and distrust in organizations: Dilemmas and approaches. In R. Kramer, M. & K.S. Cook (Eds.), *Trust and distrust in organizations: Dilemmas and approaches* (Vol. VII, pp. 1-18). New York: Russell Sage Foundation.

Kroeber, A.L., & Kluckhohn, C. (1963). *Culture: A critical review of concepts and definitions*. New York: Vintage Books.

Lahmeyer, J. (2002). *Thailand: Historical demographical data of the whole country*. Population Statistics. Available at: http://www.library.uu.nl/wesp/populstat/Asia/thailand.htm [2006, 16 May].

Lane, C. (1998). Introduction: Theories and issues in the study of trust. In C. Lane & R. Bachmann (Eds.), *Trust within and between organizations: Conceptual issues and empirical applications* (pp. 1-30). Oxford: Oxford University Press.

Library of Congress. (2006). *Thailand bibliography*. Available at: http://lcweb2.loc.gov/frd/cs/thailand/th_bibl.html [2006, 25 May].

Likhit Dhiravegen. (1973). *Political attitudes of the bureaucratic elite and modernization in Thailand.* Bangkok: Thai Watana Panich.

Ling, W., Chia, R.C., & Fang, L. (2000). Chinese implicit leadership theory. The Journal of Social Psychology, 140(6), 729-39.

Lord, R.G., & Maher, K.J. (1991). *Leadership and information processing: Linking perceptions and performance*. Boston: Unwin Hyman.

Manoonate Kamontat. (1981). *A comparative study of the attributes on the "natural opinion leaders" as identified sociemetrically by border patrol police and those as "followers" in communist infested villages in Sanangkanikom Sub-District, Ubon-ratchathani Province.* Unpublished M.A. thesis, Chulalongkorn University, Bangkok.

Mason, J.B. (1958). *Thailand bibliography.* Gainesville: University of Florida.

Mauss, M. (1990). *The gift: The form and reason for exchange in archaic societies* (W.D. Halls, Trans.). London: Routledge.

McCargo, D.J. (1993). *The political leadership of Major-General Chamlong Srimuang.* Unpublished Ph.D. dissertation, University of London, London.

Mehdi Krongkaew, Vorawoot Hirunrak, & Orathai Arj-aum. (1987). *A study on the urban poor in Thailand: Phase II.* Bangkok: Thai Kadi Research Institute, Thammasat University.

Millar, D. (1971). Patron-client relations in Thailand. *Cornell Journal of Social Relations*, 6(2), 215-25.

Mintzberg, H. (1982). If you're not serving Bill and Barbara, then you're not serving leadership. In J.G. Hunt & U. Sekaran & C.A. Schriesheim (Eds.), *Leadership: Beyond establishment views.* Carbondale, IL: Southern Illinois University Press.

Missingham, B.D. (2003). *The Assembly of the Poor in Thailand: From local struggles to national protest movement.* Bangkok, Thailand: Silkworm Books.

MOB. (1965). *The municipality of Bangkok-1965: The administration and role of Thailand's capital city.* Bangkok: Municipality of Bangkok.

MOB. (1969). *Municipality of Bangkok: The administration of the capital of Thailand.* Bangkok: Municipality of Bangkok.

Moerman, M. (1969). A Thai village headman as a synaptic leader. *Journal of Asian Studies*, 28(3), 535-50.

Montri Supaporn. (1984). *The role performance of prime ministers in the Thai political system: Styles of military and civilian rule 1932-1983.* Unpublished Ph.D. dissertation, Case Western Reserve University.

Moore, C.G. (1992). *Heart talk.* Bangkok: White Lotus.

Mosel, J.N. (1959). Thai administrative behavior. In W. Siffin (Ed.), *Toward the comparative study of public administration* (pp. 278-331). Bloomington, Indiana: Indiana University Press.

Mulder, N. (1997). *Thai images: The culture of the public world.* Bangkok, Thailand: Silkworm Books.

Mulder, N. (2000). *Inside Thai society: An interpretation of everyday life.* Chiang Mai: Silkworm Books.

Nalini Tanthuwanit, Naalini Srikasikul, Manirat Mitbrasaat, & Nisakawn Uuypat. (1998). *Wiwatanagaan chumchon ae at lae onggaan chumchon ae at nai muang: Garanii suksaa krung thep mahanakorn* [The evolution of slum communities and slum community organizations in the city: A case study of Bangkok]. In *Munithi Saphaa Wijai Lae Patana Chumchon Muang Samnakngaan Sapsin Suan Phramahakasat* [Foundation for Research and Urban Community Development of the Crown Property Bureau] (Ed.), *Kronggaan wijai lae batibat wijai wiwatanagaan chumchon ae at lae onggaan chumchon ae at nai muang: Raingaan gaan suksaa* [Research and evolution of slum communities and slum community organizations in the city project: A research report] (pp. 187-255). Bangkok: Bureau of Research Support.

Nattaya Chetchotiros. (2006). *Thailand general election 2005: Thai Rak Thai still leads in close fight for Bangkok.* Bangkok Post. Available at: http://www.bangkokpost.net/election2005/thairakthai.html [2006, 14 June].

Nelson, M. (2006). *Thai politics bibliography.* Available at: http://www.leeds.ac.uk/thaipol/Bibliog.htm [2006, 25 May].

NHA. (2006). *National Housing Authority.* Available at: http://www.nhanet.or.th/eng/aboutnha.html [2006, 5 June].

Ockey, J. (1996). Thai society and patterns of political leadership. *Asian Survey*, 36(4), 345-60.

Ockey, J. (2004a). State, bureaucracy and polity in modern Thai politics. *Journal of Contemporary Asia*, 34(3), 143-62.

Ockey, J. (2004b). *Making democracy: Leadership, class, gender and political participation in Thailand.* Honolulu, Hawaii: University of Hawaii Press.

Parsons, T. (1947). Introduction. In T. Parsons (Ed.), *The theory of social and economic organization* (pp. 3-86). New York: The Free Press.

Pasuk Phongpaichit, & Baker, C. (1996a). *Thailand: Economy and politics.* Kuala Lumpur: Oxford University Press.

Pasuk Phongpaichit, & Baker, C. (1996b). *Thailand's boom!* Chiang Mai: Silkworm Books.

Pasuk Phongpaichit, & Baker, C. (1998). *Thailand's boom and bust.* Chiang Mai, Thailand: Silkworm Books.

Pasuk Phongpaichit, & Baker, C. (2000). *Thailand's crisis.* Singapore: Institute of Southeast Asian Studies.

Pasuk Phongpaichit, & Sungsidh Piriyarangsan. (1994). *Corruption and democracy in Thailand* (2nd ed.). Bangkok: Silkworm Books.

Phillips, H.P. (1965). *Thai peasant personality: The patterning of interpersonal behaviour in the village of Bang Chan.* Berkeley: CA: University of California Press.

Piker, S. (1969). 'Loose structure' and the analysis of Thai social organization. In H. Evers (Ed.), *Loosely structured social systems: Thailand in comparative perspective.* New Haven, CT: Yale University Southeast Asian Studies.

Pira Chirasopone. (1983). *A study of agricultural opinion leaders in Thai villages.* Unpublished Ph.D. dissertation, Ohio University.

Pongsin Chuwattanakaul. (1993). *Perceived leadership style, style flexibility, and style effectiveness of government hospital administrators in Thailand.* Unpublished Ph.D. dissertation, Andrews University.

Potter, J.M. (1976). *Thai peasant social structure.* Chicago: The University of Chicago Press.

Prasan Wongyai. (1975). *Elite and power structure in Thailand.*

Pratana Pratitnayouth. (1999). *An identification of the most important perceived competencies of executives in commercial banks in Bangkok, Thailand.* Unpublished Ph.D. dissertation, Pennsylvania State University.

Punch, K.F. (1998). *Introduction to social research: Quantitative and qualitative approaches.* London: Sage.

Putnam, R.D., Leonardi, R., & Nanetti, R. (1993). *Making democracy work: Civic traditions in modern Italy.* Princeton: Princeton University Press.

Quinn, N., & Holland, D. (1987). Culture and cognition. In D.C. Holland & N. Quinn (Eds.), *Cultural models in language and thought* (pp. 3-42). Cambridge: Cambridge University Press.

Rachanee Wisessang. (1988). *Leadership styles, style flexibility, and style effectiveness of public secondary school principals in Thailand.* Unpublished Ph.D. dissertation, University of Alabama.

Radom Wongnom. (1980). *Opinion leadership and the elite in rural Thailand: A case study of two villages.* Unpublished Ph.D. dissertation, University of California, Los Angeles.

Rangsit Kosaidilok. (1993). *A descriptive study of the leadership style and ability of students in the Royal Thai Air Force Squadron Officer School.* Unpublished Ed.D. dissertation, University of San Francisco, San Francisco.

Reynolds, C.J. (2002). Introduction: National identity and its defenders. In C.J. Reynolds (Ed.), *National identity and its defenders: Thailand today* (Revised ed., pp. 1-32). Chiang Mai, Thailand: Silkworm Books.

Riggs, F.W. (1966). *Thailand: The modernization of a bureaucratic polity.* Honolulu, Hawaii: East-West Center Press.

Ritzer, G. (2000). *Classical sociological theory* (3rd ed.). Boston: McGraw Hill.

Romney, A.K., Weller, S., & Batchelder, W.H. (1986). Culture as consensus: A theory of culture and informant accuracy. *American Anthropologist,* 88(2), 313-38.

Rubin, H.J. (1979). Will and awe: Illustrations of Thai villager dependency upon officials. In C.D. Neher (Ed.), *Modern Thai politics: From village to nation* (pp. 290-317). Cambridge, MA: Schenkman Publishing.

Rubin, H.J. (1980). Rules, regulations, and the rural Thai bureaucracy. *Journal of Southeast Asian Studies,* 11(1), 50-73.

Samphan Techatik, Bricha Uytrakul, & Chuun Srisawat. (1990). *Sakayphaap lae khruakhaay phu nam thong thin: Khuu muu lae thitthaan gaanpattana phu nam chao baan pua kae banhaa nai chonabot* [The potential and networks of local leaders: A manual and direction for the development of village leaders in order to solve rural problems]. Khon Gaen, Thailand: *Sathaban Wijai lae Pattana Mahawitayalai Khon Gaen* [The Institute of Research and Development, University of Khon Gaen.

Sariya Sukhabanij. (1980). *An investigation of principal's leadership behavior as perceived by secondary school principals and teachers in Nakorn Pathom, Thailand.* Unpublished Ph.D. dissertation, University of North Texas.

Sarote Phornprapha. (1995). *The preferences of restaurant operative staff concerning leadership style: A study in Thailand.* Unpublished Ph.D. dissertation, Surrey.

Schon, D. (1982). *The reflective practitioner: How professionals think in action.* New York: Basic Books.

Schwandt, T.A. (1998). Constructivist, interpretivist approaches to human inquiry. In N.K. Denzin & Y.S. Lincoln (Eds.), *The landscape of qualitative research: Theories and issues* (pp. 221-59). London: Sage.

Schwandt, T.A. (2000). Three epistemological stances for qualitative inquiry. In N.K. Denzin & Y.S. Lincoln (Eds.), *The handbook of qualitative research* (2nd ed., pp. 189-213). Thousand Oaks, CA: Sage.

Scott, J.C. (1985). *Weapons of the weak: Everyday forms of peasant resistance.* New Haven, CT: Yale University Press.

Scott, J.C. (1990). *Domination and the arts of resistance: Hidden transcripts.* New Haven: Yale University Press.

Shin, H.-S. (1989). *Principles of church planting as illustrated in Thai Theravada Buddhist context.* Bangkok, Thailand: Kanok Bannasan (OMF Publishers).

Shore, B. (1996). *Culture in mind: Cognition, culture and the problem of meaning.* Oxford: Oxford University Press.

Siffin, W. (1966). *The Thai bureaucracy: Institutional change and development.* Honolulu, Hawaii: East-West Center Press, University of Hawaii.

Six, F. (2005). *The trouble with trust: The dynamics of interpersonal trust building.* Cheltenham, United Kingdom: Edward Elgar.

Slagter, R., & Kerbo, H.R. (2000). *Modern Thailand.* Boston, MA: McGraw Hill.

So Sethaputra. (1984). *New model Thai-English dictionary* (Vol. I). Bangkok: Thai Wattana Panich.

Somchai Rakwijit. (1971). *Kwam ben phunam nai mubaan tang phaak tawan awk chiang nua khong brathet Thai [Leadership in a northeastern village of Thailand].* Bangkok: Center of Research and Development for the Military between Thailand and America.

Somsook Boonyabancha. (2005a, 7 May 2001). *Citizen networks to address urban poverty-experiences of Urban Community Development Office, Thailand.* Available at: http://www.achr.net/networks2.htm [2005, 14 April].

Somsook Boonyabancha. (2005b). *A decade of change: From the Urban Community Development Office (UCDO) to the Community Organizations Development Institute (CODI),* [pdf]. HED Working Paper 12 on Poverty Reduction in Urban Areas. Available at: http://www.iied.org/docs/urban/urbpov_wp12.pdf [2005, 14 April].

Somsook Boonyabancha. (2005c). *The poor in Bangkok city.* Asian Coalition for Housing Rights. Available at: http://www.achr.net/th_overview.htm [2005, 14 April].

Sopon Pornchokchai. (1992). *Bangkok slums: Review and recommendations.* Bangkok: Agency for Real Estate Affairs.

Sopon Pornchokchai. (1998). The future of slums and their employment implications: The case of Bangkok. In T. Akimoto (Ed.), *Shrinkage of urban slums in Asia and their employment aspects* (pp. 415-59). Bangkok: ILO Regional Office for Asia and the Pacific.

Sopon Pornchokchai. (2003). City report: Bangkok, *Global Report on Human Settlements 2003* (pp. 32). Bangkok.

Sriwan Siribun, & Janphen Saengtianchaay. (1988). *Gan suksaa briab tiab chumchon ae at thii pattana laew lae yang mai dai pattana nai ket krung thep makah nakorn [A comparative study of congested communities that have already been developed and those that have not been developed in the Bangkok region].* Bangkok: Chulalongkorn University.

Start. (2006). *Workers seeking minimum wage hike to bt 233 per day.* Available at: http://www.start.co.th/index.php?pid=1&lang=xt&action=show&id=33&refer=1 [2006, 14 June].

Steers, R.M., Porter, L.W., & Bigley, G.A. (1996). Models of leadership. In R.M. Steers & L.W. Porter & G.A. Bigley (Eds.), *Motivation and leadership at work* (6th ed., pp. 166-85). New York: McGraw-Hill Companies Inc.

Stern, P.N. (1994). Eroding grounded theory. In J.M. Morse (Ed.), *Critical issues in qualitative research methods* (pp. 212-23). Thousand Oaks, CA: Sage.

Sternstein, L. (1973). Thailand. In G. Breese (Ed.), *Urban Southeast Asia: A selected bibliography of accessible research, reports and related materials on urbanism and urbanization* (pp. 115-34). New York: Southeast Asia Development Advisory Group of the Asia Society.

Strauss, A. (1987). *Qualitative analysis for social scientists*. Cambridge: Cambridge University Press.

Suntaree Komin. (1985). The world view through Thai value systems. In The Chulalongkorn University Social Research Institute (Ed.), *Traditional and changing Thai world view* (pp. 170-92). Bangkok: The Southeast Asian Studies Program/The Chulalongkorn University Social Research Institute.

Suntaree Komin. (1990). *Psychology of the Thai people: Values and behavior patterns*. Bangkok: National Institute of Development Administration (NIDA).

Suntaree Komin. (1994). *Value added perception of Thai effective leadership*. Paper presented at the Perception of leadership and cultural values, Symposium conducted at the Division of Organizational Psychology 23rd International Congress of Applied Psychology, Madrid, Spain.

Suntaree Komin. (28 September 2004). Meeting on term definitions. Bangkok.

Surin Maisrikrod. (1993). Emerging patterns of political leadership in Thailand. *Contemporary Southeast Asia*, 15, 80-97.

Tambiah, S.J. (1970). *Buddhism and the spirit cults in North-East Thailand* (Vol. 2). Cambridge: Cambridge University Press.

Tambiah, S.J. (1985). *Culture, thought and social action: An anthropological perspective*. Cambridge, MA: Harvard University Press.

Tanabe, S. (1984). Ideological practice in peasant rebellions: Siam at the turn of the twentieth century. In A. Turton & S. Tanabe (Eds.), *History and peasant consciousness in South East Asia* (Vol. 13, pp. 75-110). Osaka: National Museum of Ethnology.

Tawil Praisant. (1982). A brief history of the administration of Krung Thep Maha Nakon. In L. Sternstein (Ed.), *Portrait of Bangkok* (pp. xix-xxi). Bangkok: Bangkok Metropolitan Administration.

Terwiel, B.J. (1983). *A history of modern Thailand, 1767-1942*. St. Lucia: University of Queensland Press.

Terwiel, B.J. (1984). Formal structures and informal rules: An historical perspective on hierarchy, bondage, and the patron-client relationship. In H. ten Brummelhuis & J.H. Kemp (Eds.), *Strategies and structures in Thai society* (pp. 19-38). Amsterdam: Anthropological-Sociological Centre, University of Amsterdam.

Terwiel, B.J. (1991). *A window on Thai history* (2nd ed.). Bangkok: Duang Kamol.

Thinapan Nakata. (1975). *The problems of democracy in Thailand: A study of political culture and socialization of college students*. Bangkok: Praepittaya International.

Thinapan Nakata. (1987). Political culture: Problems of development of democracy. In S. Xuto (Ed.), *Government and politics in Thailand* (pp. 168-195). Singapore: Oxford University Press.

Thomas, G., & James, D. (2005). *Reinventing grounded theory: Some questions about theory, ground and discovery*. Available at: http://www.education.bham.ac.uk /aboutus/profiles/inclusion/thomas_gary/grounded%20theory%20paper%20for%20students.doc [2005, 21 October].

Thrombley, W.G., & Siffin, W.J. (1972). *Thailand politics, economy and socio-cultural setting: A selective guide to the literature*. Bloomington, Indiana: Indiana University Press.

Thrombley, W.G., Siffin, W.J., & Pensri Vayavananda. (1967). *Thai government and its setting: A selective, annotated bibliography*. Bangkok: National Institute of Development Administration.

Titaya Suvanajata. (1976). Is the Thai social system loosely structured? *Social Science Review*, 1, 171-87.

Titie Tinsulanonda. (1997). *A study of the relationship between leadership style and motivation of the Royal Thai Army officers*. Unpublished Ph.D., Nova Southeastern University.

TPRD. (2000). *The Thai government and economy*. Bangkok: Office of the Prime Minister.

Travis, M.B.J. (1964). Elite. In J. Gould & W.L. Kolb (Eds.), *A dictionary of the social sciences* (p. 234). New York: The Free Press.

Turton, A. (1976). Northern Thai peasant society: Twentieth-century transformations in political and jural structures. *Journal of Peasant Studies*, 3, 276-98.

Turton, A. (1984). Limits of ideological domination and the formation of social consciousness. In A. Turton & S. Tanabe (Eds.), *History and peasant consciousness in South East Asia* (Vol. 13, pp. 19-73). Osaka: National Museum of Ethnology.

Turton, A. (1987). *Production, power and participation in rural Thailand: Experiences of poor farmers' groups*. Geneva: United Nations Research Institute for Social Development.

Turton, A. (1991). Invulnerability and local knowledge. In Manas Chit-kasem & A. Turton (Eds.), *Thai constructions of knowledge* (pp. 155-82). London: School of Oriental and African Studies, University of London.

Unger, D. (1998). *Building social capital in Thailand: Fibers, finance, and infrastructure*. Cambridge: Cambridge University Press.

Vichai Viratkapan, Perera, R., & Watanabe, S. (2005). Factors contributing to the development performance of slum relocation projects in Bangkok, Thailand. *International Development Planning Review*, 26(3), 231-60.

Warr, P.G. (Ed.). (1993). *The Thai economy in transition*. Cambridge: Cambridge University Press.

Warr, P.G., & Bahanupong Nidhiprabha. (1996). *Thailand's economic miracle: Stable adjustment and sustained growth*. Kuala Lumpuer, Malaysia: Oxford University Press.

Weber, K.E., & Hofer, S. (1974). *Thailand research bibliography: Supplement II* (Vol. Data Paper No. 6). Heidelberg, Germany: South Asia Institute.

Weber, M. (1947). *The theory of social and economic organization* (A.M. Henderson & T. Parsons, Trans.) (Edited with an Introduction by Talcott Parsons). New York: Free Press.

Weber, M. (1949). *Methodology in the social sciences* (E. Shils & H.A. Finch, Trans.). Glencoe, Illinois: Free Press.

Weber, M. (1978). *Economy and society: An outline of interpretive sociology*. Berkeley, CA: University of California Press.

Weller, S. (1998). Structured interviewing and questionnaire construction. In B.H. Russell (Ed.), *Handbook of methods in cultural anthropology* (pp. 363-407). London: AltaMira.

Weller, S., & Romney, A.K. (1988). *Systematic data collection*. Newbury Park, CA: Sage.

Weller, S., & Romney, A.K. (1990). *Metric scaling: Correspondence analysis*. Newbury Park, CA: Sage.

Wildavsky, A. (2005). *Moses as political leader*. Jerusalem: Shalom Press.

Wilson, B. (1973). *Magic and the millennium: A sociological study of religious movements of protest among tribal and third-world peoples.* New York: Harper and Row.

Wilson, D.A. (1962). *Politics in Thailand.* Ithaca, NY: Cornell University Press.

Winthrop, R.H. (1991). *Dictionary of concepts in cultural anthropology.* New York: Greenwood Press.

Wirachai, Kowae (25 February 2006). Interview on types and bonds of relationships. Bangkok.

Withaya Sucharithanarugse. (1996). "Puak": Concept of collective behavior in Thai society, *Proceeding of the 6th international conference on Thai studies theme VII toward a new frontier of Thai studies* (pp. 219-28). Chiang Mai, Thailand.

Wolf, E.R. (1966). Kinship, friendship, and patron-client relations in complex societies. In M. Banton (Ed.), *The social anthropology of complex societies.* London: Tavistock Publications.

Wolf, E.R. (1982). *Europe and the people without history.* London: University of California Press.

World Bank. (2006). *Social capital homepage.* World Bank. Available at: http://wwwworldbank.org/poverty/scapital/index.htm [2006].

Wright, P. (1996). *Managerial leadership.* London: Routledge.

Wyatt, D. (1984). *Thailand: A short history.* New Haven: Yale University Press.

Wyatt, D.K. (1971). *Preliminary Thailand bibliography.* Ithaca, New York.

Yatsushiro, T. (1966). *Village organization and leadership in Northeast Thailand.* Bangkok: Research Division, USOM/Thailand.

Yos Santasombat. (1989). Leadership and security in modern Thai politics. In M. Ayoob & Chai-anan Samudavanija (Eds.), *Leadership perceptions and national security: The Southeast Asian experience* (pp. 83-109). Singapore: Institute of Southeast Asian Studies.

Yos Santasombat. (1990). *Amnaaj bukalikaphaap lae phu nam gan muangThai [Power and personality: An anthropological study of the Thai political elite].* Bangkok: Sathaban Thai Kadi Suksa Mahawitayalai Thaamasart.

Yukl, G.A. (2002). *Leadership in organizations* (5th ed.). Upper Saddle River, New Jersey: Prentice Hall.

Index